The Training and Practice of Psychotherapy in Post-apartheid South Africa

Zelda Gillian Knight
(Editor)

The Training and Practice of Psychotherapy in Post-apartheid South Africa

Case Studies, Controversies and Contemplations

nova
science publishers
New York

Library of Congress Cataloging-in-Publication Data

ISBN: 979-8-88697-782-0

Published by Nova Science Publishers, Inc. † New York

Dedication

This book is dedicated to all those hard-working and devoted teachers who train students in the art of psychotherapy and all the students who had the passion to learn as well as all the clients who have passed our doorways and teach us about the depths of the psyche.

Contents

Preface

South Africa has been through enormous political and societal changes since the fall of apartheid in 1994. Nelson Mandela became the first Black president and was heralded as one of Africa's finest leaders. In April 2023, it will have been 29 years of freedom from white rule and racial oppression. There have been significant advances at legislative and governmental levels to ensure and sustain a vision of a society free from oppression, racism and inequality. Many of the institutions and governing bodies of the country have been successfully integrated as a response to apartheid policies of racial segregation and discrimination.

However, in recent years, starting around 2016, South Africa has undoubtedly become a 'country in crisis'.

This crisis is the outcome of a complex interweaving of multiple socio-political processes that are embedded in deep layers of sustained corruption, 'State capture' and poor or inept governance. As I write, the previous president is in jail for corruption, and the current president has been caught breaking the law regarding not declaring foreign monies received and hiding it in one of his homes. Since apartheid, serious violent crime has increased, the unemployment rate is almost 40% and most of the citizens are still living in poverty without basic needs such as running water, adequate housing or access to medical health and mental health services. The elite few have rapidly moved up the social and financial ladder to extreme wealth and comfort, leaving behind disenfranchised citizens. The crisis in the country is a crisis of inequality. The 'haves' and 'have-nots' remain, with the gap between them widening. The cost of living has risen, school and university fees are at an all-time high and petrol prices have increased, meaning transportation of goods by roads has become expensive and food costs have increased. State hospitals are under-staffed and under-resourced, many in a state of shabbiness or disrepair and some on the brink of total collapse. Helen Joseph Hospital in Johannesburg is one such case example. With urbanization increasing, the local infrastructure is old, not maintained, overloaded and breaking down. Sewage and water systems are under strain; road maintenance is non-existent with the development of large potholes that pose a danger to citizens, lack of white painted markings on the roads, leaving South Africans to guess where the middle of the road is, and lack of working street lamps; and in some parts of the city, main arteries of roads have collapsed in the recent rains and are closed. Repair is slow, if at all.

This 'country in crisis' is located with a broader context of the ever-increasing energy crisis that means the main city of commerce – Johannesburg – is without power on a daily basis, sometimes up to 12 hours a day. As I write, we currently have no power for nine hours daily. This impacts an already weakened economy with businesses closing down or forced to offer limited services when the power is out. South Africans scramble to make a plan for electricity during these power outages. I am forced to buy expensive inverters to install in my home to assist with backup power when there is no power, and to consider the much more expensive option of solar energy installation. These two items – inverters and solar power –

are at a premium in terms of demand and supply. The government does nothing to assist citizens with alternative power and has not planned for green resources. I am one of the lucky ones who can afford at least one of these uninterrupted power technologies (inverters) to get through the day, to power my computer, to run a washing machine, to charge my phone, to cook a meal and to live and work. But the inverters need replacing every six to nine months as they cannot cope with the frequency and length of power outages. It has been announced today by the government that the country will have permanent power outages for the next two years. What they fail to say is power outages have been in existence since 2007 and have increased in length and frequency since 2015. This energy crisis reflects a lack of good planning and maintenance.

Nelson Mandela's dream of a 'rainbow nation' is an illusion. What he sacrificed for freedom is a debt that can never be repaid, but what many of the corrupt government leaders of this country have done with their bad governance and greed will take generations to fix and rebuild.

To add to the social, economic and political crisis, the COVID-19 pandemic hit us all in March 2020. The country went into lockdown for almost two years. Both economically and emotionally, the impact of this pandemic has been immense. Many people died from COVID-19, some people lost jobs and homes, some became stressed and anxious, or depressed and suicidal, some people got divorced and families broke up, some were victims of gender violence at home by intimate partners as people were forced to stay at home and some people lost hope. The president, during one of his 'Talks to the Nation' in 2021, announced that 'we have a pandemic of domestic violence against women'. Women in South Africa are more likely to die from partner murder than sickness.

A country in crisis means a country with most of its citizens simply trying to cope and survive with only the basics available.

Life is tough for many South Africans. Many citizens in other parts of the world simply don't have these kinds of societal challenges. Many other countries have managed to cope with social transitions and new governments, the COVID-19 pandemic, riots and protests and even corruption and unemployment, but many South Africans struggle to live and make a living. Some of the luckier wealthier, educated, middle class, regardless of race, have relocated to other countries, like Canada, the USA, Britain, Australia and New Zealand, taking with them their skills and expertise. While apartheid has been dismantled and some social and political progress has been made in terms of democratic freedoms and the protection of human rights, the issue of mental health in South Africa is a low priority, judging by the under-staffed state mental hospitals and its overcrowded wards. Poor people find it hard to access help for mental distress, while the elite few can access help at private clinics and hospitals.

One of the ways to alleviate mental illness remains psychotherapy. Psychotherapy has a long history in South Africa spanning more than 60 years. The implication is that for decades South Africans have traditionally sought out psychotherapy. It has been criticized that this kind of psychotherapy and its history focused on Whites to the detriment of the majority of Blacks. To this end, in the early years of psychotherapy and psychotherapy training, the main approach was psychoanalytic and cognitive therapies. Psychotherapy training has continued to remain at universities. While there are non-university-based training programs and one can train to be a psychoanalyst or even a Jungian therapist, it is the category of clinical and counselling psychologists that make up the majority of mental health practitioners.

With a society in the post-COVID-19 era and a return to the office and in-person engagement, including training and the practice of psychotherapy, the time was ripe to reflect on the state of psychotherapy in South Africa since the fall of apartheid.

It seemed to me fitting to begin the process of starting a new book that would encompass some of the aspects of the current state of psychotherapy in South Africa. The emergence of this book – *The Training and Practice of Psychotherapy in Post-apartheid South Africa: Case Studies, Controversies and Contemplations* – is an outcome of this process.

The authors in this book are all psychologists and trained in the art of psychotherapy. Some are academics at universities and train student psychologists in psychotherapy. The authors have experience with working with a diverse population group and experience with working in different psychotherapy modalities. They are all South Africans and live and work within the context described above. They try to manage the layers of meaning of the multiple shifts from in-person sessions to virtual e-platform sessions and back again to in-person sessions. Their chapters are mirrors of what they do, what they have discovered and what they feel is important or missing in the training of psychologists in psychotherapy. They have personal working experiences that reflect what they believe about the efficacy of psychotherapy.

Chapter 1 – The Current Training of Psychologists in Psychotherapy at Universities in Post-apartheid South Africa: Some Thoughts on the Integration of Transpersonal Psychotherapy into the Training Program – written by me sets the scene for training in psychotherapy. The focus of this chapter is on the current training of psychologists in psychotherapy at universities in post-apartheid South Africa. It describes the training program that students are exposed to in terms of psychotherapy training. Critical issues about this training are documented and discussed. These include issues regarding the selection process, relevancy of psychotherapy modalities, as well as contextual concerns such as the lack of psychologists. During my many years of experience as a lecturer on the training program, I have noticed the enormous gap in training of students of psychotherapy that of a psychotherapy that transcends the 'talking cure'. I offer some thoughts on the introduction to training programs at universities for these kinds of psychotherapies that bypass the intellect. To this end, I offer some of my thoughts on the integration of transpersonal psychotherapy into the training program. As a way of context, this chapter presents a brief history of psychotherapy or the world of psychotherapy.

Chapter 2 – From Freud's Reclining Couch to the Modern Digital Screen in South Africa: An Argument for the Adaptability of the Psychoanalytic Situation – is written by Kgamadi Kometsi. In this chapter, Dr. Kometsi states that the COVID-19 pandemic has forced both a reflection on and a reconsideration of how psychotherapists provide services to their patients. In particular, a reconsideration of how to provide psychoanalytical psychotherapy in this context would inevitably affect the frame. He also remarks that psychoanalytic psychotherapy has always presumed the presence of the therapist and the patient in a consultation room that is uniquely set for the psychoanalytic endeavour. This chapter aims to trace the journey of the psychoanalytic setting from Freud's reclining couch, through the post-Freudian setting requirements, and finally to the modern smart gadgets to which the pandemic forced the provisioning of psychoanalytic treatment specifically in South Africa. It uses Kohut's description of the analytic setting as a lens to reflect backwards to Freud and forward to the COVID pandemic moment. It provides an illustration of a psychoanalytic process through a vignette reflecting a psychoanalytic process that started on a face-to-face basis and was forced into becoming a virtual consultation, where it has remained until the time of writing this chapter. The chapter also reflects on the implications of these changes both against the guidelines of the Health Professions Council of South Africa (HPCSA) on telehealth and for psychoanalytic theory as it applies to the analytic setting.

Chapter 3 – A Phenomenological Case Study on the Efficacy of Somatic Experiencing (SE) as Treatment Model for Adult Survivors of Child Maltreatment: Consideration for Teaching Body-Based Trauma Therapies to Trainee Psychologists – is written by Tshepo Tlali. In this chapter, Dr. Tlali writes that the landscape of psychology has changed pointedly over the past decades. Globally, the need to cultivate short-term and responsive therapeutic interventions for a variety of mental health issues remains an integral part of any robust psychotherapy. He claims that for over a century, the conventional model of psychotherapy treatment of psychological distress remains the 'talking therapies'. By comparison, body-based psychotherapy with its numerous branches has an equally long but perhaps more controversial past. One such branch of body psychotherapy is the somatic experiencing (SE) model, which endeavours to link the mind–body gap that diffuses binary therapies. Using phenomenological case study methods, the author shall endeavour to demonstrate the effectiveness of SE therapeutic model as an efficient psychotherapeutic treatment for adult survivors of childhood maltreatment. Dr. Tlali also states that South Africa's astonishingly high incidents of interpersonal violence call for an ongoing transformation of outmoded ways of treating traumatic stress emanating from all forms of trauma. It is the broad aim of this chapter to serve as an introduction to SE therapy within the South African context, particularly in relation to the treatment of adult survivors of childhood maltreatment.

Chapter 4 – Theraplay for Children in South Africa: Therapists' Considerations for Its Use in the Local Context – written by Deidré du Toit and Ahmed Riaz Mohamed claims that attachment-based interventions and psychotherapies are targeted towards preventing and/or remediating relational challenges within caregiver–child dyads to facilitate child development and wellbeing. One such intervention is Theraplay, a dyadic attachment-focused psychotherapeutic approach. Despite its popularity among practitioners, these authors' remark that limited consideration has been given in the literature to the implementation of Theraplay in contexts outside of North America and other developed countries. Based on semi-structured interviews with six Theraplay-trained South African psychologists, this chapter explores therapists' perceptions regarding the implementation of Theraplay in South Africa. Through a thematic analysis, four main themes emerged: (1) Theraplay as a therapeutic modality; (2) South African perspective and Theraplay applicability; (3) considerations regarding resources in South Africa; and (4) caregiver accessibility and caregiver influence. The authors provide a discussion of these themes pertaining to the facilitating factors and challenges regarding the implementation of Theraplay in South Africa. Furthermore, the chapter discusses findings concerning potential adaptations to Theraplay that may enhance its applicability in the South African context. In conclusion, the chapter consolidates pertinent practice recommendations and additionally offers recommendations for future research on Theraplay in South Africa.

Chapter 5 – Process-Based Therapy and Its Potential in Accommodating a Diverse Post-apartheid South Africa – is written by Nevern Subermoney. In this chapter, he claims that post-apartheid South Africa brings with it the challenge of how to train and practice as a psychotherapist with a diversity of individuals while being sensitive to their unique history, context and goals. He proposes that a novel meta-framework for understanding evidence-based psychotherapy, process-based therapy (PBT), offers guidance on how to use the science of psychotherapy in a way that is tailored to the unique individual, their context, and their goals for therapy. Subermoney uses a multiple case-study method that is used to show how three different cases from the author's psychotherapy practice can be formulated with three different therapeutic modalities while using PBT as a meta-framework. Future research on the effectiveness and efficacy of PBT in the South African context is needed to validate the preliminary potential of this approach.

Chapter 6 – Grief: (the Lack of) Training of Psychologists in Post-apartheid South Africa – is written by Bêne Otto. In this chapter, she claims that grief is arguably the most universal human experience. This reality has been brought closer to consciousness with the COVID-19 pandemic and unprecedented loss of life, leaving behind hundreds of thousands of bereaved individuals. Death and grief remains a taboo topic which often results in misconceptions and misinformation that leads to the disenfranchising of the experience of loss. She states that despite the number of individuals affected in grief work, the training that psychologists receive in post-apartheid South Africa is minimal across universities. This chapter seeks to address this disconnect by highlighting grief theory from current thanatological literature.

I wish to thank all the authors for their valuable time in writing their chapters. I hope that this book gives them an opportunity to showcase their ideas, perspectives, hopes and longings for the profession of psychotherapy.

I hope too that this book gives some insight and food for thought for the reader into the state of training and practice of psychotherapy in South Africa today.

Zelda G. Knight
Editor
Johannesburg
30 January 2023

Book Description

This book focuses on the training and practice of psychotherapy in post-apartheid South Africa, with particular reference to case studies, controversies and contemplations. The authors are all South Africans who are trained in the art of psychotherapy and have been working with a diverse population in diverse settings. Some of the authors are academics at universities and are involved in the training of student psychologists in psychotherapy. With their unique histories and experiences, these authors together bring a vast amount of indigenous knowledge to the profession of psychotherapy. Using their own subjectivity and work experience in the field of psychotherapy, they present different perspectives on the issues, conflicts, problems, what should change, what works well and what needs to be considered in psychotherapy. To this end, this book is about new ideas and new thoughts on psychotherapy. It begins with a chapter on the current training of psychologists in psychotherapy, the critical issues in training such as selection processes as well as the identification of a gap in training leading to the suggestion for the inclusion of transpersonal psychotherapy. In the next chapter, an exploration is achieved of the shifts from the analytical couch to the virtual screen. Psychoanalytic psychotherapy has always presumed the presence of the therapist and the patient in a consultation room that is uniquely set for the psychoanalytic endeavour. This chapter aims to trace the journey of the psychoanalytic setting from Freud's reclining couch, through the post-Freudian setting requirements, and finally to the modern smart gadgets to which the pandemic forced the provisioning of psychoanalytic treatment specifically in South Africa. An argument is made for the adaptability of the psychoanalytic situation. In the following chapter, the author focuses on the efficacy of SE as a treatment model for adult survivors of child maltreatment. In this regard, a proposal is made for the consideration of teaching 'body-based trauma therapies', as opposed to those that focus only on the mind and leave the body out, to trainee psychologists. The SE model is described and its value in forging the links between the mind–body gap is shown. Using phenomenological case study methods, there is a demonstration of the effectiveness of the SE model as an efficient psychotherapeutic treatment for adult survivors of childhood maltreatment. The book also has a chapter on child therapy or 'Theraplay' – a dyadic attachment-focused psychotherapeutic approach. Based on semi-structured interviews with six Theraplay-trained South African psychologists, this chapter explores these therapists' perceptions regarding the implementation of Theraplay in South Africa. The book also details a 'process-based therapy' and its potential to accommodating a diverse post-apartheid South Africa. A novel meta-framework for understanding evidence-based psychotherapy, process-based therapy (PBT), offers guidance on how to use the science of psychotherapy in a way that is tailored to the unique individual, their context and their goals for therapy. It includes case studies from the author's psychotherapy practice to show this kind of process and therapy. In the final chapter, the concepts and perspectives on grief and grief theory are examined. Death and grief theory often results in misconceptions and misinformation that lead to the disenfranchising of the experience of loss. Despite the number of individuals affected by grief, the training that psychologists receive in post-apartheid South Africa is minimal across universities. Discussion is offered to address this disconnect by highlighting grief theory from current thanatological literature.

Acknowledgements

I wish to acknowledge all the authors' contributions to this book. Without your work and commitment to the process, this book would not have been possible. Thank you.

Chapter 1

The Current Training of Psychologists in Psychotherapy at Universities in Post-apartheid South Africa

Some Thoughts on the Integration of Transpersonal Psychotherapy into the Training Programme

Zelda Gillian Knight*

Department of Psychology, Faculty of Humanities, University of Johannesburg, South Africa

Abstract

This chapter focuses on and examines the current training of psychologists in psychotherapy at universities in post-apartheid South Africa. It describes the training programme as well as what kinds of psychotherapy modalities trainee students are exposed to in their training. It is recognized that training in psychotherapy, and even training in psychoanalysis, does occur outside of the university context. Critical issues about psychologists' training in psychotherapy are documented and discussed. These include issues regarding the selection process, relevancy of psychotherapy modalities, as well as contextual concerns such as the lack of psychologists in the country, poor access to mental health services, and language difficulties between client and therapist. During my many years of experience as a lecturer in the training programme, I have come to some realization about psychotherapy and training. One of these realizations is the enormous gap in the training of students of psychotherapy that transcends the 'talking cure'. While modalities that champion the talking cure are valuable, those that do not are equally valuable. I offer some thoughts on the introduction to training programmes at universities for these kinds of psychotherapies that bypass the intellect. I emphasize that there has been an increase in bringing the body into psychotherapy, as well as non-ordinary states of consciousness as mechanisms of healing and transformation. To this end, I offer some of my thoughts on the integration of transpersonal psychotherapy into the training programme. As a way of context, this chapter presents a brief history of psychotherapy or the world of psychotherapy.

Key Words: intervention, mental health, psychologists, psychotherapy, training, South Africa

---

* Corresponding Author's Email: zknight@uj.ac.za

Introduction: The World of Psychotherapy

The history of modern psychotherapy in the Western world is more than 130 years old. It has undoubtedly achieved a status that enables it to be a recognized profession and a scientific discipline in its own right. Psychotherapy has, however, not always been recognized in this way. With its focus on a 'talking cure' for the treatment of psychological pain and inner conflict, to some critical viewers, the science of it seemed vague, unmeasurable, and lacking in objective criteria by which to judge its merits and credibility. It seemed to elude the scrutiny of 'real' science. However, much has changed in the past 80 years. Research from all over the world that uses psychotherapy as an intervention has mushroomed and provides a sound knowledge base as to its positive effects in treating psychological distress.

It is, therefore, a tremendously fast-growing profession, and judging from the increased number of international books and academic journals on psychotherapy in the past 50 years, psychotherapy is a well-known treatment process that has become increasingly valued, effective and common in mental health programmes throughout the world. With the onset of the COVID-19 pandemic, the spotlight on psychological services to manage distress and anxiety, depression and hopelessness, brightened even more.

The underlying implication is that in modern times of the 21st century, psychotherapy, as a way to alleviate psychological distress and mental disorders, is something that many people from different ethnic backgrounds select. Such diversity of clients includes the difference in race, age and cultures, including individuals from so-called 'non-western' and collective-based cultures found in Asia (Qian, 2002) and Africa (Madu, 2002).

Few countries in the world do not know about psychotherapy, or practice it in some form. While its forms, methods and approaches may differ, reflective of different cultures, psychotherapy is no doubt a worldwide, modern professional endeavour.

In the current world of multiple modalities of psychotherapy, investigations into psychotherapy practice and training across the world have noted that cognitive behavioural therapy (CBT) is one of the most commonly recognized and used approaches in many countries (Pritz, 2002). In addition, it has been noted that 'insight therapy' has become one of the most common approaches, and exists, in varying degrees, in all five continents (Pritz, 2002). Certainly, in this context, the ideas of Sigmund Freud regarding his development of theories and the practice of his idea of psychoanalysis remain influential today.

Many other psychotherapy modalities have emerged in the past 80 years. These are mostly rooted in Western or White theories and models of mind and psychotherapeutic processes and healing. In this regard, the more established psychotherapies that have emerged are Jungian psychotherapy, existential psychotherapy, Gestalt psychotherapy, person-centred psychotherapy, psychodrama, hypnosis, systemic psychotherapy and transactional analysis psychotherapy.

Less well-known therapies but growing in popularity are those therapies that theoretically and practically move away from a theory of a 'talking cure'. These therapies are body-centred expressive therapies such as art therapy, dance therapy, breathwork therapy, clay therapy, wilderness experience therapy, mindfulness/yoga therapy, psychedelic-assisted therapy and animal-assisted therapy. These therapies attest to the growing popularity of psychotherapy as an intervention for psychological stress and mental health issues. These therapies are evidence for concepts of the mind that support the idea that psychological healing can be an experiential learning activity in which the body is engaged as well as the mind.

In a sense, these therapies encompass a spiritual dimension of the psyche or transpersonal experiences (Grof, 2019) in healing the mind. They are thus therapies that bring the soma-bodily experience alive and part of the healing process, a kind of beyond 'the skin encapsulated ego' (Watts, 1989). The transpersonal therapies that view non-ordinary states of consciousness as healing are not new but have been known and practised by ancient cultures for millennia (Grof, 2019). Methods or technologies have been developed to access these transpersonal and non-ordinary states of consciousness, ranging from psychedelic-assisted psychotherapy to Holotropic therapy (Grof, 2019). Stanislav Grof, a psychiatrist by profession, is arguably the most prominent researcher in transpersonal psychotherapy and the use of altered states of consciousness for the healing of the psyche.

At the localized level, psychotherapy training has existed in South Africa for more than 60 years. During apartheid, many of the Western psychotherapy modalities mentioned earlier such as CBT and psychodynamic psychotherapy were offered as part of the training at so-called Whites-only universities. During these painful decades of segregation and the struggle for African freedom from colonialization, the discipline of White psychology, and by implication, psychotherapy, became a mechanism of maintaining Black oppression. Furthermore, the vast majority of (Black) citizens were not only denied educational, social and economic opportunities and training afforded to Whites, but they were also denied access to good quality mental health care.

Since democracy, there has been a major diversification in the racial profile of the middle class where it once was majority White to a majority Black (Southall, 2022). Based on current trends at private mental hospitals and clinics in the Gauteng province, the Black middle class is showing interest in, and access to, psychotherapy as an intervention to psychological unwellness and mental challenges in living. This means that most clients will be Black South Africans. This implies that, as with other countries, South Africa is not unique and access to psychotherapy remains for the few (i.e., Black African middle-class citizens). While Black South Africans are also not a homogeneous group, Black clients are interested in, and support the value of, the 'talking cure'.

The current situation in South Africa is not unique in terms of individuals seeking out psychotherapy as a way to manage anxiety, depression and other mental disorders, especially during the COVID-19 pandemic and its regulated lockdown. It appears that many South Africans suffered from mental unwellness or mental disorders during the lockdown (Álvarez-Iglesias et al., 2021; De Man et al., 2022; De Backer, 2021; Nguse & Wassenaar, 2021; Posel et al., 2021) such distress and suffering extended to children and adolescents (Bloom et al., 2022) as well as caregivers (Bloom et al., 2022; Dawood et al., 2022).

With the dismantling of the apartheid system in April 1994, psychotherapy continued to be practised. Training at universities and client access to psychotherapy were now open to all citizens. The Mental Health Care Act 17 of 2002 was initiated with the aim to protect psychotherapy as a profession so that only trained and qualified professionals can legally offer and practice psychotherapy. Clinical and counselling psychologists, psychiatrists and clinical social workers became the main categories of mental health professionals that could offer psychotherapy.

A chapter on psychotherapy cannot go without something being said about the COVID-19 pandemic that essentially 'shut down the skies' and went into various forms of lockdown and quarantine measures, which resulted in individuals being separated from loved ones and friends. The pandemic ostensibly changed the socio-economic landscape of the world, including South Africa.

With people reaching for facemasks, new fears and anxieties erupted. The world was in a collective trauma, living with the fear of death from a virus that had no cure. Many South Africans experienced stress, depression, loneliness, fear and anxiety (Nguse & Wassenaar, 2021; Padmanabhanunni & Pretorius, 2021; Pillay & Barnes, 2020). Those who could sought psychotherapy. Psychotherapy suddenly became virtual as it took the shape and form of online psychotherapy. Both clients and therapists, in a kind of 'shared collective trauma', quickly learn to use various e-platforms and applications to reach each other. Psychotherapy not only became online but also opened up many emotional issues for both client and therapist about how they worked together, how they dealt with bad connectivity issues, costs of internet connection, as well as feelings of anxiety and a sense of disconnection from each other while on these virtual platforms. Some clients and therapists did manage well with online therapy and thrived on it, even choosing to continue online work after the lockdown (Knight, 2020a, 2020b).

In South Africa, as with the rest of the world, training in psychotherapy transferred to online work. For two cohorts of students representing two years of online experiences meant that all modules in the training programme, all examinations, all case presentations, and all clinical and research supervision went online. The implication is that students did not see their classmates or lecturers in-person for the entire time of their training.

It is not known how these students coped with online training as no research to date has been implemented to investigate their experiences. Informal conversations, however, indicated that some students experienced emotional difficulties with the move to online training, while others seemed to flourish.

The Current State of Psychologists' Training in Psychotherapy in South Africa

This section of the chapter focuses only on the current state of psychologists' training in psychotherapy in South Africa. Training in psychotherapy does occur outside of the university context, and there are many programmes on offer in many modalities of psychotherapy. There is thus a rich and abundant collection of courses, training programmes, study groups, organizations and associations to which psychotherapy is promoted and mental health practitioners can access.

The current state of psychologists training in psychotherapy in South Africa has a long history dating back to the 1960s. Much of the curriculum in psychotherapy was CBT and psychodynamic. Psychologists' training in psychotherapy was and remains a part of a broader university-based Master's training programme that includes other mental health competencies such as psychological diagnostics, assessment and testing. The Professional Board of Psychology regularly monitors the training at all universities that offer it. This Board is a branch of the overarching organization for the regulation, registration, qualification checking, monitoring and training of health professions including psychologists known as the Health Professions Council for South Africa (HPCSA).

Training for clinical and counselling psychologists who are the two main psychology categories of registration with the HPCSA that offer psychotherapy as a profession is a two-year Master's level coursework training programme. The Master's level of training in psychotherapy forms one module among other requirements, including a research thesis, which makes up 50% of the overall final mark for the first year. The Professional Board of Psychology, a branch of the HPCSA, regulates the training in the first year. This same Board regularly visits universities offering such training to inspect, monitor, assess and accredit the quality and content of the programme. The implication is that training is largely standardized. The Board thus sets the designated time allocated to training in psychotherapy in any training programme.

The Master's level of training in psychotherapy exposes student psychologists to a wide range of theoretical approaches. While there is some exposure to African approaches to mental health, mental illness and psychotherapy, the psychotherapy approaches taught in universities remain largely Westernized approaches. The two most common Westernized approaches are psychodynamic and CBT. Psychoanalytic-based psychotherapies have theoretical and practice roots in the British School of Object Relations theories and Self Psychology perspectives, to the more recent developments in psychoanalysis, such as relational psychoanalysis. CBT has roots in American views of the mind and beliefs about the relationship between cognitions and behaviour.

Training in psychotherapy at universities for psychologists now requires at least two other psychotherapy modalities. These two psychotherapy modalities that students are exposed to are drawn from a pool of Western perspectives such as solution-focused therapy, narrative therapy, existential psychotherapy, person-centred psychotherapy or Gestalt therapy.

In the M1 year, students have an opportunity to work therapeutically with a range of client populations while under guidance or weekly supervision by an experienced and registered psychologist. This exposure to clients in the first year of training is also part of the Board's recommendations in terms of M1 student training and skill acquisition in preparation for the following 12-month internship year.

In the second year, students do an internship year. The Professional Board monitors the quality of training at these internship sites. During this internship year, students are exposed to psychotherapy training in various settings such as in a psychological ward at a government hospital, in a counselling centre at a university or in a non-profit organization (NGO). The psychology students see clients for psychotherapy under the weekly supervision of a trained psychologist. Quarterly reports on the students' progress, including their skills in psychotherapy with a range of diverse clients, are compulsory and form part of the monitoring and measurement of their competencies. The Board mandates the involvement of the university lectures in the internship year. Such involvement is normally attendance at the quarterly meetings, engagement with the student and supervisors on the progress of the student, and identifying both strengths and weaknesses of the interns.

At the end of the internship year, students write a Board exam, which includes questions on psychotherapy as an intervention. They must pass the exam in order to register with the HPCSA. Clinical students, however, process onto a third year, referred to as a 'community year'. In this community year, clinical students are assigned to outlying or rural areas where resources are limited. Once completed, clinical students can register with the HPCSA as clinical psychologists. Counselling students can register with the Board as Counselling Psychologists after passing the Board exam.

Once registered, all professional psychologists who provide psychotherapy in South Africa must maintain their competencies and skills by attaining Continued Professional Development (CPD) points. This is achieved by attending professional activities that aim to upgrade skills. These activities are regulated by the Board of Psychology. Service providers for these training activities are registered mental health practitioners. Training in ethical practice is compulsory. The Board through random audits monitors individual compliance for CPD points.

Critical Issues About Psychologists' Training in Psychotherapy

As far back as 2002, I wrote the following:

> The history and development of psychology as a profession and discipline, and the application of its theoretical principles to the practice of psychotherapy, as well as its relevance to the South African context, has been a complex and contentious matter in South Africa.
> *(Knight, 2002, p. 593)*

In this regard, psychology was criticized for its role in the maintenance and practice of racism during the apartheid era (Cooper, 2014; De la Rey & Isper, 2004; Dawes, 1985; Manganyi, 2016).

Padmanabhanunni and colleagues (2022) joined in these critical voices and noted that psychology has had a contentious history in South Africa since the 1920s. Intelligence tests in South Africa were used to justify apartheid practices of racial segregation on the grounds of supposed racial differences in mental test scores (Padmanabhanunni et al., 2022). In this context, Padmanabhanunni and her colleagues highlighted that these intelligence tests were based on White South African norms and subsequently used to show that other race groups were inferior. This eventually laid the foundation for the justification of segregationist education policies (Padmanabhanunni et al., 2022).

Apartheid ideologies also controlled the training and practice of professional psychology and for many years excluded the entry of Black South Africans into the profession (Padmanabhanunni et al., 2022; Pillay & Siyothula, 2008; Pillay & Kramers-Olen, 2014; Pillay & Nyandeni, 2021). The role of psychology in perpetuating racist, exclusionary policies has been extensively documented elsewhere (Cooper et al., 1990; Dawes, 1985; Manganyi, 2016; Mayekiso et al., 2004). The implication is that during apartheid era, professional psychology and thus psychotherapy training was only available to White South Africans (Mayekiso et al., 2004; Padmanabhanunni et al., 2022; Pillay & Siyothula, 2008; Pillay & Nyandeni, 2021). Once apartheid ended in 1994, new ideologies of transformation and redress of past injustices began to take root.

At the level of professional training at universities, however, such transformation is slow. For example, at the curriculum level of training, African-centred psychologies and traditional healing perspectives struggled and jostled for positions in undergraduate and post-graduate curricula and programmes in psychology and psychotherapy. To this end, professional psychology and psychotherapy continue to be criticized today as being at odds with the majority of South African lived experiences, and thus it appears that this 'political crisis in psychology' still persists.

The investigation by Pillay and Siyothula (2008) showed that a few universities, led by the Medical University of Southern Africa (MEDUNSA), the Universities of the Witwatersrand, North West (Mafikeng Campus), Natal, Durban-Westville and the North (currently Limpopo), were among the main role-players, training 150 (56.4%) of the 266 Black African clinical psychologists in the post-apartheid period until 2006. Given the history of MEDUNSA and its creation in 1976 specifically to boost the training of Black healthcare professionals in the country, the fact that the institution topped the list of training institutions for Black African clinical psychologists suggests that it has been meeting its mandate (Pillay & Nyandeni, 2021).

In this regard, a new study by Pillay and Nyandeni (2021) was essentially a follow-up study to the one in 2008. This new study showed little change in access to training of Black South

Africans since apartheid's exclusionary policies. In their investigation, Pillay and Nyandeni noted that the licencing register of the HPCSA was examined during the period from 2007 to 2018 to ascertain the number of Black South Africans trained as clinical psychologists. They discovered that no real change had occurred in the number of trained Black students from the previous period (1994–2007) which was the focus of the previous research in 2008. This new study (2021) showed that of the 2,883 clinical psychologists licensed in the study period (2007–2018), only 426 (14.8%) were Black Africans, despite this group constituting 80.7% of the South African population.

The implication is that there has not been much change in the selection of candidates by universities for training in terms of demographics. This finding can be examined against the background of the findings of Mayekiso et al. (2004) who published self-reported data by eight universities on the race distribution of students admitted into their programmes. They found that in the 11-year period 1994–2004, the eight training programmes reported between 9% and 31% of their student intake being Black Africans. Pillay and Nyandeni (2021) point out that this trend is troubling and must alert the profession of psychology and training institutions to the need for more concerted action.

It is also noted that even though psychology has come a long way since its complicity in apartheid, pleas for action have been made regarding the transformation of the discipline (Cooper & Nicholas, 2012; Pillay et al., 2013). For some, such as Pillay and colleagues, the initiatives have not really translated into improved equity in training numbers within clinical psychology (Pillay & Nyandeni, 2021). Moreover, the nature of the selection process has normally included role-play activities and group work activities which some candidates may have been exposed to and others not. This kind of selection process has been contentious. For this reason, at the University of Johannesburg, Counselling Master's training no longer uses role-plays.

In addition, bearing in mind that it was once a trend for some universities to select candidates currently in personal psychotherapy. At some universities, this practice has now been excluded because personal psychotherapy is hard to access as a criterion for suitability for training. In addition, psychotherapy is expensive, and some candidates who cannot afford it may be at a disadvantage.

Some universities have reviewed their selection processes over the years, such as the University of Johannesburg, The University of the Witwatersrand (WITS), and Nelson Mandela University. Some positive changes have occurred that are more inclusive of diversity and less invasive in terms of personal information of a sensitive nature.

The main aim for some universities nowadays for selection criteria is not to identify how much trauma candidates have experienced to judge their capacity for empathy but to explore candidates' capacity for research and work in communities. For example, at the University of Johannesburg, selection processes include students providing a concept paper or research proposal.

The main takeaway is that not only should there be some critical scrutinization of the implicit ideas and assumptions that influence the choice of some applicants over others (Padmanabhanunni et al., 2022), but there should also be a careful consideration of the assumptions that influence the choice of selection activities over other activities.

The implication is that to some extent, psychotherapy as a profession in post-apartheid South Africa remains at odds with many aspects of South African life and society. Universities are not training enough Black South Africans (Pillay & Nyandeni, 2021). This translates into the fact that the majority of practitioners of psychotherapy are not Black South Africans. This means that in many cases Black clients may not find Black psychotherapists. Not only is this worrisome, but it means that psychotherapy is taking place in a language other than the mother tongue of the clients.

In addition, the majority of South Africans, who are living in poverty, cannot easily access good quality mental healthcare. Resources are limited in the government sector. Poorer citizens who can access some limited psychotherapy sessions in the public domain often do so in understaffed and under-resourced government hospitals. For even fewer and more wealthy citizens, access to psychotherapy is often with private psychologists or psychiatrists in private practice and private clinics and facilities. These few wealthy South Africans (15% of the population of 70 million) have access to medical insurance for psychotherapy or they are able to afford the rates and thus are self-funded. The implication is that there is still an interest in seeking psychotherapy as an intervention for psychological challenges, but it is expensive if accessed privately and limited to a few sessions at some state hospitals.

This means that mental healthcare services have not been an investment by the government and thus have remained inaccessible for the majority of the population (Nguse & Wassenaar, 2021). In the absence of government investment and an affordable mental healthcare funding model, access to good quality mental health service and care will remain something only for the privileged (Padmanabhanunni et al., 2022).

Not only is access to psychotherapy mostly limited to the privileged few, but it is also limited to where you live. There is a disproportionate distribution of psychologists, and thus access to psychotherapy, in urban areas as compared to rural areas. Most practising psychologists in South Africa are located in two highly urbanized provinces, namely Gauteng and the Western Cape (Padmanabhanunni et al., 2022). The implication is that citizens in rural areas will struggle to access mental health services and psychotherapy. The scarcity of available and accessible psychology practitioners, as well as the lack of resources, remains a problem, particularly within the public healthcare sector (Padmanabhanunni et al., 2022).

This 'unequal area access' is coupled with another challenge of there being a shortage of psychologists in South Africa compared to other countries. The statistics show that there are only 2.5 psychologists per 100,000 of the South African population, which is well below the global average of 33.3 psychologists per 100,000 of the population (Padmanabhanunni et al., 2022; Siyothula, 2019). This shortage directly influences access to mental health services (Padmanabhanunni et al., 2022).

This state of affairs 29 years after the inauguration of a Black The African National Congress (ANC) government is dismal in terms of improving the (mental) lives of South Africans. A shortage of psychologists should be laid at the doorstep of the Health Department which offers so few paid internship sites for clinical and counselling psychologists. To extend this thought it is necessary to criticize the government for poor performance in the provision of good quality mental health service and care. While the South African government has attempted to address the limitations of mental health services through the decentralization of psychology in government hospitals to community-based health clinics (Padmanabhanunni et al., 2022), it can be concluded that this initiative has largely failed.

Questions about the relevancy of Westernized or Euro-centric models of mind and theories of psychotherapy have been around for many decades (De la Rey & Isper, 2004; Long, 2016; Pretorius, 2012; Schneider et al., 2021). The discussion necessarily turns towards the lived experiences of the majority of citizens who are not European, and the issues of these theories' applicability to their belief systems, culture and cosmology about mental health and mental illness. It is unlikely that the Euro-centric models of mind and psychotherapy will be completely excluded from training programmes. There is a need to move to incorporate and integrate different African-centred systems and theories of psychopathology and healing in training programmes rather than demonize some theories or idealize other theories over others.

While there is much to celebrate in South Africa, the road to mental health services and psychotherapy for all citizens remains bumpy and uneven. A troubled past does not mean that there is no troubled present. South Africa's so-called rainbow nation is in trouble. The economy is weak and is weakening annually. The country faces an ever-increasing energy crisis, with daily load-shedding of up to 12 hours of outage a day in Gauteng, a crumbling infrastructure with potholes in major roads, sewage and water systems overloaded as a result of increased urbanization, a housing crisis, as well as public concern for governmental corruption, state capture and bankrupt parastatal agencies such as the national airline.

The story of South Africa is not all gloom. It is a more racially integrated society, with equal opportunities for the previously disadvantaged. It has a focused celebration of human diversity and protection of human rights that includes laws that protect the individual's right to choice, such as sexual orientation, gay marriage and abortion. South Africa has one of the most advanced constitutions in the world in terms of human rights.

As indicated, psychotherapy itself has been in existence in South Africa for 60 years. This means that it developed during the apartheid era for essentially the consumption of a White consumer with Western values and mores. It is important to acknowledge the history of psychotherapy as it remains present in what kinds of psychotherapy modalities are offered. While other African-centred perspectives on mental health are slowly being introduced into the training at universities, they remain largely fringe or supplementary. In South Africa, as in other parts of the world, CBT and psychodynamic psychotherapy remain the most common and thus particularly dominant discourse in training in psychotherapy.

Some Thoughts on the Integration of Transpersonal Psychotherapy into the Training Programme

During my more than 20 years of experience as a lecturer on the training programme teaching psychodynamic psychotherapy and publishing in the area, I have come to some realization about psychotherapy and training. One of these realizations is the enormous gap in the training of psychologists in psychotherapies that transcend talk and the so-called 'talking cure'. While modalities that champion the talking cure are valuable, those that do not are equally valuable. These kinds of psychotherapies understand the healing potential of working with psychological and emotional problems through the body and, thus, bypass the intellect and talk about feelings rather than feeling feelings. There has been an increase in bringing the body into psychotherapy, meaning that the body contains memories and feelings and is the site of the unconscious. These body therapies thus support processes of an experiential nature. Closely related to experiential work and the unconscious is transpersonal psychotherapy and the value of non-ordinary states of consciousness. In my personal experience of transpersonal experiences from both Holotropic breathwork with Stan Grof as a facilitator and my personal psychotherapy in which I went through these transpersonal experiences, as well as my own years of research, I have come to appreciate the immense healing potential of these transpersonal experiences. For many years, I have not been involved in transpersonal work. I do, however, feel that there is a new zeitgeist emerging, or perhaps it is a returning of a keen professional interest in transpersonal psychology and psychotherapy. Many of my Master's students who have qualified under me as psychologists are inquiring about transpersonal psychotherapy or psychotherapy that includes experiences of a non-ordinary state of consciousness. I think that there is now a ripe clinical training environment that introduces transpersonal psychotherapy to the training programme of psychologists in psychotherapy.

In my extensive experience in teaching psychodynamic psychotherapy, I have come to appreciate the diversity of theories of psychotherapy, and thus theories of how healing occurs and what is good and not good therapy, what works and does not work. At a more specific level of training in psychotherapy, it is unlikely that CBT and psychodynamic therapy will be discarded too soon. It has much to offer theoretically and practically. Students and clients work well in these paradigms, and their efficacy has been demonstrated. However, I think there is a case for the integration of transpersonal psychology and transpersonal psychotherapy into the curriculum. This modality encompasses theories of the mind and psychotherapy that are suitable for most clients in most cultures (Grof, 2019).

Transpersonal psychology reconceptualizes models of the mind and psyche.

Some time ago, when I was a young and inexperienced lecturer in the early 1990s at Rhodes University, a Master's degree coursework programme was initiated that had a focus on transpersonal psychology. Students were encouraged to consider engaging in breathwork therapy or Holotropic therapy, as developed by Stan and Christina Grof in the 1970s. During Holotropic breathwork, clients can, in a safe controlled environment, and with no psychedelic assistance, access experiences of non-ordinary states of consciousness. Sessions are normally two to three hours long and can accommodate up to 100 people or more, if organized well, in one group at one time. These states of consciousness or spiritual transcendent experiences are reported by the thousands of clients who have done Holotropic breathwork over the years as powerfully healing and transformative (Grof, 2019). Holotropic breathwork requires facilitators who are trained and qualified in doing Holotropic breathwork. Most of these students reported that these experiences were emotionally and psychologically healing. In conjunction with one or two follow-up supportive psychotherapy sessions to integrate these experiences, the students reported that they would like training in this field and possibly offer it to their clients.

In the early 1990s, I travelled to Ireland and San Francisco to participate in Holotropic breathwork workshops with Stan and Christina Grof as facilitators. This kind of psychotherapy was experienced as powerful and transformative. At a personal level, I can attest to its value as a therapy for psychological healing. As a result of my positive exposure to transpersonal psychology and transpersonal psychotherapy, influenced by many more experiences of transpersonal psychotherapy in my own personal psychotherapy, I began to do my own research in the field. This research took several years and culminated in a PhD with the main topic in transpersonal psychotherapy. I also began to do other kinds of related research with African shamans that used methods to access experiences of non-ordinary states of consciousness. I participated in some of these shamanic rituals and ceremonies as a guest participatory researcher. These were also transformative and healing.

I am thus able to suggest, based on my personal experience and my research, that university training programmes for psychologists in psychotherapy should consider including transpersonal psychology and transpersonal psychotherapy. This kind of psychotherapy has the potential for long-lasting psychological healing (Grof, 2019). While there are risks to any psychotherapy process, such as the emergence of psychosis or suicidality or disintegration and depersonalization, to not offer some training in transpersonal psychology and transpersonal psychotherapy is to do a disservice to trainee psychologists and the wider public. The massive amount of research done these past 60 years on the potential healing processes that arise from careful and safely initiated experiences of non-ordinary states of consciousness cannot be ignored.

What is transpersonal psychology? Transpersonal psychology views the human psyche differently from Western theories of mind, and thus, the practice of transpersonal psychotherapy is different. Most of these Western theories of psychology, psychotherapy and psychiatry do not recognize nor support the emergence of non-ordinary states of consciousness for the healing of psychological trauma and pain. Transpersonal psychology and psychotherapy, on the other hand, call for psychotherapeutic work to access experiences of non-ordinary states of consciousness, and thus it is experiential and body-orientated. It describes a cartography of the human psyche that includes many different kinds of transpersonal experiences such as pre-natal experiences or experiences in the womb, birth experiences and their four stages, near-death experiences, spiritual experiences, out-of-body experiences, experiences that transcend time and space, such as experiences of identification with animals, with other people, with groups and racial consciousness, with mythological realms of other cultures, and so-called past life experiences or identification with historical periods of time (Grof, 2019).

Grof states that the psyche is infinitely larger than we believe. All these different kinds of experiences of non-ordinary states of consciousness are understood within transpersonal psychology as contributing to the formation of the human psyche and it is healing of trauma, rather than limiting the psychic and its development to post-natal biographical experiences only (Grof, 2019). Western psychology (psychoanalysis, object relations, self psychology, CBT) thus constricts psychic experience to the post-natal biographical level. It does not view birth as trauma and ignores birth experiences entirely in its understanding of the human psyche. Western psychology, psychotherapy and psychiatry have no category for spiritual experiences and will pathologize them as psychotic.

While psychedelic-assisted psychotherapy can be used in transpersonal psychotherapy, this kind of psychotherapy advocates more strongly for the use of breathwork. The implication is that it is a psychotherapy that initially transcends verbalization or the so-called 'talking cure' method. It does, however, require training by a qualified professional experienced in these kinds of experiences. While most if not all universities will not have these transpersonal professionals on campus, it is possible to invite them into the classrooms of trainee psychologists. It will take some decisions from the Head of Departments, Programme Directors and the Professional Board of Psychology to be convinced and supportive of the benefits of transpersonal psychotherapy.

Students who are trained in transpersonal work and theory that underlies it can offer it to the public. There would have to be some inclusion and exclusion criteria for the public as transpersonal psychotherapy is not suitable for everyone. These counterproductive characteristics include those persons with a history of psychosis, suicidality and addictions. The clients included in transpersonal psychotherapy sessions (Holotropic breathwork) will have to access a few follow-up psychotherapy sessions for support for the integration of these transpersonal experiences. These follow-up psychotherapy sessions are important because simply having non-ordinary states of consciousness is not enough.

Trainee psychologists should have an option to not have induced experiences of non-ordinary states of consciousness. They should, however, be exposed to transpersonal theory as it is possible that their clients may have such experiences and that these experiences should be recognized for possibly being spiritual experiences. It is advisable that trainee psychologists have some sessions of Holotropic breathwork if they feel ready and if it is something they feel they want to have more advanced training in. Advanced training and qualification in Holotropic breathwork would have to be outside of the university context, but initial exposure to transpersonal theory and practice could take place in the M1 year of study.

Conclusion

This chapter has highlighted the phenomenon of globalized psychotherapy, a history spanning decades. It has indicated that psychotherapy has achieved a status that enables it to be a profession practised by trained professionals who recognize its potential as a powerful process of psychological and emotional healing and transformation. It is, therefore, an evidence-based profession that seeks to alleviate mental distress. There are many modalities of psychotherapy that have emerged in the past 80 years. In more recent decades, less well-known therapies have emerged that are more body-focused and bypass the traditional idea of talking cure.

Psychotherapy training has existed in South Africa for decades, but it has a dark history. Typical current discussion regarding training involves the relevancy of Western models of mind and psychotherapy, poor mental health service delivery, the inequality of those who can access therapy and those who cannot, as well as selection processes and curriculum development. With a focus on training that must accommodate multiple cultures, it becomes imperative to find and train students in a diverse range of psychotherapies for a diverse range of clients. While African psychology and concepts of mental illness and treatment are less in the wings of the stage that is curriculum development, I think there is also room for much more. I would like to see trainee psychologists exposed to transpersonal approaches to healing and transformation, with their rich history of research. I believe it will expand their understanding and knowledge of the human psyche, the human capacity for healing and human spiritual experiences that can facilitate personal growth.

References

Álvarez-Iglesias, A., Garman, E., & Lund, C. (2021). Effects of COVID-19 on the economy and mental health of young people in South Africa: Opportunities for strengthening social protection programmes by integrating mental health. *South African Journal of Psychology, 51*(2), 199–204. https://doi.org/10.1177/00812463211015348

Bloom, J., Lachman, A., Gaxo, E., Pillay, J., & Seedat, S. (2022). Child, adolescent, and caregiver mental health difficulties and associated risk factors early in the COVID-19 pandemic in South Africa. *Child & Adolescent Psychiatry & Mental Health, 16*(1), 1–14.

Cooper, S. (2014). A synopsis of South African psychology from apartheid to democracy. *American Psychologist, 69*, 837–847. https://doi.org/10.1037/a0037569

Cooper, S., & Nicholas, L. (2012). An overview of South African psychology. *International Journal of Psychology, 47*, 89–101.

Cooper, S., Nicholas, L. J., Seedat, M., & Statman, J. M. (1990). Psychology and apartheid. In L. J. Nicholas & S. Cooper (Eds.), *Psychology and apartheid* (pp. 1–21). Madiba.

Dawes, A. (1985). Politics and mental health. *South African Journal of Psychology, 15*, 55–61.

Dawood, B., Tomita, A., & Ramlall, S. (2022). 'Unheard,' 'uncared for' and 'unsupported': The mental health impact of Covid-19 on healthcare workers in KwaZulu-Natal Province, South Africa. *PLoS One*, *17*(5), 1–17. https://doi.org/10.1371/journal.pone.0266008

De Backer, L. (2021). COVID-19 lockdown in South Africa: Addiction, Christian spirituality and mental health. *Verbum et Ecclesia*, *42*(1), 1–8. https://doi.org/10.4102/ve.v42i1.2135

De la Rey, C., & Isper, J. (2004). The call for relevance: South African psychology ten years into democracy. *South African Journal of Psychology*, *34*, 544–552. http://doi.org/10.1177/008124630403400403

De Man, J., Smith, M., Schneider, M., & Tabana, H. (2022). An exploration of the impact of COVID-19 on mental health in South Africa. *Psychology, Health & Medicine*, *27*(1), 120–130. https://doi.org/10.1080/13548506.2021.1954671

Grof, S. (2019). *The way of the psychonaut vol. 1: Encyclopedia for inner journeys.* Multidisciplinary Association for Psychedelic Studies.

Knight, Z. (2020a). Empathy as core to the development of holding and recognition: The case of Garret. *Research in Psychotherapy: Psychopathology, Process and Outcome*, *23(*2), 180–188. https://doi.org/10.4081/ripppo.2020.457

Knight, Z. G. (2002). The history, development and current trends of psychotherapy in South Africa. In A. Pritz (Ed.), *Globalized psychotherapy* (pp. 593–612). Facultas Universitatsverlag.

Knight, Z. G. (2020b). Living under lockdown in the shadow of Covid-19 pandemic in South Africa: Anxious voices from the unplanned shift to online therapy. *Research in Psychotherapy: Psychopathology, Process and Outcome*, *23*(3), 202–210. https://doi.org/10.4081/ripppo.2020.487

Long, W. (2016). On the Africanization of psychology. *South African Journal of Psychology*, *46*(4), 429–431. https://doi.org/10.1177/0081246316650853

Madu, S. (2002). Psychotherapy and African traditional healing: Attempts to cooperate and integrate. In A. Pritz (Ed.), *Globalized psychotherapy* (pp. 793–804). Facultas Universitatsverlag.

Manganyi, N. C. (2016). *Apartheid and the making of a Black psychologist: A memoir.* NYU Press.

Mayekiso, T., Strydom, F., Jithoo, V., & Katz, L. (2004). Creating new capacity through postgraduate selection. *South African Journal of Psychology*, *34*, 657–671.

Nguse, S., & Wassenaar, D. (2021). Mental health and COVID-19 in South Africa. *South African Journal of Psychology*, *51*(2), 304–313. https://doi.org/10.1177/00812463211001543

Padmanabhanunni, A., & Pretorius T. (2021). The unbearable loneliness of COVID-19: COVID-19-related correlates of loneliness in South Africa in young adults. *Psychiatry Research*, *296.* http://doi.org/10.1016/j.psychres.2020.113658.

Padmanabhanunni, A., Jackson, K., Noordien, Z., Pretorius, T., & Bouchard, J. (2022). Characterizing the nature of professional training and practice of psychologists in South Africa. *Annales Medico-Psychologiques*, *180*, 360–365.

Pillay, A. L., & Siyothula, E. T. B. (2008). The training institutions of black African clinical psychologists registered with the HPCSA in 2006. *South African Journal of Psychology*, *38*, 725–735.

Pillay, A. L., Ahmed, R., & Bawa, U. (2013) Clinical psychology training in South Africa: A call to action. *South African Journal of Psychology*, *43*(1), 46–58 https://doi.org/10 1177/0081246312474411

Pillay, A., & Kramers-Olen, A. (2014). The changing face of clinical psychology intern training: A 30-year analysis of a programme in Kwazulu-Natal, South Africa. *South African Journal of Psychology*, *44*, 364–374. https://doi.org/10.1177/0081246314535683

Pillay, A., & Barnes, B. (2020). Psychology and COVID-19: Impacts, themes and way forward. *South African Journal of Psychology*, *50*, 148–153. https://doi.org/10.1177/0081246320937684

Pillay, A., & Nyandeni, N. (2021). Is post-apartheid South Africa training more black African clinical psychologists and addressing the historical imbalance? *South African Journal of Psychology*, *51*(1), 147–157. https://doi.org/10.1177/0081246320977985

Posel, D., Oyenubi, A., & Kollamparambil, U. (2021). Job loss and mental health during the COVID-19 lockdown: Evidence from South Africa. *PLoS One*, *16*(3), 1–15. https://doi.org/10.1371/journal.pone.0249352

Pritz, A. (2002). Introduction into globalized psychotherapy. In A. Pritz (Ed.), *Globalized psychotherapy* (pp. 13–21). Facultas Universitatsverlag.

Pretorius, G. (2012). Reflections on the scope of practice in the South African profession of psychology: A moral plea for relevance and a future vision. *South African Journal of Psychology*, *42*, 509–521.

Qian, M. (2002). Psychotherapy in Asia. In A. Pritz (Ed.), *Globalized psychotherapy* (pp. 465–480). Facultas Universitatsverlag.

Schneider, M., Greif, T., Galsky, A., Gomez, D., Anderson, C., & Edwards D. (2021). Giving psychology trainees a voice during the COVID-19 pandemic: Trainee mental health, perceived safety, and support. *Training Educational Professional Psychology*, *15*, 76–85. https://doi.org/10.1037/tep0000343

Siyothula, E. (2019). Clinical psychology service distribution and integration into primary healthcare in KwaZulu-Natal, South Africa. *South African Journal of Psychology*, *49*, 391–402. https://doi.org/10.1177/0081246318815337

Southall, R. (2022). The middle class and suburbia: Desegregation towards non-racialism in South Africa? *Journal of Contemporary African Studies*, 1–15. https://doi.org/10.1080/02589001.2022.2083589

Watts, A. (1989). *The book: On the taboo against knowing who you are.* Vintage Books.

Chapter 2

From Freud's Reclining Couch to the Modern Digital Screen in South Africa

An Argument for the Adaptability of the Psychoanalytic Situation

Kgamadi Kometsi*

Department of Psychology, Faculty of Humanities, University of Johannesburg, South Africa

Abstract

The COVID-19 pandemic has forced both a reflection on and a reconsideration of how psychotherapists provide services to their patients. In particular, a reconsideration of how to provide psychoanalytic psychotherapy in this context would inevitably affect the frame. Psychoanalytic psychotherapy has always presumed the presence of the therapist and the patient in a consultation room that is uniquely set for the psychoanalytic endeavour. This chapter aims to trace the journey of psychoanalytic setting from Freud's reclining couch, through the post-Freudian setting requirements, and finally to the modern smart gadgets to which the pandemic forced the provisioning of psychoanalytic treatment specifically in South Africa. It uses Kohut's description of the analytic setting as a lens to reflect backward to Freud and forward to the COVID pandemic moment. It provides an illustration of a psychoanalytic process through a vignette reflecting a psychoanalytic process that started on a face-to-face basis and was forced into becoming a virtual consultation, where it has remained until the time of writing this chapter. The chapter also reflects on the implications of these changes both against the guidelines of the Health Professions Council of South Africa (HPCSA) on telehealth and for psychoanalytic theory as it applies to the analytic setting.

Key Words: COVID-19, digital screen, Freud, psychotherapy, therapist

Introduction: The Problematic of Treatment through Cyberspace

The different theoretical approaches on which the practice of psychotherapy is based all have guidelines as to how to conduct psychotherapy. Although there are specific differences between them, delineating each occurrence of psychotherapy accordingly, what they do have in common is the assumption that a therapist and a patient or patients will come together for the purpose of this activity. Until recently, the possibility of providing psychotherapy using

---

* Corresponding Author's Email: kkometsi@uj.ac.za

a virtual platform was unimaginable for most practitioners and their patients. This is particularly the case for psychoanalysis and psychoanalytic psychotherapy. Due to its original practice and development in Vienna, thinking about psychoanalysis always evokes images of a patient lying on a couch, facing away from the analyst, and free-associating. That this is something that could be attempted successfully on a virtual platform, with the analyst and the patient being on two different continents (Neumann, 2013), was simply beyond even the stretch of the imagination. Through the lens of the psychoanalytic setting, my main focus here is to reflect on the journey of analysis and psychotherapy from patients lying on the couch and facing away from the therapist, to patients and therapists countenancing one another through the screen of a smart device. In the first instance, and as part of the problematic raised by this transition, I explore the implications of this journey on the integrity of a psychoanalytic psychotherapeutic process, as well as the ethical considerations that apply. In the end, I use the process of one of my patients to illustrate my reflections on the viability of psychoanalytic treatment away from Freud's reclining couch more concretely. As part of this reflection, and in the section entitled 'The declaration of the process as psychoanalytic', I also make a brief reference to what about the process with this patient qualifies it as psychoanalytic psychotherapy even as it takes place via the screen of a smart device. In part, this is crucial given the challenges that Schoan et al. (2018) raise regarding possibilities and impossibilities of transference and countertransference processes as the psychoanalytic treatment begins to negotiate its encounters with technological developments.

Introducing an edited book entitled *Psychoanalysis Online*, Scharff (2013) suggests that amongst others, what motivated the offering of psychoanalysis and psychoanalytic psychotherapy on virtual platforms (in this case, she refers to the various offerings of Skype) was the mobility of persons in an increasingly globalizing world. The challenge of this mobility arose when a person who is in treatment or analysis had to relocate or travel. Instances where treatment ends up being stopped prematurely due to a patient relocating have been reported even in the early writings and articulations of the psychoanalytic theory (Klein, 1960), and clearly this is an undesirable eventuality, particularly for the well-being of the patient. Two other reasons implied in Scharf's (2013) introduction of her book are the scarcity of qualified psychotherapists or analysts away from traditional psychoanalytic centres (most of the European countries, the United Kingdom, and the United States) and the need to keep up with technological developments. Availing psychotherapy on a virtual platform under these circumstances improves the accessibility of services for patients and contributes to the psychoanalytic training of persons without requiring them to relocate in order to access the training. The advantages of finding an alternative way in which those who need to travel may still continue with their analytic process were apparent even then, at the beginning of the last two decades. The impact of the rural–urban divide and the first-world–third-world inequities on the accessibility of psychotherapy can be managed by mobilizing the use of technology. Although amongst the effects of technological developments, one may also count the exacerbation of the gap of inequality between those who can access technology and those who cannot, its potential to avail psychotherapy beyond the therapy room remains an important contribution. Other challenges and disadvantages abound too, and it is through the lens of ethical considerations that I look at these below. Some challenges, such as the differential access to technological artefacts, may be seen as structural. However, there are challenges that supports the therapist's ability to provide psychotherapy. Brahman (quoted in Schoan et al., 2018, p. 38) refers to these as *mediation artefacts* (technological glitches that manifest in virtual treatments)

Before a dedicated focus on the case material referred to above and concluding reflections on the resultant implications of its consideration, this chapter also reflects on developments impacting the psychoanalytic setting during the most acute pandemic phases of COVID-19 in South Africa. (Knight (2020) captures the facts and experiences of the 2020 lockdown most vividly.) Unlike the context of Scharf (2013) and her colleagues, shifting the treatment of patients to a virtual platform was not an option that was slowly considered and gradually applied. As will be discussed below, the COVID-19 moment forced an alternative treatment setting on the therapeutic pair.

Ethics, Security and Safety: Considerations Then

Psychotherapy, particularly psychoanalytic psychotherapy with its emphasis on creating a safe enough setting to facilitate the emergence of repressed material, requires the promise of confidentiality and privacy. During in-person consultations, it is the responsibility of the therapist to ensure confidentiality and privacy. The use of teletherapy or other virtual platforms puts at least part of the responsibility in the hands of the patient, making this a shared responsibility (Kadish, 2018). Martin (2013) recommends that a therapist should discuss the limits to confidentiality and privacy posed by virtual consultations. She says 'Be honest about the risks to privacy and confidentiality … You cannot give an absolute guarantee of privacy' (Martin, 2013, p. 79). These issues must be raised right from the onset, to ensure that the patient makes an informed decision in initiating virtual psychoanalytic treatment. Martin (2013) raises other factors as well, including reimbursement for teletherapy sessions by medical aid, billing transparently to avoid being accused of fraud, permission to treat the patient if they reside under a different professional and legal jurisdiction, and issues of access given that 'no matter how sophisticated the programme you choose may be, all computerized activities are vulnerable to failure' (79). In the instance of the latter, the extent to which the therapist will expect payment should be clear, as well as alternative ways in which the patient may reach the therapist in the event that the virtual platform of choice fails to work.

Given the focus of this chapter, for many therapists in South Africa, including me, literature on the use of technology to facilitate a session for psychoanalytically informed psychotherapy was not commonplace. The few exceptions though useful (e.g. Kadish et al., 2018) were pre-COVID-19 and during COVID-19. Contrastingly, this chapter assumes a retrospective view of the process, underlining the reality that COVID-19 imposed a need to explore alternative means to provide treatment to patients some of whom were at crucial phases of their processes. Scharf (2013, p. xix) captures the reality that we faced as therapists succinctly when she says: 'For most of us who are not experts in technology, it is hard to know what to believe, particularly when experts argue among themselves, and the various mental health professions having differing standards of practice'. I must qualify here that, unlike virtual psychoanalytic psychotherapy treatment, telemedicine has been in existence since the 1960s, initiated by the National Aeronautics and Space Administration in collaboration with the US Department of Public Health and Lockheed and the Nebraska Psychology Institute (LeRouge & Garfield, 2013). Even then, these authors reflect on the barriers against the adoption into mainstream medicine, referring to these barriers as the 'telemedicine chasm'. It is the somewhat rigid expectations relating to the psychoanalytic frame that hitherto had positioned psychoanalysis and virtual consultations as mutually exclusive. Scharf (2013, p. 61) cites Argentieri and Mehler (2003) in capturing the negative sentiment virtual platforms received from the psychoanalytic community as a vehicle for analysis: 'Some have said that any analytic work done by and analyst working with an analysand on the telephone may do some good but it cannot be analysis: it must be supportive psychotherapy'. It is to the psychoanalytic setting that I turn in a discussion below, delineating the facility of the psychoanalytic frame to change, particularly the aspect that is of particular interest for this chapter, being the psychoanalytic situation (Wolf, 1988).

The Metamorphosis of the Clinical Setting

For some practitioners of psychoanalysis, the concepts of psychoanalytic setting and psychoanalytic situation are coterminous (Stone, cited in Modell (1988) and Goldsmith, 2018)). For instance, both these authors cite Stone (1961) to define the psychoanalytic setting as 'the common and constant features of the analytic setting, procedure and personal relationship in both conscious and unconscious meanings and function'. However, for Wolf (1988), the psychoanalytic setting consists of three aspects, namely the psychoanalytic situation, psychoanalytic ambience and the psychoanalytic process. The central difference between these conceptualizations of the psychoanalytic setting is that Stone's (as cited in Modell, 1988, and Goldsmith, 2018) definition fuses what Wolf (1988) disaggregates as the psychoanalytic situation and the psychoanalytic ambience. In both conceptualizations, it is apparent that the psychoanalytic process is seen as a separate process which is nonetheless dependent on both the psychoanalytic situation and the psychoanalytic ambience. Using Wolf's (1988) conceptualization, it is specifically the psychoanalytic situation aspect of the psychoanalytic setting that I wish to reflect on adding to the argument that the psychoanalytic ambience and process (psychoanalytic endeavour) are possible notwithstanding what I believe to be constant changes of the psychoanalytic setting over time. A more specific definition of the psychoanalytic situation for purposes of this chapter derives from Wolf (1988, p. 87) and asserts as follows: 'the analyst and analysand, the arrangements of time, place, fees and other obligations and, in general, anything observable and reportable by an outside party'. By contrast, the psychoanalytic ambience and the psychoanalytic process refer to how the analyst and analysand experience the psychoanalytic situation at the subjective, intrapsychic level and the psychological changes initiated and maintained in and by both participants (Wolf, 1988), respectively.

To qualify the assertion that I made above, suggesting that the psychoanalytic endeavour survives and even thrives notwithstanding the psychoanalytic situation changes, I would need to turn to a brief discussion of the history of the psychoanalytic setting. Most literature seems to credit the origins of the psychoanalytic setting as set out by Freud to its hypnosis historical links as well as the clinical laboratory (Mayer, 2006; Goldsmith, 2018), settings where Freud worked prior to developing free association as a technique.

Historicizing the Notion of the Setting

Keeping in mind the disaggregated conceptualization of the psychoanalytic setting as proposed by Wolf (1988), where the main focus of this chapter is the psychoanalytic situation, in the ensuing historicization of the psychoanalytic setting I do not emphasize this differentiation. Instead, I only enunciate this differentiation where there is a clear conflation of the psychoanalytic situation, ambience and process. Similarly, it would seem Mayer (2006, p. 39 and p. 54, respectively) specifies the concept of the psychoanalytic situation by using phrases such as 'concrete features of the actual setting' and 'the concrete spatial setting of psychoanalytic treatment'. For this part, I rely significantly on Mayer's (2006) engagement with the concept of the psychoanalytic setting. In an article the declared aim of which is to 'elucidate [the] peculiar way of "losing" or forgetting objects or the actual material components that make up the psychoanalytic setting', Mayer (2006) traces the beginnings of what we now know as the psychoanalytic situation to a single desk on which Freud sat to engage in self-analysis. It is a well-known fact that the beginnings of the psychoanalytic theory reflect the important contribution of Freud's self-analysis. What is particularly instructive for this chapter is Mayer's (2006) suggestion that the private communication between Freud and Wilhelm Fliess represented a form of analysis, which he refers to as 'epistolary analysis'. Based on just this, it should become apparent that from the beginning, the psychoanalytic setting was not intended to be static, that its evolution has remained a constant through time, and that this evolution should not necessarily obstruct psychoanalytic data (which is different from psychological data). I discuss this differentiation further when I explore what qualifies as psychoanalytic endeavour below.

Imagining the perspective of one of Freud's first patients, Mayer (2006, pp. 37–38) creates a visual imagery of Freud's consultation room as follows:

> Roman, Greek, and Chinese antiquities, mostly sculptures were displayed in showcases or on the shelves of the library, and the portraits of Egyptian mummies and pictures of mythological scenes covered the walls. On their first visit, many patients got the impression that Freud was not a physician, but rather the curator of some off archeological museum.

Beyond this, Mayer (2006) cites Freud's letter to Fliess in 1897 which explicates that Freud carried out the analyses while walking with his patients. One could add to this the fact that Freud gave his patient (Rat Man) a meal without anticipating that this would interfere with the psychoanalytic setting (Goldsmith, 2018). As it were, it was only in 1904 that Freud articulated what has become the familiar arrangement in the psychoanalytic consultation room, including the requirement that a patient should recline on a sofa (couch). Mayer (2006) points out that the couch as an essential aspect of the psychoanalytic setting seems to have escaped scrutiny as a cultural artefact of Freud's time. The argument of this chapter is that psychoanalytic endeavour is not immune to cultural developments, including technological developments. This chapter also accepts that contestations regarding the inclusion of technology in the psychoanalytic endeavour have been part of the process from the early years of the development of psychoanalysis. (Mayer (2006) cites Freud's banning of the Zurich psychiatric clinic's and Stekel's private practice innovations of the setting, and Scharff (2013) notes challenges against availing psychoanalytic treatment on virtual platforms.)

I have discussed the psychoanalytic setting above as that which relates to analysis. Although there are some important differences between what constitutes analysis and psychoanalytic psychotherapy, e.g. the use of the couch, frequency of sessions and relative activity of the analyst or therapist (Goldsmith, 2018) or both, the psychoanalytic setting is of significant importance and plays a similar role. In psychoanalytic psychotherapy, the patient and the therapist tend to sit face to face, whereas the use of the couch specifically is associated with analysis. Wolf (1988) suggests that some analysts conduct productive analysis in face-to-face encounters. He states that self-psychologically oriented psychoanalysts tend to use face-to-face encounters and patients reclining on the couch in combination, depending on the psychoanalytic process for the patient at a given time (e.g. regression, intensive clinical work). These developments and variations in conceptualizing the psychoanalytic setting illustrate its dynamism, even as the goal of providing effective treatment to the patient remains central.

I have labelled the changes and challenges in conceptualizing the psychoanalytic setting as being akin to a metamorphosis, only to the extent that they relate to the *psychoanalytic situation* as articulated by Wolf (1988) or the concrete spatial setting of psychoanalytic treatment according to Mayer (2006). From analysis being possible as a solitary process (self-analysis), to the epistolary analysis enabled by private correspondence between Freud and Fliess, through to the reclining couch at the close of the 19th century, and now possibilities enabled by technological developments and the experience of the COVID-19 pandemic: the change is as metamorphic as it is phenomenal. However, the appreciation hereof does not throw caution to the wind given the centrality and significance of the psychoanalytic setting as a whole, to the psychoanalytic endeavour. Goldsmith (2018) highlights the risk of paying too little attention to the psychoanalytic setting and treating it as just a basic arrangement for treatment to occur 'without much further meaning in and of itself' (p. 1). He suggests that initially Freud did not elaborate on this important concept, assuming that for 'classical patients' the psychoanalytic situation specifically need not become the focus of the treatment. In the end, Freud did elaborate on this concept, a process that was continued by other thinkers due to experience with patients who challenged or breached the psychoanalytic setting, underlining its clinical significance in its own right.

A Note on the COVID-19 Moment and Ethics in South Africa and the HPCSA Ethical Guidelines

Recent experiences with the COVID-19 pandemic shocked the world and exposed the fragilities of protections we take for granted, including those that are promised by national health systems in the case of South Africa (Rispel et al., 2021). Prior to the detection of the first case of COVID-19 in South Africa in March 2020 (Van Deventer, 2020), the growing incidence of COVID-19 in China and Europe then did not evoke proactive action aimed at fighting a pandemic in South Africa. It would seem that the country was seduced into a feeling of false security, given that other pandemics (e.g. Ebola, H1N1) did not impact South Africa in a manner that required changes that we came to see in the case of COVID-19. The COVID-19 moment in South Africa was characterized by the government declaring a National State of Disaster, imposing a total lockdown on the country, with progressive relaxations and tightening of lockdown restrictions over time as influenced by the intensity of the spread of the virus. Although the provisioning of health services, including psychotherapy, was exempted from the lockdown measures, such measures were still seen as amongst the strictest globally (Van Deventer, 2020). The healthcare system in South Africa was ill-prepared for the changes required by the reality of the devastating virus at the time. Medical aid companies (medical insurance) gave mixed responses to whether they would fully fund treatment conducted via virtual platforms, prompting the Council for Medical Schemes to issue a circular encouraging these companies to fund telemedical consultations (or psychotherapy on virtual platforms) appropriately, to avoid overcharging patients and to not apply a blanket termination policy on those who are not able to pay for medical aid (Circular 25 of 2020).

The Health Professions Council of South Africa approved guidelines for telemedicine in 2014 (HPCSA Booklet No. 10). However, in the wake of the COVID-19 pandemic, certain accommodations had to be explicated. For instance, the HPCSA defines telemedicine as follows in Booklet 10: *The practice of medicine using electronic communications, information technology or other electronic means between a healthcare practitioner in one location and a healthcare practitioner in another location for the purpose of facilitating, improving, and enhancing clinical, educational and scientific healthcare and research, particularly to the under serviced areas in the Republic of South Africa.* As may be appreciated, the guidelines applied to the medical field (and not to psychology or psychotherapy), and permission was restricted to communication between two healthcare practitioners, and not between a practitioner at one location and a patient unaccompanied by another healthcare practitioner at another location. In essence, the Telemedicine guidelines prohibited routine virtual consultations. During the COVID-19 moment in South Africa, the following changes were made: 'Telemedicine' was changed to 'Telehealth' in order to accommodate Telemedicine, Telepsychology, Telepsychiatry and Telerehabilitation. For Telemedicine, this permission applies only to already-established doctor–patient relationships and is discouraged for new patients. This qualification does not apply to Telepsychology and Telepsychiatry. These permissions stand to be reviewed at the end of the COVID-19 pandemic. Additionally, the overarching responsibilities of practitioners during the COVID-19 moment include adhering to established standards as far as it is practical; departing from established procedures responsibly, reasonably, and in the best interests of patients; and lastly, practising within the scope of practice except for in emergency situations (HPCSA Booklet 10, & HPCSA Communication to practitioners, 26 March 2020). These are the broad conditions under which I undertook the treatment of a patient as discussed below. The chapter thus far suggests that in addition to misgivings that some psychotherapists and analysts have regarding psychoanalytic treatment on virtual platforms, this work has to consider applicable ethical guidelines as well, which change in line with societal forces such as the pandemic of COVID-19 in this case. The chapter explicates both the COVID-19 moment as described above and applicable ethical prescriptions and accommodations to provide a context within which the provision of psychotherapy on virtual platforms and considerations for the psychoanalytic setting articulated themselves in South Africa. The overview of the treatment process discussed below elucidates these articulations

Psychoanalytic Treatment on a Virtual Platform

My patient (named *Thabiso*[1] *(T)* for this chapter) was a mid-thirties adult male whose parents had translocated to Johannesburg from the rural Eastern Cape when he was still a baby, joining other paternal family members that had moved to Johannesburg earlier. His stated reason for seeking therapy was that his process with another therapist had reached a plateau, in part due to cultural differences. He reported that he found himself spending time in his sessions explaining content that related to his culture, and thereby felt he was not being understood. T also referred to his experience of a racially mixed school, and the impact that race had on his life, including at

1 Permission was obtained from the client to use the pseudonym – Thabiso – for the case material described in this chapter.

his previous workplaces. T had a disrupted caregiving surround due to parental conflict and his father's drinking and subsequent abandonment of his family home. His mother held a leadership role in the local municipality and was respected and admired by the community, including T's friends. T, on the other hand, felt detached from his mother and did not feel he was cared about for himself.

When he commenced therapy with me, both his parents had passed away and there had been efforts at mending the relationship with his mother prior to her passing on. Such an opportunity was not available with his father, who had passed away when T was still much younger. He had undergone treatment for substance abuse following a long period of abuse since adolescence, and therefore, part of the treatment was to provide support for his recovery. Before the substance abuse treatment, he had engaged in behaviour that he acknowledged as having been self-destructive and dangerous while under the influence of the substance. It was only in the second session that T revealed that he had been sexually abused as a child. When the COVID-19 moment happened at the beginning of 2020, T had completed 24 weekly sessions with me, extending over eight months (inclusive of the end of the year break).

Sexual Abuse and Thoughts About the Suitability of Virtual Treatment

Intuitively, I would have felt that providing psychotherapy to a patient who had suffered childhood sexual abuse over a virtual platform would be contra-indicated. This is more the case if the conceptualization of the treatment is psychoanalytic with the anticipated increase in distress as the process continues to elucidate the defences (Malan, 1990) and the original trauma behind them. I derived cautious comfort from the reflection that I had seen the patient for a number of sessions when the reality of COVID-19 imposed a reconsideration of how we continued the treatment. Consequently, I believed that the working relationship had been established reasonably well and that it would contain the transition adjustment challenges adequately. Further reflections on this in hindsight suggest that transitions from in-person consultations to virtual platforms are possible. Bakalar (2013) reports an instance where after two years of psychoanalytic psychotherapy she recommended a switch from in-person consultation to telephone therapy, and with that, a switch from psychoanalytic psychotherapy to analysis proper (over the phone) four times a week. In regard to sexual abuse specifically, Schaffer (2013) quotes Zalusky (2005) to endorse the suitability of virtual consultations with severely traumatized patients on the basis that 'the telephone may allow a necessary space in which they can begin to tackle the fears associated with intimacy' (p. 71). This might have been true of my patient T as well, but in addition, the convenience and familiarity of his own home as part of the psychoanalytic situation provided a much-needed place of safety, from which to engage in his own treatment. It is important noting that my intuitive thoughts about child sexual abuse as contra-indicated for treatment on a virtual platform were informed by the clinical picture of child sexual abuse that we know. Sexual abuse has a debilitating effect on the victim, and amongst the symptoms that T presented with, in which Parker and Turner (2013, citing Kendall-Tacket, 1993) lists, the following could readily be identified: aggressive or disturbed behaviour, depression, self-harm (self-destructive behaviour), substance misuse and relationship problems. Some of these effects were discernible only in his history and did not form part of the current presentation (e.g. substance abuse and self-destructive behaviour).

The Declaration of the Process as Psychoanalytic

I pause here to provide an outline of what qualifies T's treatment as psychoanalytic, emphasizing the severity of psychological harm caused by sexual abuse, and the need for an ongoing sense of safety to facilitate some alleviation of attendant symptoms. I believe there are different ways in which a process may be declared as psychoanalytic. I raise a few points below, in no exhaustive manner, but enough to delineate the psychoanalytic aspects of the treatment process with T. Bearing in mind the criticism by Argentieri and Mehler (2003, cited in Scharff, 2013, p. 61) that 'treatment done by an analyst working with an analysand on the telephone may do some good, but it cannot be analysis: it must be supportive psychotherapy', I disagree with this criticism firstly because even at the point of conceptualization, the debilitating effect of child sexual abuse suggests that a sense of safety will be cardinal for the victim, with the associated feelings of being damaged and ashamed. Getting to a place where firstly an acknowledgement to self that the abuse happened would require enormous effort at providing a safe enough environment, where feelings of self-blame may also be dealt with. A part of what T was looking for in changing therapists and commencing the process with me might have been about a search for this safety. According to Kohut's psychology of the self, T might have been searching for an essential alikeness (even only as perceived based on the common racial and gender identities), which, given the unresolved nature of the impact of sex abuse on him, would be a primitive self-object need. Wolf (1988) refers to this self-object need as the alter ego need. Entrusting the secret that T had borne from his early childhood to a space where he felt 'being misunderstood' at an extra-verbal level of expression would be unlikely, if at all. In quoting Rycroft (1985), Modell's (1988, p. 584) description of psychoanalytic treatment (including over a virtual platform) is instructive:

> psychoanalytic treatment is not so much a matter of making the unconscious conscious, or of widening and strengthening the ego, as of providing a setting in which healing can occur and connections with previously repressed, split-off and lost aspects of the self can be re-established. And the ability of the analyst to provide such a setting depends not only on his skill in making 'correct interpretations' but also on his capacity to maintain a sustained interest in, and relationship with, his patients.

Breaking off treatment at the onset of the COVID-19 moment would have set back the analytic process for T, specifically because I hypothesize that having completed a rehabilitation programme prior to commencing therapy with me, he had taken care of one manifestation of the impact of his trauma of abuse and was well on track to continue with the process of healing by allowing himself to countenance what had happened to him and the cost of his survival up to that point. Despite his readiness, it still had to be a safe space for him to dare try to access the reaches of his inner life from a different vantage point. Continuing treatment over a virtual platform enabled my ongoing empathic immersion into my patient, frequently, over a long period of time, allowing for the acquisition of access to the patient's inner life (Wolf, 1988).

The Three Main Phases of the Treatment Process

At the point of writing this chapter, I had seen T for over a period of three years, at a frequency of once a week, until recently where in acknowledgement of the significant changes that have taken place, the frequency dropped to once every two weeks. In illustrating the unfolding of the psychoanalytic process with T from an in-person process and its continuation on a virtual platform, I have divided the phases of his treatment into three main parts, excluding the latter part which I will discuss separately.

The first part may be referred to as the *in-person pre-COVID-19 phase*. As stated above, the first session dealt with T's personal and family history, and it was in the second session where T revealed the sexual abuse by a family member, without providing any further details about it. The impact that this had on the process was a sense that the secret was being dropped as if to eject it into my care even as I had no further information about it except for 'I was sexually abused as a young child'. In subsequent sessions and talking around what we had come to call 'the secret', T expressed that he wished it had been 'just an irritation' dreading to talk any further about it, but also fantasizing about the implications of not talking about the impact of the sexual abuse that he had carried on his own for over two decades. He had not talked to anyone about 'the secret' until when he entrusted it to me. In a later session, T acknowledged that he needed to check the safety of the therapeutic relationship before exploring 'the secret' any further, expressing the fear that talking about it might lead to family disintegration and that it might lead to him acting out in ways he could not imagine. Towards the middle of this phase, which spanned a total of 24 sessions, T indicated that he was ready to talk about 'the secret' adding to the picture his sense that some in the family might have had knowledge of what had happened to him, a view that he continued to refrain from exploring until the end of this phase. Instead, T initiated a break-up with his girlfriend, recoiled inwards and engaged in behaviour that would limit interaction with others at work (wearing headphones). Through all this time, T expressed a wish that the impact of the sexual abuse should stop as contained in this question: 'Will I always be dealing with these concerns?' Part of the reason for breaking up with his girlfriend was his feeling that his needs were not responded to, while at the same time, it was clear that he held back from expressing his needs, feeling that the expression of his needs might overwhelm others. Instead, he seemed to yearn for a visceral 'hearing' of his unexpressed needs, and a tactile response to these, 'I need a hug'. One may read from this a certain degree of regression, interfering with T's experience of genital relationships as per Freud's psychosexual stages. The phase concludes with what I learned was a misinformed pursuit on my part, of getting T to express his needs so they could stand a chance of being responded to. At that point, I might have missed the communication implied by the regression, as well as T's apparent resistance in one session where he gave monosyllable responses.

At the beginning of the next phase that I will call *transitioning into virtual consultations*, I had become aware of being 'misattuned' towards the end of the first phase and had adopted Casement's (1985) notion of *learning from the patient*. T had ended the last phase having started to talk about the family that he had yearned for, in terms of both his family of origin and his family of procreation. He engaged in the mourning of the losses that robbed him of having a family he yearned for. What also stood out as a strong theme at least at the beginning of this phase was T's opting not to pursue relationships in a sense that Kohut's (1971) conceptualization of these as sources of self-object experiences implied. I chose to try and understand what this meant for T without challenging it as a reflection of his lack of faith in the capacity of relationships to respond to his needs nor as an expression of fear engendered in the fact that the length of time during which he had not had his needs met might have led to the intensification of this needs, leading to his fantasy that their expression would destroy the 'other', that his needs were un-*meet-able*. I explored the implications of solitude as a source of a cohesive, vitalized and invigorated self by reading Storr's (1988) *Solitude*. In the end, I was still convinced as

Storr (1988) indeed suggests that the capacity to be alone assumes the pre-existence of attuned, responsive relationships to enable this capacity in the first place. This phase ended with T starting a couple of relationships at different times, almost unexpectedly given his wish to pursue a cohesive self that did not involve the expression of his needs and therewith, the establishment of relationships. Was the turning away from relationships and the abdicating of the responsibility to express his needs a communication of T's fear rather than a genuine belief in embracing life alone? In hindsight, it certainly looks like this might have been the case. But more importantly, I believe by walking 'one step behind him' and not ahead of him, I might have reduced the threat of inadequacy in T, thereby answering what I believe to be his original question when he commenced treatment with me: 'Can I rely on the safety of this space?' This contributed to the commencement of the third main phase that I discuss below.

I call the third phase the *return to the secret*. The exploration of relationships that did not work led the process back to the incomplete exploration of T's feelings relating to the sexual abuse. With the one relationship, he got a sense that it had arrived at a connection that was real enough for the girlfriend to have sensed that T was withholding something that impacted the experience of the relationship. We called this 'the wall', implying that in its development, the relationship had come up against something that T was keeping away from scrutiny, even as its impact was palpable. Inevitably the relationship ceased to be fulfilling, with T appearing to opt for giving up the relationship rather than allowing his girlfriend access to what was behind 'the wall'. In what seemed to be akin to a mourning process, T started exploring who he could have been had he not been sexually abused as a child. He engaged in the exploration of what the trauma had cost him, fantasizing about being more outgoing and having a family of his own. Rage and sadness characterized this phase, with T not wanting his whole life to only be understood in terms of the abuse, as he felt this would make him appear weak (or turn him into a perpetual victim). He skipped a session towards the end of this phase, explaining that he had needed a break following the return to 'the secret'.

The Last Phase and the 'Unexpected' Resolution and New Beginnings

Conventional wisdom suggests that arriving at a point where trauma may be metabolized through representations and verbal articulations might be a good place to start imagining a resolution for the victim. T started off this phase expressing wishes to eject 'the secret' into the family, and to relocate somewhere remote and far away where he could have an opportunity to start life anew and unburdened by 'the secret'. Part of his fantasy was that he had carried the impact of 'the secret' on his own for decades and that it was the perpetrator's turn to feel its impact and to answer questions. In earlier phases, T had mobilized the idea of a family romance (Verges, 1999), both relating to the family of origin and the family of procreation, to shore up a subjective reality that was receding. The recession of his subjective reality was particularly activated by his perception that the perpetrator lived life unaffected by the trauma inflicted on T. Phantasies of revenge, escape and starting a life unburdened with the impact of the trauma of sexual abuse hardly represent the expected resolution of trauma. However, what was equally unexpected was a genuine satisfaction with having talked about the abuse with me in this process, and not wishing to extend revealing 'the secret' to any other person further. There is no evidence that talking about it beyond this point and also facing the perpetrator would guarantee a better outcome. This is where T felt he had attained enough progress to want to start living.

To this end, he had reprocessed the idea of escaping to a faraway remote town and had come to an understanding that what he really wanted was something that would resonate with his wish to start living anew in a significant way. He had been talking about buying himself a house and had started with this process at the last meeting I saw him. He wished to leave his current place, a place from which all the virtual sessions had taken place. To the extent that I was anticipating that T could have benefitted from a different way of talking about 'the secret', including with his one sibling that he was particularly close to, the apparent resolution as it turned out, felt unexpected, and yet genuine. This resonates with Verma's (2018) assertion that 'as psychotherapists it is never our task to find and answer. We might stumble across one serendipitously, which is great'. She emphasizes instead that the task of a psychotherapist is to always be aware, to think and to relate to another in a genuine and present way. This point links to what I believe to be the unpredictability of the course of psychotherapy with any patient, which I expatiate below in reference to T's treatment process.

Clinical Implications

In this process with T, I have come to appreciate even more the fact that there is no predetermined course in which a patient's process will unfold. In this context, and when T ejected 'the secret' into my care as I saw it, I felt unprepared to deal with what had to happen next. I wondered if it could have been a more familiar process if there had been a gradual build-up towards the revelation of 'the secret' which would then increase the likelihood of a catharsis-like experience for the patient when 'the secret' finally comes out. In a systematic review of studies conducted on the treatment of children and adolescents who have been sexually abused, Parker and Turner (2013) suggest that the commencement of psychotherapy tends to be a result of some personal or relationship conflict that causes distress. To the extent that these conflicts originate from past experiences and evoke anxiety and psychic pain, they would be covered with defence mechanisms, with the implication that it would require a concerted effort both from the therapist and the patient to uncover the original trauma. In the case of T, the ejection of 'the secret' (albeit without much detail and further exploration at the time) took the wind out of my sail. Faced with having to readjust to the process that did not include a build-up towards T telling about 'the secret', I had to be content with Rycroft's (1985) assertion that psychoanalytic treatment is about providing a setting in which 'healing can occur and connections with previously repressed, split-off and lost aspects of the self can be re-established' (cited in Modell, 1988, p. 584). T came to the process of seeking a safe space, and a relationship that would be both sustained and interesting. This is what I offered through the in-person sessions initially, and on the virtual platform subsequently and on the main. At the beginning of the phase dealing with the 'unexpected' resolution and new beginnings, T had a much more sobered conceptualization of relationships, characterized by the wish to get to know the other, rather than a preconceived idea that the other should coincide with. T's relation to his own needs was less terrifying for him, and the extreme fantasies of escape had attenuated. He appreciated his own limits regarding the creation of a family of origin that would be different from the family that was the site of his trauma. T had begun the process of mourning the life he could have had had he not experienced the sexual abuse trauma. Mourning the life and experience that he did not have also allowed T space to start embracing the life that was possible at present. Wolf (1988, p. 103) characterizes the end of the therapeutic process in a befitting way when he says 'we have not got much to show for our efforts, except that our patients lead fuller, more creative and more satisfying lives. And that is a lot'. Through the process both in-person and on a virtual platform, T made a modest but significant shift, occasioned by a relatively less burdened self.

Conclusion

This chapter set out to make a positive, albeit cautious, argument for a more nuanced response to providing psychoanalytic psychotherapy on virtual platforms. It focused more on the psychoanalytic situation that virtual platforms have become a part of and illustrates the viability of a psychoanalytic treatment on a virtual platform through a reflection on one patient's process. The chapter was less of a discussion of technique, which I admit could have been of equal importance. The chapter concurs with Scharff (1988) that ideally and where possible, psychoanalytic treatment should take place in-person. Both technological developments with all their implications with inequality and the emergency-like conditions of the COVID-19 moment in South Africa compel psychoanalytic practitioners to reexamine the ideal of in-person treatment as sacrosanct and unchangeable for 'proper' psychoanalytic treatment to take place. Mayer's (2006) genealogical reflection on the concept of the psychoanalytic setting (of which the psychoanalytic situation is a part) provides strong evidence that the psychoanalytic setting was never cast in stone; instead, it has responded and absorbed aspects of the cultural developments of the time and place in which psychoanalytic treatment is provided. The all-familiar psychoanalytic couch is a cultural artefact the inclusion of which in the psychoanalytic situation requires further exploration. Psychoanalytic treatment over a virtual platform, especially where there has been prior in-person as was the case in the treatment of T, points to both the survival of the 'play within play' characteristic of psychoanalytic treatment, and the unique relationship or object tie that develops only in a setting where the psychotherapist and the patient meet for the purpose of psychoanalytic treatment. I conclude by quoting a part of Mayer's (2013, p. xix) introduction to the seminal work on psychoanalysis online that she contributed with her colleagues: 'We certainly want to do no harm, and so we cannot afford to have false confidence in the privacy of the virtual setting. Yet we do not want to deny our patients access to care and continuity when they must travel or relocate'. Knight (2020) writes about 'new anxieties' that her patients presented with during a process that was forced onto a virtual space not by travel or relocation, a process that nonetheless continued, these challenges notwithstanding. I add to this that continuing psychoanalytic treatment under the conditions of a pandemic like COVID-19 in South Africa, the extant socio-economic inequalities, the distance from the main psychoanalytic centres, and the ethical prescriptions and accommodations that apply in this context accentuates the need to view technological artefacts with caution, but also with less suspicion.

References

Bakalar, N. L. (2013). Transition from in-person psychotherapy to telephone psychoanalysis. In J. S. Scharff (Ed.), *Psychoanalysis online* (pp.103–118). London: Routledge.

Casement, P. (1985). *On learning from the patient*. London: Routledge.

Council for Medical Schemes: Circular 25 of 2020: COVID-19 lockdown measures. Retrieved from https://www.google.com/search?q=Council+for+Medical+Schemes%3A+Circular+25+of+2020%

3A+COVID-19+lockdown+measures&rlz=1C1GCEV_enZA862ZA862&oq=Council+for+Medical+Schemes%3A+Circular+25+of+2020%3A+COVID-19+lockdown+measures&aqs=chrome..69i57.2119j0j15&sourceid=chrome&ie=UTF-8 Accessed October 11, 2022.

Goldsmith, G. N. (2018) Retrieved from https://nanopdf.com/download/the-therapeutic-setting-in-psych-oanalysis-and-psychotherapy_pdf Accessed September 30, 2022.

Health Professions Council of South Africa. (2014). General Ethical Guidelines for Good Practice in Telemedicine. Retrieved from https://docs.mymembership.co.za/docmanager/editor/34/UserFiles/hpcsa%20booklet%20general%20ethical%20guidelines%20for%20good%20practice%20in%20telemedicine.pdf Accessed July 15, 2022.

Health Professions Council of South Africa. (2020) Guidance on the Application of Telemedicine Guidelines During COVID-19 Pandemic. Retrieved from https://www.psyssa.com/wp-content/uploads/2020/03/APPLICATION-OF-TELEMEDICINE-GUIDELINES-FINAL-1-002.pdf Accessed August 15, 2022.

Kadish, Y., Schoan, J., Green, J., Hanson, S., & Kuhn, J. (2018). Psychotherapy in the age of technology: The ethical challenges of online treatments for South African clinicians. *Psycho-analytic Psychotherapy in South Africa, 26*(1), 30–53.

Klein, M. (1960). *The psychoanalysis of children.* New York: Grove Press.

Knight, Z. (2020). Living under lockdown in the shadow of the COVID-19 pandemic in South Africa: Anxious voices from the unplanned shift to online therapy. *Research in Psychotherapy: Psychopathology, Process and Outcome, 23*, 202–210.

Kohut, H. (1971). *The analysis of the self: A systematic approach to the psychoanalytic treatment of narcissistic personality disorders.* International Universities Press.

LeRouge, C., & Garfield, M. J. (2013). Crossing the telemedicine chasm: Have the U.S. barriers to widespread adoption of telemedicine been significantly reduced? *International Journal of Research in Public Health, 10*(12), 6472–6484.

Malan, D. H. (1990). *Individual psychotherapy and the science of psychodynamics.* London: Butterworth.

Martin, A. C. (2013). Legal, clinical, and ethical issues in teletherapy. In J. S. Scharff (Ed.), *Psychoanalysis Online* (pp. 75–84). London: Karnac Books.

Mayer, A. (2006). Lost objects: From laboratories of hypnosis to the psychoanalytic setting. *Science in Context, 19*(1), 37–64.

Modell, A. H. (1988). The centrality of the psychoanalytic setting and the changing aims of treatment. *The Psychoanalytic Quarterly, 57*(4), 577–596.

Neuman, D. A. (2013). The frame for psychoanalysisin cyberspace. In J. S. Scharff (Ed.), *Psychoanalysis Online,* (pp. 171–182). London: Karnac Books.

Parker, B. & Turner, W. (2013). Psychoanalytic/psycho-dynamic psychotherapy for children and adolescents who have been sexually abused: A systematic review. *Campbell Systematic Reviews, 9*(1), i–158.

Rispel, L. C., Marshall, C., Matiwane, B., & Tenza, I. S. (2021). Innovations, contestations and fragilities of the health system response to COVID-19 in the Gauteng Province of South Africa. *PLos One, 16*(12), e0261339.

Scharff, J. S. (2013). Clinical issues in analysis over the telephone and the internet. In J. S. Scharff (Ed.), *Psychoanalysis online*, (pp. 61–74). London: Karnac Books.

Scharff, J. S. (2013). Introduction. In J. S. Scharff (Ed.), *Psychoanalysis online*, (pp. xvii–xxi). London: Karnac Books.

Schoan, J., Kadish, Y., Green, J., Hanson, S., & Kuhn, J. (2018). Psychotherapy in the age of technology: The ethical challenges of online treatments for South African clinicians. *Psycho-analytic Psychotherapy in South Africa, 26*(1), 30–53.

South Africa's Response to Covid-19 pandemic. https://a2ii.org/en/blog/south-africas-response-to-the-covid19-response.

Storr, A. (1988). *Solitude*. London: Fontana Paperbacks.

Verges, F. (1999). *The family romance of French colonialism and metissage*. Durham: Duke University Press.

Verma, M. (2018). Screen relations: The limits of computer-mediated psychoanalysis and psychotherapy. *Psychoanalytic Psychotherapy.* https://doi.org/10.1080/02668734.1440457

Wolf, E. S. (1988). *Treating the self – Elements of clinical self psychology.* New York: The Guilford Press.

Chapter 3

A Phenomenological Case Study on the Efficacy of Somatic Experiencing (SE) as a Treatment Model for Adult Survivors of Child Maltreatment

Consideration for Teaching Body-Based Trauma Therapies to Trainee Psychologists

Tshepo Tlali*

Department of Psychology, Faculty of Humanities, University of Johannesburg, South Africa

Abstract

The landscape of psychology has changed pointedly over the past decades. Globally, the need to cultivate short-term and responsive therapeutic interventions for a variety of mental health issues remains an integral part of any robust psychotherapy. For over a century, the conventional model of psychotherapy treatment of psychological distress remains the 'talking therapies'. By comparison, body-based psychotherapy with its numerous branches has an equally long but perhaps more controversial past. One such branch of body psychotherapy is the somatic experiencing (SE) model, which endeavours to link the mind–body gap that diffuses binary therapies. Using phenomenological case study methods, the author shall endeavour to demonstrate the effectiveness of the SE therapeutic model as an efficient psychotherapeutic treatment for adult survivors of childhood maltreatment. South Africa's astonishingly high incidents of interpersonal violence call for an ongoing transformation of outmoded ways of treating traumatic stress emanating from all forms of trauma. It is the broad aim of this chapter to serve as an introduction to SE therapy within the South African context, particularly in relation to the treatment of adult survivors of childhood maltreatment.

Key Words: body-based therapies (somatic therapies), emotional, sexual, sexual abuse, trauma psychotherapy

Introduction

Conventional treatment of psychological distress in Western cultures has historically been associated with methodologies related to dialogue and talk therapies (Cloitre et al., 2011). More

* Corresponding Author's E-mail: ttlali@uj.ac.za

specifically, the therapeutic interventions commonly used rely strongly on the patient's ability to express their distress and their dysfunction. Over the years, there has been steady acknowledgement and growth of body-based (also known as somatic therapies) psychotherapy with its numerous branches (Carroll, 2014; Epstein, 2014; Ogden et al., 2006; and Sigurdardottir & Halldorsdorsdottir, 2018). These alternative approaches to psychological treatment have been termed complementary and alternative methods (CAMs)[1] in recent literature. These include (but are not limited to) mind–body approach therapies, including somatic experiencing (SE) (Payne et al., 2015; Brom et al., 2017), brainspotting (Fuzicawa, 2015; Hildebrand et al., 2017; Marx, 2020), eye movement desensitization reprocessing (EMDR) (Tarquinio, 2021; Rothschild, 2003), media-focused expressive therapies, and mindfulness and psychedelic-assisted therapy (Desai et al., 2012, 2013). Although various studies have been conducted on CAMs, there is a paucity of research on the efficacy of body-based therapies when it comes to the treatment of developmental (complex) trauma (Anderson et al., 2017; Brom et al., 2017). This glaring gap in the use and application of body-based therapies can be attributed to the fact that most of the clinical and counselling psychology training programmes (both in South Africa and in Western countries) do not teach these alternative trauma treatment methods. Although most studies have found somatic therapies to be highly effective with acute stress disorder and posttraumatic stress disorder (PTSD) as well as with dissociative disorders (Kuhfub et al., 2021; McMahon, 2017; Reuille-Dupont, 2020; Winblad et al., 2018), most psychologists in South Africa remain ill-equipped and reticent to use most of these alternative trauma treatment models to treat patients presenting with an assortment of trauma-related disorders.

Current Trauma Models Used in the South African Context

The body and emotions are intimately related to each other since an alteration of the emotions can cause physical pain, and vice versa. Not all psychologically traumatized patients can benefit from the conventional trauma interventions (that tend to focus on emotional catharsis and cognitive processing of the trauma memories) as some of the patients experience these models as too intrusive, retraumatizing and emotionally trained (Masson et al., 2016). Yet most professional training institutions do not incorporate teaching of somatic therapies as one of the models for trauma treatments. Due to multiple shortcomings of psychotherapy therapeutic intervention with severely traumatized patients, most of these patients suffer variable residuals and complications of the unresolved trauma that is mostly stuck and/or trapped in the bodies and in the senses (Beethoven de Haan et al., 2021). Furthermore, Johnson and Naidoo (2017) asserted that due to high stress levels and burnout among high-risk and trauma-affected patients, most of these patients seek alternative trauma treatment models that are less retraumatizing and perhaps that are more suitable to them. There is a glaring gap in the scholarly body of work on the psychological treatment of childhood maltreatment or developmental trauma in the adult population (Beethoven de Haan et al., 2021). This dearth of the scholarly and empirical body of work relating to body-based therapies mirrors the non-teaching of these trauma treatment models in most clinical and counselling psychology training programmes in South Africa. The few academic written work on body-based

1 Complementary and alternative medicine (CAM) is a group of diverse medical and healthcare systems, therapies and products that are not presently considered to be part of conventional medicine (Barnes et al., 2002: 54).

psychotherapy includes the two Psychology Honours essays (Zentgraf, 2018; Marx, 2020) that I have supervised and one doctoral thesis by Silva (2018), whose thesis employed SE and logotherapy to explore how unresolved trauma contributes towards stuckness within intrapersonal and interpersonal relationships. Of these Psychology Honours essays, Heinrich Reinhard Zentgraf (2018) wrote his research essay on the introduction to SE therapy in the South African context, specifically investigating the SE application to patients suffering from PTSD. On the other hand, Zandrea Marx (2020) explored the application and the effectiveness of brainspotting with patients diagnosed with complex PTSD. The findings of these two essays were significant and revealed a positive and high efficacy of these body-based treatment models with both traumatic stress disorders, namely PTSD and Complex posttraumatic stress disorder (CPTSD). Notwithstanding, the lack of scholarly research, including empirical research on body-based psychotherapies, there are a handful of psychotherapists who are trained and are competent in a variety of alternative individual psychological trauma treatment models such as mindfulness (meditation, progressive relaxation techniques and yoga (Masson et al., 2016)), brainspotting (Grand, 2013), SE (Levine, 2010) and EMDR (Grand, 2011; Tarqunio et al., 2020). Often time, most psychotherapists in the South African context tend to treat their patients using cognitive processing theories due to the perceived unorthodox nature of these alternative treatment models (Marx, 2020). According to van Rooyen (2016), some of the most used individual trauma treatment modalities that are used with individuals who have experienced trauma include the following:

- Cognitive behavioural therapy (CBT) and trauma-focused cognitive behaviour therapy
- Exposure therapy (ET)
- Narrative exposure therapy
- EMDR therapy
- Psychodynamic trauma therapy

In addition to cognitive processing trauma models, several trauma treatment models tend to focus on debriefing models of traumatized individuals, grief and PTSD (Edwards, 2005; Kaminer & Eagle, 2010). The skewed attention given to teaching and developing acute trauma models for trauma individuals is understandable due to the high prevalence rates of interpersonal trauma in the South African context (Gouws, 2021; Ramafoko, 2020). To this end, Eagle (1998) proposed an integrative trauma treatment model for traumatized individuals while Edwards (2005) developed a model for treating PTSD. Furthermore, several individual trauma interventions are used with traumatized individuals in the South African context, and these include narrative trauma therapy (de la Porte & Ndzeku, 2016), strength-based trauma interventions, an integrated approach (Masson et al., 2016) and the University of the Witwatersrand (WITS) trauma treatment model (Eagle, 1998).

The Aims

Given the reported successes of CAM treatment models with both acute trauma and dissociative disorders, by using a case study research method, this chapter argues for the incorporation of CAMs in the clinical practice of psychology and in the graduate training programmes for psychologists in South Africa. To respond to the observation asserted above, the author aims to demonstrate the effectiveness of SE as a form of body-base therapy in the treatment of adult child maltreatment survivors. Not only is it evident that the research on CAMs is rapidly expanding but also that the integration into professional psychological practice is becoming a common practice (Cayton et al., 2014; Wynn, 2015). One such branch of body therapy, somatic psychology, endeavours to link the mind–body gap that diffuses binary therapies that were created by the lineage of Cartesian dualism (Dika, 2020; Thibaut, 2018). In this equation of dichotomous orientation of psychotherapy as a vehicle for the treatment of psychological disorders, the human body seems to be completely neglected (Anderson et al., 2017).

Somatic Experiencing

Somatic experiencing (SE) is a form of resiliency-focused body-oriented psychotherapy founded and developed by Peter Levine more than 45 years ago. It is the product of decades' worth of interdisciplinary research and clinical application in psychology, medical biophysics, neuroscience, healing practices and the physiology of stress, which ultimately adapts a psychobiological approach to treat traumatic stress and related symptoms (Winblad et al., 2018). SE differs starkly from traditional therapies, which attempt to elicit affective transformation through 'talk therapy', by focusing on a somatic method with the purpose of addressing dysregulation within the autonomic nervous system (ANS) (Payne, 2015a). SE's therapeutic approaches focus on the psychophysiological consequences of the traumatic event, and it aims to achieve this by using "felt sense" or interoceptive cues by the patient, which act as a "map" to unresolved traumatic experiences (Brom et al., 2017; Kuhfub et al., 2021). That is, during therapy, the SE practitioner (SEP) will use physiological clues to afford their patients to track and evoke the completion of previously incomplete survival responses related to a traumatic event, thereby inducing the patient's ANS to restabilize (Payne et al., 2015b). This way of treating trauma that also encompasses targeting early experiences of that trauma that are stuck in the ANS is referred to as a bottom-up approach to trauma treatment because it addresses somatic symptoms of trauma that affect the central nervous system (Ogden et al., 2006; Zandberg et al., 2017). According to Levine and Frederick (1997) and Price and Hooven (2018), the natural trauma adaptation (including dissociation, PTSD) originate from a permanent overreaction of the innate stress system due to the overwhelming character of the traumatic event. SEPs argue that in traumatic situations, people are unable to complete the initiated psychological and physiological defence reaction, and this leads to persistent somatic and emotional dysregulation of the nervous system.

Therefore, the primary goal of SE is to modify the trauma-related stress response (Kuhfub et al., 2021). To achieve this, SE's major interventional strategy builds on bottom-up processing. This means that the client's attention is directed to internal sensations both visceral (interoception[2]) and musculoskeletal (proprioception[3] and kinaesthesis[4]), rather than primarily cognitive or emotional experiences, which is in direct contrast with the top-down trauma treatment

2 Interoception refers to the detection and perception of signals from the inner body (Brom et al., 2017; Payne et al., 2015a).

3 Perception or awareness of the position and movement of the body. Proprioception, also referred to as kinaesthesia, is the sense of self-movement, force and body position. It is sometimes described as the 'sixth sense'. Proprioception is mediated by proprioceptors, mechanosensory neurons located within muscles, tendons and joints (Payne et al., 2015a).

4 Kinaesthesis refers to the sensation by which bodily position, weight, muscle tension, and movement are perceived (Payne et al., 2015a).

models. In doing so, patients are trained to gradually reduce the arousal associated with the traumatic event by increasingly tolerating the inner physical sensations and related emotions that were previously intolerable and activating. Simultaneously, the ability to gradually tolerate the felt sense of trauma is helpful in activating the internal and external resources, such as identifying parts of the body or visual or auditory memories that are associated with a positive and reassuring feeling (Silva, 2014; Ogden et al., 2006). The resulting increase in interoceptive and proprioceptive awareness leads to 'discharge process' after which trauma-related activation is resolved (Brom et al., 2017; Payne et al., 2015a). Furthermore, unlike cognitive and behavioural therapeutic, specifically exposure-based intervention, SE therapeutic intervention deliberately shuns direct and intense evocation of traumatic memories instead it focuses on renegotiation and modifying the client's traumatic stress related to the trauma in an adaptive and holistic manner (Levine, 1997, 2010). As mentioned above, SE is based on a generalized psychophysiological model of resilience (Levine, 1997). Thus, the psychophysiological dysregulation that occurs in a traumatic situation tends to be associated with many other psychological disorders such as panic disorder, dissociation, depression, PTSDs and somatic symptom disorders. In this way, the bottom-up approach aims to promote patients' ability for self-regulation, thereby contributing to stress reduction and an improvement in trauma symptoms. Levine (2010; p. 74) outlined nine steps in SE and has emphasized that the first three steps are important to follow sequentially to establish a stable foundation for later work with the patient's trauma.

1. Establish an environment of relative safety.
2. Support initial exploration and acceptance of sensation.
3. Establish 'pendulation'[5] and 'containment' – likened to the innate power of rhythm.
4. Use titration to create increasing stability, resilience and organization. Titration is about carefully touching into the smallest "drop" of survival-based arousal, and other difficult sensations, to prevent retraumatization.
5. Provide a corrective experience by supplanting the passive response of collapse and helplessness with active, empowered and defensive responses.
6. Uncouple or separate the conditioned association of fear and helplessness from the biologically immobility response.
7. Resolve hyperarousal states by gently guiding the "discharge" and redistribution of the vast survival energy mobilized for life-preserving action while freeing that energy to support higher-level brain functioning.
8. Engage self-regulation to restore "dynamic equilibrium"[6] and relaxed alertness.
9. Orient to the here and now, contact the environment and reestablish the capacity for social engagement.

Furthermore, SE incorporates a therapeutic technique known as the SIBAM model (Levine, 2010). This model allows the therapist to track the patient' felt experiences and here-and-now emotional and physical (behavioural) sensations as informed by the "*bottom-up*" processing framework (Silva, 2014). The SIBAM model stands for Sensation, Imagery, Behaviour, Affect,

---

5 Pendulation – The technique of moving from a resource, which promotes relaxation and discharge, to the experience of a small piece of traumatic material that is still upsetting. Then back and forth to make the process of trauma resolution less painful and more manageable (Heller & Heller, 2001; p. xviii).

6 Dynamic equilibrium refers to a state of balance between continuing processes.

Meaning model and is intended as a bottom-up model to allow for intimate observations of these five channels of processes (Levine, 2010; p. 139). In this model, "Sensations" involve tracking physical sensations in the body, or "interoceptive" awareness. Levine observed that these sensations arise from nerve impulses sent from the interior body to the brain stem, the most primitive part of the brain. "Imagery" prompts the therapist and the patient to observe external stimuli including sight, taste, smell, hearing and tactile sense (Levine, 2010; p. 142). The "Behaviour" component of the SIBAM model involves tracking behavioural responses by observing body language that gestures emotions, postures, autonomic signals such as heart rate and respiration, as well as internal organ sounds such as stomach gurgling, *burping and farting* (*italic my emphasis*). The "Affect" channel incorporates reading the emotional sensation of the patient through facial expressions, posture, as well as subtle nuances known as "contours of feeling" (Levine, 2010; p. 150). Lastly, the "Meaning" channel includes tracking the patient's beliefs about what their experience means to them as well as core beliefs, which are also aspects of cognitive therapies. The SIBAM model is incorporated into SE's phase-based approach as the therapist tracks the patient's behaviour during every session and phase of the therapeutic interaction to track subtle cues and responses to adjust their approach to each individual patient.

The Human Body and Childhood Maltreatment

The body and emotions are intimately related to each other since an alteration of the emotions can cause physical pain, and vice versa. In so many ways, child maltreatment (and by implication, the body of adult survivors of child maltreatment) can be likened to an abandoned archaeological site. The complex psychopathology of adults with PTSD from childhood experiences has been considered detrimental to the effectiveness of treatment (Cloitre et al., 2011). In this sense, for most patients who are adult survivors of childhood maltreatment, the enduring effects of their abuse represent the sediment of the unconscious trauma that lies deep in their bodies. The human body means different things to different people and disciplines. In the field of psychotherapy, the body represents a variety of images, including sex and erotica (Epstein, 2014; Ogden, 2014). Fuentes et al. (2017) argue that in psychoanalysis, the body is an erogenized body and it is constituted as an object for another self. Similarly, in phenomenology, the body represents the self, rather than a living body and a material body (Berndtsson, 2018). Both positions enable us to understand how this conceptualization of the body is essential in any human field. Carroll (2014) provides a variety of conceptualization of the body and assert that the body can refer to how mothers and babies communicate before talking takes place or to somatization as represented by the presence of illnesses, eating disorders and medically unexplained symptoms as well as to the myriad of feelings, sensations and impulses that emerge in the countertransference (p. 11). This conceptualization of the body resonates with Bowlby's suggestion that attachment behaviour has a survival value, which encompasses caring protection from any external threat that gets activated by conditions such as sickness, fear, anger and fatigue (White, 2014). For others, the body refers to the cultural object fought over in a political process involving power, gender, sex, human rights and aesthetics (Mbembe, 2018). Additionally, offers the following definition of the body.

> The body, as represented in the brain, may constitute the indispensable frame of reference for the neural processes we experience as mind … our very organism [the body] is used

as the ground reference for the constructions we make of the world around us and for the construction of the ever-present sense of subjectivity (p. xviii).

In recent years, there has been greater recognition of the importance of the body in psychotherapy due to the interdisciplinary dialogue and advances in neurobiology, attachment, intersubjectivity and relational psychoanalysis (Stern, 2010; Stolorow, 2001; Wachtel, 2010). For the purposes of this, I will confine my discussion of the idea of the body to the initial relationality thesis of Stephen A. Mitchell's four modes of relating as put forth in his book, *Relationality: From Attachment to Intersubjectivity* (2000). He identified the following four modes of relationality as applicable to all forms of psychotherapy. Mitchell defines them as:

- Nonreflective behaviour
- Affect permeability
- Self-other configuration
- intersubjectivity

I have adapted this framework partially to bring the *body* to live and not just as a measly representation of a proverbial abandoned archaeological site or primal scene as symbolized by either flight/fight or collapse/freeze/dissociative responses to traumatic experiences. Furthermore, since the human body holds the trauma (Ogden, 2014), I hope to demonstrate that these modes or lenses (of relating) can be used to comprehend how psychotherapists can intensify the therapeutic contact with their patients. According to Michelle, the first mode refers to the observable aspects of human behaviour in the way the patient's interaction, attitude and demeanour manifest. To elucidate this point, think of a severely traumatized patient who exhibits either the signs and symptoms of hyperactivation and/or hypoactivation as a result of past childhood maltreatment. In this intersubjectivity therapeutic space, the psychotherapists' personal movement, demeanour and communication are equally important. This mode of relating is comparable directly with embodied awareness and interaction of the two bodies that form the therapeutic dyad (Ogden, 2014). The second mode of relating encompasses the whole range of human mood and affect that is felt, explored and elaborated in therapy. Carroll (2014) likens this mode of relating to affect regulation because it includes the therapist's role in coregulation and self-regulation, conveying empathy and *tracking the patient's body* (*italics my emphasis*). Stabilizing, orienting and tracking (awareness of the patient's here-and-now over and/or under-activation) are some of the core skills employed by SEPs. The third mode refers to the symbolic aspects of self and others as they are evoked, enacted and embodied in a therapeutic relationship (Mitchell, 2000). Historically, this has been understood as a transference and countertransference matrix. This third mode can essentially provide an understanding of bodies as sites of projections, confusion or creations of the self and other identities within the therapeutic relationship. Lastly, the fourth mode describes the mutual recognition of self-reflective, agentic persons (Mitchell, 2000; p. 54). In this way, the therapist's and patient's bodies act as both resources and containers for mutual meetings as can be imagined in somatic transference and countertransference.

Child maltreatment is not a new phenomenon. It first appeared in the mental and public health literature in the 1960s, and since then there has been a steady increase in efforts aimed at understanding this phenomenon by many mental health professionals, researchers, medical practitioners, lawmakers and the criminal and justice system (Miller-Perrin & Perrin, 2012; Gilbert et al., 2015). Similarly, the media has also mobilized efforts to highlight and expose the plight of millions of children who are maltreated by adults, particularly in the context of caregiving and family set-up (Centers for Disease Control & Prevention, 2019). Although the terms 'child abuse' and 'child maltreatment' are sometimes used interchangeably, *child maltreatment* is considered an umbrella term that encompasses both child abuse and neglect. According to Wekerle (2019), child maltreatment "includes all forms of physical and emotional maltreatment, sexual abuse, neglect, and exploitation that results in actual or potential harm to the child's health, development or dignity" (p. 4). Juxtaposing Wekerle et al.'s (2019) definition of child maltreatment against Knefel et al. (2019) and Cicchetti and Rizley (1981) who describe child maltreatment as 'any recent act or failure to act on the part of the parent or caretaker which results in death, serious physical or emotional harm, sexual abuse, or exploitation or failure to act which can cause an imminent risk of serious harm to a child'. By doing so, one will notice the emphasis placed by the latter authors on the role of caregivers and parents in the equation of maltreatment, thus rendering child maltreatment as relational and interpersonal problems between the child and the caregiver (Briere & Scott, 2006). In the same vein, child maltreatment is not a phenomenon that can be confined to a family system only as most forms of child maltreatment are largely a reflection of systemic and chronic patterns of dysfunctional relating that may also be isolated and episodic pervasive and rampant (Messman & Bhuptani, 2017).

According to Ritacco and Suffla (2012), child maltreatment is a multi-faceted experience as it predominantly occurs in a psychologically and emotionally toxic environment and it may involve a variety of abuses, such as sexual abuse, incest, physical and psychological abuse, neglect and abandonment. Knefel et al. (2019) argue that neglect occurs when a child's parents and other caregivers are not providing the requisites for a child's emotional, psychological and physical development and occurs for a wide range of reasons (p. 5). Neglect can also be further split into four additional subcategories, which include physical neglect, emotional neglect, medical neglect and educational neglect (Cicchetti & Rizley, 1981). Physical neglect occurs when a child's needs for food, clothing, shelter, cleanliness and medical care, safe living conditions and protection from harm are not adequately met (Saison et al., 2011). Emotional neglect happens when a child's need to feel loved, wanted, safe and worthy is not, while emotional neglect can range from parents and/or caregivers being unavailable to active rejection (Wekerle, 2019). On the other hand, physical abuse and/or injury (ranging from bruises to severe fractures or death) because of punching, beating, kicking, biting, shaking, throwing, stabbing, choking, hitting (with a hand, stick, strap or another object), burning or otherwise harming a child (Hughes et al., 2017). These acts of commission by a caregiver cause actual physical harm or have the potential to harm the child's physical and emotional integrity. According to Wekerle et al. (2019), sexual abuse occurs when a child is used for sexual purposes by an adult or adolescent. Sexual abuse can include both touching and non-touching behaviours. Non-touching behaviours can include voyeurism (trying to look at a child's naked body), exhibitionism or exposing the child to pornography (Kloppen et al., 2016).

Closely related to the experiences of child maltreatment is the concept of adverse childhood experiences (ACEs) (Knefel et al., 2020). Contend that childhood adversities, including ACE, can overactivate the child's stress response system, wearing down the body and brain over time. This overactivation is referred to as toxic stress and is the primary way in which adversity damages a child's development and well-being (Messman & Bhuptani, 2017). While the focus of this chapter is on child maltreatment, I think it would be pertinent to briefly define and explain ACE as it is closely related to child maltreatment and in some instances, the two terms may be used interchangeably. Furthermore, expatiating what is meant by ACE will assist in broadening our understanding of the long-term effects of child maltreatment on the life of an adult survivor. Additionally, ACEs can have a tremendous impact on future violence victimization and perpetration, and lifelong health and opportunity (CDC, 2019). While there is no consensus on the definition of ACE (Kalmakis & Chandler, 2015), most researchers tend to agree that 10 major components of ACE include emotional abuse, physical abuse, sexual abuse, emotional neglect, physical neglect, parental separation or divorce, persistent exposure to domestic violence, household substance abuse, and presence of mental illness in the household as well as a criminal household member (Watkins et al., 2018; Briere & Lanktree, 2012).

A Phenomenological Case Study

In this chapter, I employ a single case study research method as a vehicle to, closely and in greater detail, demonstrate the application of the SE treatment model to the case of one of my patients, named Setadimo. A case study allows the examination of complex cases to deepen our understanding of unique phenomena, a research method involving an up-close, in-depth and detailed examination of a subject of study (Mills et al., 2010). A single case study involves an analysis of a person that is being studied holistically. Like most case studies, Setadimo's case is founded on the phenomenological tradition that argues that reality is individually constructed due to the lived experience of the narrator. Within phenomenology, emphasis is placed upon seeing all individuals in their context, as well as the understanding that each person perceives the world in a unique way, and that individual perception is moulded by past experience and the interpretation of that experience. Similarly, this chapter employs the case study method to showcase how Setadimo interpreted or internalized her experience of trauma and others (her stepfather and her mother) and the world around her (her immediate community). I use SE trauma treatment model not only as a lens through which I conceptualized her suffering (psychopathology) but also as a treatment model that aided me to manage her psychological anguish. Setadimo was seen as in an acute medical hospital following a suicide attempt and she presented with an atypical clinical syndrome involving severe vegetative symptoms of depression, with suicide ideations, auditory and visual perceptual disturbances, and PTSD. Upon assessment it soon became evident that she was not experiencing psychosis as the referring physician reported instead, she was experiencing severe and unbearable intrusive auditory and visual flashbacks of certain traumatic experiences of seven years of sexual, emotional and physical abuse at the hands of her stepfather. Therefore, the material for this chapter is gleaned from various moments of my consultation with her as an inpatient in a private psychiatric facility in Johannesburg.

Ethical Aspects of Study

After her discharge from the private psychiatric facility, we continued our therapeutic consultations. At this point, her acute psychiatric symptomology was in partial remission, and all her areas of functioning were intact. However, she was still on psychotropic medication and was seeing her psychiatrist once in three months for reviews. It was during one of our sessions in which she recounted her long journey of psychiatric treatment that saw her consulting more than five psychiatrists and four voluntary psychiatric admissions at different private psychiatric facilities, when asked her for permission and consent to use my clinical material of our psychological sessions for an academic case study. Without thinking twice, she acquiesced to my humble request arguing that documenting what she called my treatment method will be of assistance to other patients who may have suffered similar trauma. Despite the verbal consent to use my clinical material for academic case study, I still insisted that she should give it some thought and when she was certain she can simply complete a consent form that I had handed her.

Setadimo: The Case Material

Setadimo is a 26-year-old African female who works as a junior Information Technician (IT) in a medium logistics company. She has been with this company for a little over 18 months and reports that she enjoys her time at work as it makes her forget about her haunted and miserable life. She is single with no children and says that she has not dated since her second year of varsity. She states that she stopped dating after two failed relationships which she described as retraumatizing and emotionally draining.

Reason for Referral

Setadimo was referred to me by her physician in one of the private hospitals in Johannesburg following a parasuicide (suicide attempt) the night before. The physician was also concerned about her eccentric and bizarre behaviour, which reckoned that it could be psychosis.

Observation

While Setadimo seemed oriented to all spheres, she appeared preoccupied, distracted and paranoid as well as panicky. She also looked a bit dishevelled and sloppy. She further seemed to be guarded with personal information (as if she was uncomfortable with me) and from time to time she would voluntarily place both hands on her ears as if to shut out my voice or the external noise. When I asked her about this behaviour, she responded by saying that she is haunted by the voices of her childhood trauma and wishes to shut them off. "This has been a story of my life" she added. Furthermore, psychological and medical investigations excluded any form of psychosis and medical as well as substance-induced psychological and/or medical condition(s). Following the initial examination, I referred her for inpatient psychiatric treatment in one of the private psychiatric clinics where I work. While admitted to the clinic, she was seen by a psychiatrist and yours truly for individual psychotherapy sessions and attended group therapy sessions.

History of the Presenting Problem

Setadimo recounted that she has a long history of psychiatric admissions. She says she was first admitted to a private psychiatric facility when she was 18 years old while in grade 12 and twice during undergraduate studies. In all her admissions, she asserts that she was either diagnosed as borderline personality disorder (in crisis), bipolar disorder or with depression and panic attacks or with generalized anxiety disorder or dissociative disorder or PTSD. She reports that in most cases her admissions would be necessitated by some psychological distress, such as uncontrollable panic attacks, maddening feelings of guilt, stifling emptiness and on other occasions it would be necessitated by debilitating depressive episodes (without any specific trigger), or prolonged periods of isolation, disorientation and indifference to the world around her. She referred to the latter experience as the 'wondering child' or 'the zombie me'.

She reported that while most of her psychiatric admissions were helpful in alleviating or lessening the debilitating symptoms of panic attacks, flashbacks, and intrusive visual and auditory replays of all the horrible words that were said to her, it was mostly temporary and it necessitated heavy reliance on prescriptive psychotropic medication. However, she was quick to add that psychotherapy was less effective because most psychologists that she has seen over the last seven years of her life seemed more concerned with diagnosing her and imposing on her to retell her trauma over and over. Despite having told them about her persistent and violent childhood maltreatment, including multiple rapes, at the hands of her stepfather, none of the psychologists seemed to know what to do with this information. All they did was to ask the details of the abuse and how often it happened and if I told my mom, etc. Another psychologist disclosed that she also experienced the same thing, and she was now fine, while another psychologist asked her to write a letter to her stepfather and to my mother. Both my psychologists told me that it was important that she retell her trauma over and over as it has cathectic worth.

Background

Setadimo reports that she is the only child of her mother and that her mom and her stepfather never had children of their own. She says that her mother worked as a professional nurse some 60-odd kilometres away from home. As a nurse, she worked seven days and would be off duty for another seven days. During the seven days she was on duty she would be away from home the whole time and only came home on her off-duty days. When her mother was away, she was left in the care of her stepfather. She reports that it did not take long before her stepfather (who worked as a school educator) turned her into his wife. She reports that molestation that quickly escalated into full-blown penetration starting from the age of seven years old until she was 17 years old, when she left home for varsity.

At first, she resisted, but she would be tied to the bed and beaten for hours, while she was insulted and called names and she was also deprived of food. She reports that at other times she would try to run away from home, but her stepfather would search for her until he finds her. Neighbours would help him to search for this 'naughty child' without knowing what was going on. The stepfather would tell neighbours lies, such as "I don't like school, or I don't want to do the house chores, or I am sleeping with boys".

The only time she had a break from her stepfather was when her mother was on her off-duty days. However, this did not bring any form of solace, or sense of security, as her mother "did not see her silent cries for help, nor did she see that I had lost weight and wetted my bed, I did not play with other children and that my schoolwork was dismal". She felt unwanted, unseen and abandoned by her mother who seemed smitten in love with her stepfather. She reports that as time went on, especially in her teen years, the sexual abuse would continue even when her mother was present. This happened when her father insisted on fetching her from school and on their way back home, he would park the car in the bushes to have sexual intercourse with her in the car. It was particularly, in her teens when she started enjoying sexual intercourse (and on several occasions she had orgasm during sexual encounter with the stepfather) with her stepfather and felt self-anger and guilty for enjoying sex with him. Other times, she would feel horny and be turned on during the school lessons and this confused her greatly because she hated having sexual intercourse with her stepfather.

SE Application to Setadimo's Case

Unlike most common trauma treatment models (whether for children, adolescents or adults) that tend to have a set protocol for treating patients with an assortment of trauma disorders (see Table 3.1), SE is rather more dynamic and complex in its application. While there might be some imbrication between treatment principles and other trauma treatment models in some instances, SE has a vast array of techniques for different clinical symptoms, and it needs specialized training to understand the complex interaction of body and mind. One of the main aims of SE is to uncover and address somatic sensations linked to traumatic emotions and memories. This therapeutic approach primarily addresses the physiological outcomes of humans' fight, flight and freeze responses to perceived danger.

From my first interaction with Setadimo, I was aware of how not in control of her body sensations (*bodily dysregulated*) because she was so used to them and felt defeated by her body. She seemed to be in a state of perpetual hyperarousal to the external stimuli (which she mostly misinterpreted as danger) and thus she appeared stuck in a state of hyperactivation. In this state, she appeared to be constantly tormented by an avalanche of stimuli from which she had no control, Setadimo's senses seemed to be misreading and misinterpreting most external stimuli as intrusive, daunting and incapacitating. This is usually a very terrifying experience to most people especially because it appears to emanate internally. Along with this internal world that she seemed to have no control over were overwhelming feelings of powerlessness, guilt and defeat. Hence, her sense of disorientation, dissociation, and multiple and unpredictable anxiety attack. As an SEP, I got a sense that her waking life is characterized by an endless state of intrusive traumatic memories, and her body was the canvass upon which the past traumatic experiences, both interoceptive and proprioceptive, played themselves out. In my understanding of human physiology, I understood that it is not uncommon for severely traumatized people to lose their ability to regulate (modulate) their bodies and thus they are more vulnerable to experiencing fluctuating states of hyperarousal (i.e., experiencing 'too much' activation) and/or hypoarousal (i.e., experiencing 'too little' activation as manifested as numbness, psychomotor retardation). The above clinical description of Setadimo reminds us of Epstein's (2014) comment

> most of our clients have some form of traumatic experiences, [rich tapestry of relational patterns] where their early relationships were either avoidant, ambivalent, or disruptive and unpredictable. Their environment did not provide them with the secure and safe holding they needed (p. 109).

In this instance and given the chaotic affective and somatic (activated) states, she presented with agitation, hyperventilation, uncontrolled and unpredictable anxiety attacks, and perceptual disturbance. This oscillation between hyper- and hypoarousal states is quite common among traumatized patients as they fumble their way to control their physiological reaction (Ogden et al., 2006). A perfect example of dysregulated bodily sensations would be an instance in which Setadimo described how she found herself being sexually turned on when she meets an old domineering male figure. Put simply, Setadimo was confused and felt betrayed by her body (her vagina gets extremely wet and her body tenses up) when she was confronted by older males in a position of authority. She described this reaction, which occurred frequently, as confusing, sick and bizarre.

Thus, the first line of intervention was to create a safe and trusting therapeutic milieu. This meant that I had ensured that I build a sound therapeutic alliance that would allow her to feel safe (Silva, 2014). Using mindfulness[7] insights, the SE approach to healing child maltreatment (developmental) and relational trauma considers a felt sense of safety as a primal need for the mainstay of a trusting relationship. As SEP I was acutely aware that I would achieve nothing without allowing her to feel safe with me.

Furthermore, I was also under no illusion that it would take some time to get Setadimo to be somatically settled as she paid close attention to every move I made and scanned every word I uttered as part of her test and externalizing her trust issues. During this initial phase, I engage her in a lot of grounding exercises, including orienting and relaxation exercises. I also provided her with much-needed information on my thoughts regarding her current somatic and cognitive processes (mindfulness). As could be witnessed by her body posture and demeanour, Setadimo seemed to react well to orienting activities, including tracking her body for any minute sensations (which basically brought the here-and-now cognitive and somatic awareness to the fore) because she calmed down significantly and was able to make eye contact with me. I commended her greatly for the little successes such as the ability to slow her body sensations down, the ability to be emotionally present in the session and making eye contact with me. Her ability to slow down and calmly engage with me signified two important things, namely, she has expanded her window of tolerance towards external stimuli and she was ready to engage in what Stephen Porges calls social engagement.[8] Meaning that in the context of non-threatening situations, she would be able to engage and disengage with the environment and in social relationships by regulating her heart rate by mobilizing the sympathetic nervous system. Consequently, this enabled her to achieve body awareness and could identify the change in pace in her body, which allowed her to slowly and meaningfully (with 'very little' overt signs of activations) talk about

7 Souza et al. (2019) describe mindfulness as a technique that involves awareness, attention, and memory and practical utility is to continuously identify one's own feelings, emotions and thoughts to remove memories associated with trauma (p. 242). Because survivors of childhood trauma and/or prolonged exposure to trauma tend to process their feelings and emotions, think, behave in an auto-pilot manner, these patients are oriented and are taught to concentrate (on internal bodily sensation – interoceptive) what they are doing or feeling and become aware of the evolution of their bodily sensations and behaviours. Therefore, this requires them to shift from reactive, automatic and unconscious responses to conscious ones (Vasquez-Dextre, 2016).

8 Porges' (2018) social engagement system (or theory) involves the vagus nerve that influences our heart rate and breathing, and is involved in how we perceive, react to and recover from stress. When the vagus nerve is activated, we able to feel confident, our heart rate and breathing slows down, our blood pressure drops, and our stress response switches off and in this way, we are able to social better. Therefore, in a state of social engagement, our bodies enter a state of physical calm. We feel safe enough to move closer to another person, making intimacy possible.

her current presenting problem and the history of the presenting problem. However, I took notice of her poor levels of tolerance for the distress that often leads to what Ogden et al. (2006) refer to as a form of "compartmentalization" (p. 4) or activation (Payne et al., 2015b; Silva, 2014) and due to decreased window of tolerance and compromised resiliency (Heller & Heller, 2001). In this instance, one of the long-term therapeutic goals would be to assist her to expand her window of tolerance and provide her with the ability to tolerate distressing external stimuli that often lead to activation.

Creating a conducive and safe environment in the trauma treatment of traumatized patients goes hand in hand by establishing and maintaining healthy emotional and physical boundaries in the intersubjective space (Mitchell, 2000; White, 2014) between the client and me. I also had to be comfortable in my own body and regulate my own somatic (bodily) countertransference (Egan & Carr, 2008; Gubb, 2014) so that I could convey a sense of calmness to her. This was achieved by asking the client to sit comfortably while inviting her to engage in a series of *interval breathing exercises* to aid in bringing awareness to her own body sensations and reactions. In tandem with the grounding exercises, I was also tracking her body for any signs of activation and deactivation and inviting her to be aware of any changes (calming and/or unsettling) in her body sensations. According to Levine (1997, 2010), the ability to scan and track one's body sensations has a number of benefits including aiding the traumatized person to calm her/himself down (body regulation) and reclaim their bodily self-control. Moreover, orienting and teaching her that scary sensations (in a form of acute and stifling panic attacks) that she was experiencing are not life-threatening but simply the 'misfiring of her body's autonomous nervous system'. When in a state of traumatization, a person can enter a 'trauma vortex' whereby they feel trapped in a loop of reliving the experience. It is important to move in and out of this vortex in treatment to prevent retraumatizing them and bring the person back to there here and now.

Further consideration of intervening using the SE therapeutic approach was to track her felt bodily and visceral sensations to determine parts of her body and sensations that are hyperactivated and/or hypoactivated. Usually, her auditory and visual illusions or senses were mostly affected (highly activated) in that she experienced unbearable and intrusive voice of her tormentor (stepfather) and experienced disturbing visual images (mostly intrusive) of herself being chained on one leg of the bed screaming and begging for mercy. At this point, it would be important to remind the reader that Levine (2010) and Porges (2015) argue that the traumatic experiences of traumatized individuals are reified and captured in their senses. This means that traumatized individuals with unresolved trauma suffer a profound deficit in the ability to integrate their experiences of trauma resulting in disintegrated emotions, thoughts, memory and somatosensory (Ogden et al., 2006). In this instance, it makes sense that Setadimo tended to experience frenzied and random auditory and visual illusions when under severe distress. To assist her to integrate these experiences of trauma, I started working with her on the less traumatic events to allow her some kind of mastery over small 'traumas' and from time to time I slowly introduced more threatening memories of trauma (pendulation). This process required me to be vigilant of any activation and/or numbing experiences when moving between the two traumas (peripheral versus threatening memories of trauma) and it was repeated over a number of sessions.

In addition, the haunting delusions seemed to be coupled with a replay of the ferocious sexual acts (including seeing an erected penis and being forced to engage in oral sex) that were perpetrated on her frozen, helpless body. It is these intrusive visual images and rerunning of sexual groaning and heavy breathing (that she would hear whenever she was being raped) that look as if to drive her to the brink of madness and had distorted her perception of the world. She described these experiences as schizophrenic because of how powerful she would experience them and her failure to stop seeing or her hearing them. Over a number of sessions, I used the SE's technique of 'freeze frame' which afforded Setadimo an opportunity to capture a disturbing moment by "stopping" or "freezing" it like a frame in a movie. The use of stopping the image or action gives the body time to contact and complete its normal biological defence mechanism of fight or flight. This was the most difficult task for her to do as it evoked a lot of pain and emotions associated with this traumatic exposure, but with time and increased window of tolerance, she seemed to be less evoked by replaying these moments.

On the other hand, her hypoactivation manifested in what she described as a sense of emotional deadness, powerlessness and emotional exhaustion as well as depersonalization and derealization that rendered her unable to connect with other human beings. She described herself as a 'wondering girl' and a 'walking zombie' with little to no tolerance for interpersonal relationship skills and attachment ability due to high levels of activation associated with interpersonal connectedness. In her case, she lost the ability to acquire the necessary interpersonal skills, which were thwarted in her childhood due to the prolonged history of child maltreatment. The feelings and experiences of fatigue represented her sense of resignation and powerlessness to protect herself against the emotional, sexual and physical assaults when confronted with threatening external stimuli for which escape was perceived to be impossible. Confronting unresolved and threatening memories and/or experiences (stored in all senses) has the power to assist traumatized individuals to discharge (release) emotional pain associated with unresolved traumatic experiences. This ability is akin to the behaviour of the animals in the wild that get to shake off the trapped (conserved) energy of the threat that has disappeared. According to Levine (2010), once these discharges of trauma have happened the individual regains the ability to feel again and to feel alive to appreciate the here-and-now experiences. Remember the experiences of dissociation, numbing or derealization are mostly learned early in life and are related to the limbic brain that served a protective purpose in those early stages of trauma. Therefore, this freeze reaction on her part is similar to functioning in an auto-pilot mode because it served a protective function (of feeling dead and numb inside). This way no one will take interest in her or her sexuality.

Furthermore, in Setadimo's case, her somatic symptoms are possibly a source of reciprocal affliction in that her physical pain contributes to, understandably, unpleasant moods which likely result in certain behaviour and consequent anxiety, thereby causing more unnecessary muscular tension and pain. Hence, by assisting Setadimo to become as relaxed as possible (positive feelings playing a key role) helped her to gain a deep-seated state of inner awareness that acts as an initial resourcing used for parasympathetic discharge within SE treatment. Central to her treatment was to provide Setadimo with psychoeducation on what she can expect throughout the treatment. For instance, instead of the typical practice of retelling her life story, I would often halt Setadimo mid-sentence to prevent her from overactivating her sympathetic nervous system and encourage her to use the story and specific content to track bodily sensations/responses and how they manifest as physiological arousal. I also assured her that an important part of interoceptive awareness is to remain present (in the here-and-now), which allows her body (and by extension her nervous system) to integrate the material necessary to transform trauma.

Once Setadimo became comfortable and confident in her ability to move between arousing (trauma vortex) and non-arousing content, I slowly introduced corrective experiences (Olssen,

2013). One of SE's aims is to assist the patient to renegotiate interrupted survival responses. In Setadimo's case, I argue that her past multiple rapes which were accompanied by physical and emotional abuse are associated with interrupted survival responses, which now manifest in an array of symptoms such as anxiety, depression and difficulty sleeping. I believe that the steady acquisition of resources reinforced somatically through pendulation, completion of stuck trauma or energy (internalized self-beliefs) and resourcing allowed Setadimo to experience her body's self-protective capacity (resilience) as an active participant to the threat. Throughout our sessions, I systematically moved closer to the centre memory (associated with the most traumatic event) and the missing survival response thwarted becomes apparent (Levine as cited in Payne et al., 2015a). Heller and Heller (2007) mentioned that one effective strategy for the therapist is to allow clients to move the trauma memory as far back as necessary for them to feel safe and to rebuild their sense of resiliency and self-control.

By steadily moving closer (framing the most threatening memories of the trauma) to the core of her traumatic experience allowed her body to ample warning of the approaching threat and allows her body to respond in the manner it wishes (survival responses mainly aimed at fight or flight). Throughout Somatic Experiencing Therapy (SET), I encouraged Setadimo to notice her body's embodied experiences, and how the body wished to respond (in SE terms, it is normally referred to *as to allow the body to do what it wants to do*). Small tremors, shaking, yawning, or burping and crying may be evoked due to this experience that signals the experience of discharge of struck energy. Payne et al. (2015a) state these small discharges would be indicative of her nervous system's physiological response to reset the sympathetic overactivation and gives way to the larger goal at hand, namely self-regulation and completion. Given the experiential nature of SET, Setadimo was frightened, uneasy and sometimes confused during treatment, which was something I was anticipating. I constantly had to remind her how the body reacts in response to threats and encourages her to allow these uncomfortable feelings to manifest.

Continuing from the above, SET further aims to uncoupling of fear as manifested in the traumatized individuals' immobility response that is normally characterized by dissociation and numbing and general somatic fatigue (Olssen, 2013). The uncoupling mechanism (separating mumbled chain of thoughts and/or behaviour) aids to bring a shift in somatic awareness between arousing and non-arousing memories. The coupling and uncoupling mechanisms are informed by SE's conception of the body as essentially programmed to enact the appropriate responses as it defends or protects or mobilizes itself for extreme kinetic action. According to Levine (2010), the energy released in the process of reacting to traumatic exposure refers to biological energy, such as neuroendocrine substances and those associated with the amplification of muscular activation. One key aspect within the SE treatment was to notice the subtle kinaesthetic markers and to bring Setadimo's attention to them, as well as the accompanying tremors and oscillations, which serve as a sign of her nervous system's effort to restore equilibrium to an overactivated ANS.

Finally, I introduced the SIBAM technique to help Setadimo to complete the correction of her autonomous system (i.e., assisting to strike a balance between the sympathetic and parasympathetic nervous systems). The use of the SIBAM may look easy on paper but it is one of the most important SE technique that requires utmost attention and skill because of the possibility of reactivating the patient. I would like to compare the use of the SIBAM technique to psychoanalytic interpretation because both these techniques require skills and timing. In this instance, I work with one (in a graded manner) traumatic experience and one sense. Keeping in mind that at this stage, Setadimo has acquired and regained functional body regulation and mastery over her body sensations due to a series of completion of thwarted trauma responses and releasing of stuck energy and has furthermore expanded her window of tolerance of previously threatening trauma memories as well as having mastered her social engagement response to any external stimuli, I would now, for example, work with one particular trauma imagery and assist to track her body sensation while holding (visualizing) the trauma.

The following are some of the key terms used in SE treatment (Table 3.1).

SE as a Viable Model of Childhood Maltreatment and Developmental Trauma

The aim of this chapter was to demonstrate the potential use of SE therapeutic models as one of the viable trauma therapeutic modalities within the South African context. While the actual complexity of the treatment process has been oversimplified in this chapter, SET is normally a very brief and direct therapeutic treatment model for individuals who have suffered severe and unresolved childhood interpersonal trauma. It offers the practitioner the rear spectacle of seeing the past trauma been enacted in here- and-now and the discharge of that emotional pain associated with trauma evaporates. However, one must be a skilful SEP to sensitively hold the traumatized individual's pain while at the same time allowing them slowly (in titrated fashion) confront their intractable and long-held somatic dysregulation which has made it possible all along for traumatized patients to either be hyperactivated or hypoactivated. In all my years of using SE therapeutic methods in treating survivors of child maltreatment, I have become extremely confident in treating trauma patients of all stripes. In my experience, most clients tend to find it very effective in helping them to connect with their pain and assortment of unresolved feelings and thoughts associated with child maltreatment. However, at first, most clients find it a bit strange when they are not allowed to rumble on and on about their problems and instead, they are directed to feelings, thoughts and sensations associated with what they want to talk about. For most clients, they found SE not only unusual, but they also find it extremely difficult to embody their feelings and thoughts. Some found the full manifestation of the somatic sensation to be threatening as if they were experiencing a full-blown panic attack but significantly, they would almost immediately report marked changes in how they experience their feelings outside therapy

In this way, SE offers a unique contribution to the therapeutic application related to anxiety reduction and resilience increase by expanding on the available coping skills and expanding the window of tolerance to traumatic events. However, as Payne et al. (2015b) note, what separates SE from other therapies is its extensive utilization of meditative practices. In that sense, SE aims to achieve a bidirectional relationship to conducting therapy. Comparatively, SET also adheres to certain conventions of so-called "mainstream" procedures by attending to the humanistic side of psychotherapy, which is aimed at reducing client's distress and inciting exploration of unfamiliar concepts. Moreover, SET is not void of constituent CBT elements found in exposure-based therapies as much of the literature asserts (see for example Rossi, 2014; Silva, 2014). Rather, as demonstrated in Setadimo's case, it shows that individuals that have been subjected to prolonged child maltreatment tend to experience stunted emotional and psychological growth as well as physical dysregulation. Accordingly, the utilization of mild exposure and meditative-type practices seek to address negative emotions and behavioural symptoms related to

Table 3.1 Key SE terminologies

Key SE Phrases	Explanation of the Phrase
Activation/arousal	Hyperarousal or overcharge of the nervous system.
Autonomic nervous system	The part of the nervous system responsible for involuntary functioning such as breathing, heart rate, perspiration, appetite, trembling, sleep, shaking, sex drive, etc.
Boundaries	The sense of personal space and containment that allows you to feel safe.
Boundary rupture	A feeling that you are no longer protected or sheltered from events and objects around you or being flooded by outside stimuli.
Compartmentalization	The propensity of traumatized individuals to alternate between (1) emotional and bodily numbing and avoidance of cues reminiscent of the trauma and (2) intrusive relieving of the trauma via flashbacks, dreams and thoughts and somatic symptoms.
Creative self-regulation	The body's capacity to modulate activation and to remain balanced. Modulation of activation means that the body has the energy it needs to face challenged or danger as well as the capacity to discharge and rest after a challenge has been met.
Discharge	Release of energy through the body.
Dissociation	Disconnection, "zoned" or "spaced" out.
Freeze frame	The technique in which you capture a dangerous moment by stopping or "freezing" it like a frame in a movie. This use of stopping the image or action gives the body time to contact and complete its normal biological defence mechanism of fight or flight.
Linking	The snapshot the mind takes of a traumatic event that then causes us to associate any element in that "snapshot" with danger, i.e., if we were hit by a white car on a highway in the mountains when it was raining, we may associate all these elements (white cars, driving in the mountains, driving on highways, rainstorms) with treat afterwards which may trigger anxiety reactions.
Pendulation	The technique of moving from a resource, which promotes relaxation and discharge, to the experience of a small piece of traumatic material that is still upsetting. Then back and forth to make the process of trauma resolution less painful and more manageable.
Non-sequential	Not in the order the event originally took place.
Oasis	An inner experience of safety that a person can rely on for support is needed when beginning to work on difficult trauma material. You never work with the traumatic experience without first establishing this stable foundation called an oasis.
Overactivation	Overarousal and overcharge in the nervous system.
Overwhelmed	A state of feeling there is more than you can cope with at any given moment.
Range of resilience	The range within a person based on genetics, family history, support system, etc., which allows a person to deal with life's difficulties without being overwhelmed.
Reptilian brain	Core brain often referred to as "primitive" because it is the oldest part of our brain. Expert in survival, self-preservation and instincts.
Resiliency	The capacity to cope with life challenges and remain connected to yourself in an integrated way. The capacity to "bounce back" after difficulty.
Resource	Anything that makes you feel safe and comfortable, helps discharge tour tension or arousal, and riggers a relaxation response.
Survival mode	The state of hyperarousal where you are continuously mobilized to meet threat.
Titration	A healing process where you deal with the trauma one small, manageable step at a time, piece by piece, bit by bit.
Working the periphery	Begin with the least traumatic material and slowly move towards the more traumatic material.

Adopted from: Heller and Heller (2001). *Crash Course: Self-Healing Guide to Auto Accident Trauma and Recovery* (pp. xviii–xx). Berkeley: California.

a dysregulated ANS, specifically those regarded as high levels of distress. Consequently, one traumatic response discussed in relation to SET and notably associated with child maltreatment assault is tonic immobility (Levine & Frederick, 1997). This involuntary inhibition of motor and vocal response to child maltreatment is one imperative focal point considered within the SET approach, although it should be noted that the CBT variation of prolonged exposure was originally designed for the treatment of rape victims and has been found to be highly supported by Randomized Clinical Trials (RCT) studies (Akobeng, 2005; Chia, 2000; Souza et al., 2019). As with any theoretical approach, several inconsistencies become apparent throughout the literature on SE. As previously discussed, many publications on SE lay claim to a non-exposure or non-cognitive approach (see for example, Levine, 2010; Silva, 2014; Payne et al., 2015b).

Strengths

Albeit speculative and therefore limited, several studies mentioned earlier support SET as an effective intervention for traumatic experiences, which highlights several strengths for the current review. Firstly, the data from several outcome-based studies conducted on different continents (see Leitch, 2007; Leitch et al., 2009; Brom et al., 2017) suggest that, although founded and developed in a Western climate, the SET approach provides positive evidence for cross-cultural relevance to non-western societies, as well as not being restricted by language barriers such as those who are from non-English speaking countries. This entails that within the diversified context of South Africa, further development and application of SE interventions may be more accessible to a wider variety of groups, previously out of reach of the appropriate means for treatment. This is because (a) the use of SE's focus on interoceptive awareness rather than complex cognitive jargon was found in other theories (Corey et al., 2017), and (b) SE can be used in conjunction with other practices already shown to be effective is anticipated research gaps. Therefore, creating an army of SE therapists in the South African context by teaching this model of body-based trauma treatment to the new generation of clinical and counselling psychologists would be of great benefit to many patients who live with the lingering effects of childhood maltreatment. By becoming more aware of her physical responses to stress, Setadimo learned how to control her emotions through relaxation techniques. Upon termination of our sessions, she expressed that she felt free and more engaged with life. She reported that she felt less inclined to resort to physical pain and mental stress.

Limitations

A clear limitation of this review is noted by the lack of available literature on SE, with approximately three unpublished sources, four and five masters and doctoral dissertations, respectively, as well as 13 peer-review publications as of 2018. Most of these papers also focused on the qualitative aspects of research found in the relevant literature on SET, as opposed to quantitative or mixed methods. Additionally, despite several active SEPs within South Africa (currently estimated at 15 engaged in practice), none of the literature on violence, trauma or alternative therapies included this consideration. Restrictions associated with narrative reviews further limit this study by being non-predictive at its outset, not being protocol-based (simple description of findings), partially objective in its approach and open to author bias.

References

Akobeng, A. K. (2005). Understanding randomized controlled trials, Arch Dis Child, 90, 840–844. https://doi:10.1136/adc.2004.058222.

Andersen, T. E., Lahav, Y., Ellegard, H., & Manniche, C. (2017). A randomized controlled trial of brief somatic experiencing for chronic low back pain and comorbid posttraumatic stress disorder symptoms. *European Journal of Psychotraumatology*, *8*, 1331108. https://doi.org/1080/20008198 .2017.1331108

Barnes, P. M., Powell-Griner, E., McFann, K., & Nahin, R. L. (2002). Complementary and alternative methods use among adults: United States, 2002. *Seminars in Integrative Medicine*, *2*, 54–71. https://doi.org/10.1016/jsigm2004.07.003

Barratt, B. (2010). *The emergence of somatic psychology and body-mind therapy*. Palgrave Macmillan. http://www.cmej.org.za/index.php/cmej/article/view/2678/2775.

Berceli, D., & Napoli, M. (2006). A proposal for a mindfulness-based trauma-prevention program for social work professionals. *Journal Evidence-Based Complementary Alternative Medicine*, *11*, 153–165.

Berndtsson, I. C. (2018). Considering the concepts of the lived body and the lifeworld as tools for better understanding the meaning of assistive technology in everyday life. *ALTER, Journal of Disability Research*, *12*(33), 140–152. https://doi.org/10.1016/j.alter.2018.01.001

Blaustein, M. E., & Kinniburgh, K. M. (2010). *Treating traumatic stress in children and adolescents: How to foster resilience through attachment, regulation, and competence*. New York: Guilford Press.

Boterhoven de Haan, K. L., Lee, C. W., Correia, H., Menninga, S., Fassbinder, E., Köehne, S., & Arntz, A. (2021). Patient and therapist perspectives on treatment for adults with PTSD from childhood trauma. *Journal of Clinical Medicine*, *10*(5). https://doi.org/10.3390/jcm10050954

Briere, J. N., & Lanktree, C. B. (2012). *Treating complex trauma in adolescents and young adults*. Los Angeles, CA: SAGE.

Breslau, N., Wilcox, H. C., Storr, C. L., Lucia, V. C., & Anthony, J. C. (2004). Trauma exposure and posttraumatic stress disorders: A study of you in urban America. *Journal of Urban Health*, *81*, 530–544.

Briere, J. N., & Scott, C. (2006). *Principles of trauma therapy: A guide to symptoms, evaluation, and treatment*. Thousand Oaks, CA: Sage.

Brom, D., Stokar, Y., Lawi, C., Nuriel-Porat, V., Ziv, Y., Lerner, K., & Ross, G. (2017, June). Somatic experiencing for posttraumatic stress disorder: A randomized controlled outcome study. *Journal of Traumatic Stress*, *30*, 304–312.

Cahill, S. P., Rothbaum, B. O., Resick, P. A., & Follette, V. M. (2010). Cognitive-behavioral therapy for adults. In E. B. Foa, T. M. Keane, M. J. Friedman, & J. A. Cohen (Eds.), *Effective treatments for PTSD: Practice guidelines from the international Society for traumatic stress studies* (pp. 139–222). New York: Guilford Press.

Carroll, R. (2014). Four relational modes of attending to the body in psychotherapy. In K. White (Ed.), *Talking bodies: How do we integrate working with the body in psychotherapy from an attachment and relational perspectives* (Chapter 2, pp. 11–40). London: Karnac Publishers.

Cayton, J., Neuendorf, R., Senders, A., & Wahbeh, H. (2014). Complementary and alternative medicine for post-traumatic stress disorder symptoms: A systematic review. *Journal of Evidence Based Complementary and Alternative Medicine*, *19*(3), 161–175. https://doi.org/10.1177 /2156587214525403

Centers for Disease Control & Prevention. (2019). *Preventing adverse childhood experiences: Leverage the best available evidence*. Atlanta, GA: National Centre for injury Prevention and control centers for Disease Control & Prevention. http://www.cdc.gov/violence-prevention/pdf/preventingACES -508.pdf,co-

Chia, K. S. (2000). Randomization: magical cure for bias. *Annals Academic Medicine*, Singapore, *29*, 563–564.

Cicchetti, D., & Rizley, R. (1981). Developmental perspectives on the etiology, intergenerational transmission, and sequelae of child maltreatment. *New Directions for Child Development*, *11*, 31–35.

Cloitre, M., Courtois, C. A., Charuvastra, A., Carapezza, R., Stolbach, B. C., & Green, B. L. (2011). Treatment of complex PTSD: Results of the ISTSS expert clinician survey on best practices. *Journal of Trauma Stress*, *24*, 615–627.

Cloitre, M., Hyland, P., Bisson, J. I., Brewin, C. R., Roberts, N. P., Karatias., et al. (2019). ICD-11 posttraumatic stress disorder and complex posttraumatic stress disorder in the United States: a population-based study. *Journal of Traumatic Stress*, *32*(6), 833–842. https://doi.org/10.1002/jts.22454

Cohen, J. A., Mannarino, A. P., Kliethermes, M., & Murray, L. A. (2012). Trauma-focused CBT for youth with complex trauma. *Child Abuse and Neglect*, *36*(6), 528–541.

Corey, G., Nicholas, L. J., & Bawa, U. (2017). Theory and practice of counselling and psychotherapy. (2nd Ed.), Cengage Learning: Cape Town, South Africa.

Courtois, C. A. & Fiord, J. D. (2013). Treating complex trauma: a sequenced relationship-based approach. New York: Guilford

Cusack, K., Jonas, D. E., Forneris, C. A., Wines, C., Sonis, J., Middleton, J. C., … Gaynes, B. N. (2016). Psychological treatments for adults with posttraumatic stress disorder: A systematic review and meta-analysis. *Clinical Psychology Review*, *43*, 128–141.

de la Porte, A., & Nzeku, M. (2016). Narrative practices in trauma care, support, and counselling. In A. Herbst & G. Reitsma (Ed.), *Trauma counselling: Principles and practice* (Chapter 10, pp. 183–204). Cape Town: JUTA Publishers.

Desai, R., Libby, D., & Pilver, C. (2012). Complementary and alternative medicine in VA specialized PTSD treatment program. *Psychiatric Services*, *63*, 1134–1136.

Desai, R., Libby, D., & Pilver, C. (2013). Complementary and alternative medicine use among individuals with posttraumatic stress disorder. *Psychological Trauma*, *2*, 277–285.

Dika, T. R. (2020). The origins of Cartesian dualism. *Journal of the American Philosophical Association*, *6*(3), 335–352. https://doi.org/10.1017/apa.2019.47

Eagle, G. T. (1998). An integrative model for brief term intervention in the treatment of psychological trauma. *International Journal of Psychotherapy*, *3*(2), 135–145.

Eagle, G. T., & Kaminer, D. (2015). Traumatic stress: Established knowledge, current debates, and new horizons. South African. *Journal of Psychology*, *45*(1), 22–35. https://doi.org/10.1177/0081246314547124

Edwards, D. (2005). Treating PTSD in South African contexts: A theoretical framework and a model for developing evidence-base practice. *Journal of Psychology in Africa*, *15*(2), 209–220. https://doi.org/10.4314/jpav152.30660, https://www.researchgate.net/publication/29807414

Egan, J., & Carr, A. (2008). Body-centred countertransference in female trauma practitioners. *Irish Association for Counselling and Psychotherapy*, *8*, 24–2.

Epstein, O. B. (2014). Touching trauma: working relationally and safely with the unboundaried body. In K. White (Ed.), *Talking bodies: How do we integrate working with the body in psychotherapy from an attachment and relational perspectives* (Chapter 6, pp.109–124). London: Karnac Publishers.

Felitti, V. J. (2002). The relation between adverse childhood experiences and adult health: Turning Gold into lead. *The Permanente Journal*, *6*(1), 44–47.

Foa, E. B., Doron, M., & Yadin, E. (2011). *Prolonged exposure: The treatment guide for PTSD* (3rd ed.). New York: Oxford University Press.

Foa, E. B., Gillihan, S. J., & Bryant, R. A. (2013). Challenges, and successes in dissemination of evidence-based treatments for posttraumatic stress: Lessons learned from prolonged exposure therapy for PTSD. *Psychological Science in the Public Interest*, *14*, 65–111.

Ford, J. D. (2021). Progress and limitations in the treatment of complex PTSD and developmental trauma disorder. *Current Treatment Options in Psychiatry*, *8*, 1–17. hppts://doi.org/10.1007/s40501-020-00236-6

Ford, J. D. (2021). Progress and limitations in the treatment of complex and developmental trauma disorders. *Current Treatment Options in Psychology*, *8*, 1–17.

Fuentes, P. M., Carmen Rojas Hernández, M. D., Santasilia, S., & Fuentes, F. M. (2017). The body as constitutive element phenomenology and psychoanalysis on our view of ourselves and others. *Life Sciences, Society and Policy, 13.* https://doi.org/10.1186/s40504-017-0051-0

Grand, D. (2011). Brainspotting a new brain-based psychotherapy approach. *Trauma and Gewalt, 3,* 276–285.

Gilbert, L. K., Brejding, M. J., Merrick, M. J., Parks, S. E., Thompson. W. W., Dhingra, S. S., & Food, D. C. (2015). Childhood adversity and adult chronic disease: An update from ten states and the district of Columbia, 2010. *American Journal of Preventative Medicine, 48*(3), 345–349.

Goldenson, J., Kitollari, I., & Lehman, F. (2021). The relationship between ACEs, trauma-related psychopathology, and resilience in vulnerable youth: Implications for screening and treatment. *Journal of Child and Adolescent Trauma, 14,* 151–160.

Gouws, A. (2021, April 21). South Africa is notorious for its high levels of gender-based violence. IOL. Retrieved October 11, 2022, from https://www.iol.co.za/capetimes/opinion/south-africa-is-notorious-for-its-high-levels-of-gender-based-violence-81ebad46-e4ec-4a86-b678-5e9bc8b22b02

Gubb, K. (2014). Craving interpretation: A case of somatic countertransference. *British Journal of Psychotherapy, 30*(1), 51–67. https://doi.org/10.1111/bjp.12062

Heller, D. P., & Heller, L. S. (2007). Somatic experiencing in the treatment of automobile accident trauma. *US Association for Body Psycho-Therapy Journal, 3,* 42–52.

Heller, D. P., & Heller, L. S. (2001). *Crash Course: Self-healing guide to auto- accident, and trauma, and recovery.* Berkeley, CA: North Atlantic Books.

Herbst, A., & Reitsma, G. (2016). *Trauma counselling: Principles and practice in South today.* Cape Town: Juta & Company (PTY), Ltd.

Hinton, D. E., Pich, V., Chhean, D., Safren, S. A., & Pollack, M. H. (2006). Somatic-focused therapy for traumatized refugees: Treating posttraumatic stress disorder and comorbid neck- focused panic attacks among cambodian refugees. *Psychotherapy: Theory, Research, Practice, Training, 43*(4), 491–505. https://doi:10.1037/0033-3204.43.4.491

Homann, K. (2010). Mind in the body: Concepts of neuroscience in dance/movement therapy practice. *American Dance Therapy Association, 32,* 80–99. https://doi.org/10.1007/s10465-010-9099-6

Hughes, K., Bellis, M. A., Hardcastle, K. A., Sethi, D., Butchart, A.., Mikton, C., … Dunne, M. P. (2017). The effects of multiple adverse childhood experiences on health A systemic review and meta-analysis. *The Lancet Public Health, 2*(8), e356–e366. https://doi.org/10.1016/S2468-2667(17)30118-4

Johnson, S., & Naidoo, A. (2017). A body-based group intervention for teacher stress and burnout in high-risk schools. *Acta Psychopathologica, 3*(6), 79. https://doi.org/10.4172/2469-6676.100151

Kalmakis, K. A., & Chandler, G. E. (2014). Adverse childhood experiences: towards a clear conceptual meaning. *Journal of Advance Nursing, 70*(7), 1489–1501. doi:10.1111/12329

Kaminer, D., & Eagle, G. (2010). *Traumatic stress in South Africa.* Johannesburg: Wits University Press.

Kaminer, D., & Eagle, G. T. (2015). Interventions for posttraumatic stress disorder: A review of the evidence base. *South African Journal of Psychology, 47*(1), 7–22. https://doi.org/10.1177/0081246316646950

Kaminer, D., Owen, M., & Schwartz, B. (2018). Systematic review of the evidence based for treatment of common mental disorders in South Africa. *South African Journal of Psychology, 48*(1), 32–47. https://doi.org/10.1177/0081246317704126

Keeshin, B. R., & Strawn, J. R. (2012). Treatment of children and adolescents with posttraumatic stress disorder (PTSD): A review of current evidence. *Child and Adolescent Psychopharmacology News, 17*(2), 5–10.

Kloppen, K., Haugland, S., Svedin, C. G., Mæhle, M., & Breivik, K. (2016). Prevalence of child sexual abuse in the Nordic countries: A literature review. *Journal of Child Sexual Abuse.* https://doi.org/10.1080/10538712.2015.1108944 to link to this article: http://doi.org/10.1080/10538712.2015.1108944

Knefel, M., Lueger-Schuster, B., Karatzias, T., Shevlin, M., & Hyland, P. (2019). From child maltreatment to ICD-11complex post-traumatic stress symptoms: The role of emotion regulation and revictimization. *Journal of Clinical Psychology, 75*(3), 392–403. https://doi.org/10.1002/jclp.22655

Kuhfuß, M., Maldei, T., Hetmanek, A., & Baumann, N. (2021). Somatic experiencing – Effectiveness and key factors of a body-oriented trauma therapy: A scoping literature review. *European Journal of Psychotraumatology, 12*(1). https://doi.org/10.1080/20008198.2021.1929023

Leitch, L. M. (2007). Somatic experiencing treatment with tsunami survivors in Thailand: Broadening the scope of early intervention. *Traumatology, 13*(3), 11–20.

Leitch, M. L., Vanslyke, J., & Allen, M. (2009). Somatic experiencing treatment with social service workers following Hurricanes Katrina and Rita. *Social Work, 54*(1), 9–18. https://doi.org/10.1093/sw/54.1

Levine, P. (1997). *Waking the tiger: Healing trauma.* Berkeley: North Atlantic Books.

Levine, P. A. (1977). Accumulated stress, reserve capacity and disease (Unpublished dissertation). Ann Arbor, MI: University of California.

Levine, P. (1997). *Waking the tiger: Healing trauma.* Berkeley: North Atlantic Books.

Levine, P. A., & Frederick, A. (1997). *Waking the tiger; healing trauma.* Berkeley, CA: North Atlantic Books.

Levine, P. A. (2010). *In an unspoken voice: How the body releases trauma and restores goodness.* Berkeley, CA: North Atlantic Books.

Lewis, A. (2009). Assessing childhood trauma: A holistic perspective. *Child Abuse Research in South Africa, 10*(1), 14–26.

Manyemaa, M., Norrisa, S. A., Said-Mohameda, R., Tollman, S. T., Twine, R., Kahn, K., & Richter, L. M. (2018). The associations between interpersonal violence and psychological distress among rural and urban young women in South Africa. *Health & Place, 51*, 97–106. https://doi.org/10.1016/j.healthplace.2018.03.003

Marks, S. (2017, April 20). Psychotherapy in historical perspective. *History of the Human Sciences, 30*(2), 3–16. https://doi.org/10.1177/0952695117703243

Marx, Z. (2020). Introduction to Brainspotting therapy: Application to Complex PTSD within a South African context. Psychology Honours Essay, University of Johannesburg.

Masson, F., Graham, T., & Langa, M. (2016). An integrated approach to working with trauma. In A. Herbst & G. Reitsma (Eds.), *Trauma counselling: Principles and practice in South Africa Today* (Chapter 12, pp. 232–240). Cape Town: Juta and Company (PTY), LTD.

McMahon, S. (2017). The body recovers: Practitioner perspective on somatic experiencing, Unpublished MA Dissertation, St. Catherine University. Retrieve from Sophia, the St Catherine University repository website. https://sophia.stkate.edu/msw_papers/768

Messman, T. L., & Bhuptani, P. H. (2017). A review of long-term impact of child maltreatment on posttraumatic stress disorder and its comorbidities: An emotion dysregulation perspective. *24*(S1). https://doi.org/10.1111/cpsp.12193

Mitchell, S. A., & Black, M. J. (1995). *Freud and beyond: A history of modern psychoanalytic thought.* New York: Basic Books.

Mitchell, S. A. (2000). *Relationality: From attachment to intersubjectivity.* New York: Taylor & Francis.

Miller-Perrin, C. L., & Perrin, R. D. (2012). *Child maltreatment: An introduction.* Los Angeles, CA: SAGE Publications.

Modell, A. H. (2007). The body in psychoanalysis and the origin of fantasy. In J. P. Muller & J. G. Tillman (Eds.), *The embodied subject: Minding the body in psychoanalysis* (pp. 1–15). Jason Aronson.

Ogden, P. (2014). Wisdom of the body, lost and found: The nineteenth John Bowlby Memorial lecture. In K. White (Ed.), *Talking bodies: How do we integrate working with the body in psychotherapy from an attachment and relational perspectives* (Chapter 6, pp. 109–124). London: Karnac Publishers.

Ogden, P., Minton, K., & Pain, C. (2006). *Trauma and the body: A sensorimotor approach to approach to psychotherapy.* New York: WW Norton Company.

Olssen, M. C. (2013). Mental health practitioners' views on why somatic experiencing works for treating trauma. Master of Social Work Clinical Research Papers. Paper 244. http://sophia.stkate.edu/msw_papers/244

Payne, P., Levine, P. A., & Crane-Godreau, M. A. (2015a). Somatic experiencing: Using interoception and proprioception as core elements of trauma therapy. *Frontiers in Psychology, 6*, 93. https://doi.org/10.3389/fpsyg.2015.00093

Payne, P., Levine, P. A., & Crane-Godreau, M. A. (2015b). Corrigendum: Somatic experiencing: using interoception and proprioception as core elements of trauma therapy. *Frontiers in Psychology, 6*, 93. https://doi.org/10.3389/fpsyg.2015.00423

Price, C. J., & Hooven, C. (2018). Interoceptive awareness skills for emotion regulation: Theory and approach of Mindful Awareness in Body-Oriented Therapy (MABT). *Frontiers in Psychology, 9*. https://doi.org/10.3389/fpsyg.2018.00798

Porges, S. W. (2018). Polyvagal theory: A primer. In S. W. Porges & D. Dana (Eds.), *Clinical Applications of the polyvagal theory: The emergence of polyvagal-informed therapies*. New York: WW Norton.

Porges, S. W. (2001). The polyvagal theory: phylogenetic substrates of a social nervous system. *International Journal of Psychophysiology, 42*, 123–146. https://doi.org/10.1016/S0167-8760(01)00162-3

Porges, S. W. (2003). The polyvagal theory: Phylogenetic contributions to social behavior. *Physiology and Behavior, 79*, 503–513. https://doi.org/10.1016/S0031-9384(03)00156-2

Porges, S. W. (2015). The polyvagal perspective. *Biological Psychology, 74*(2), 116–143. https://doi.org/10.1016/j.biopsycho.2006.06.009

Racco, A., & Vis, J. (2015). Evidence-based trauma treatment for children and youth. *Child and Adolescence Social Work Journal, 32*, 121–129. https://doi.org/10:1007/510560-014-0347

Ramafoko, L. (2020, December 4). Gender-based violence. *Mail & Guardian*. Retrieved October 11, 2022, from https://mg.co.za/special-reports/2020-12-04-gender-based-violence/

Ritacco, G., & Suffla, S. (2012). A critical review of child maltreatment indices: Psychometric properties and application in the South African context. *African Safety Promotion Journal, 10*(2), 3–17.

Rossi, C. P. (2014). SE™ beginning level training effect on professional and personal life of students (Unpublished doctoral dissertation). Charisma University: Grace Bay, Providenciales.

Rothschild, B. (2003). *The body remembers: Casebook: Unifying methods and models in the treatment of trauma and PTSD*. New York: W. W. Norton & Company.

Reuille-Dupont, S. (2020). Blending disciplines: Using exercise science to explain somatic psychology. *International Body Psychotherapy Journal, 19*(1), 82–93. https://www.ibpj.org/issues/IBPJ-Volume-1-2020.pdf.

Schnyder, U., & Cloitre, M. (Eds.). (2015). *Evidence based treatments for trauma-related psychological disorders: A practical guide of clinicians*. Switzerland: Springer International Publishing. https://doi.org/10.1007/978-3-319-07109-1

Sigurdottir, S., & Halldorsdottir, S. (2018). Screaming body and silent healthcare providers: A case study with a childhood sexual abuse (CSA) survivor. *International Journal of Environmental Research and Public Health, 15*, 94. https://doi.org/10.3390/ijerph15010094. www.mdpi.com/jpurnal/ijerph

Silva, S. M. G. (2014). Engaging touch & movement in somatic experiencing trauma resolution approach (Unpublished doctoral dissertation). New York: Author.

Schmidt, N. B. (2021). Exploring human freeze responses to a threat stressor. *Journal of Behavior Therapy and Experimental Psychiatry, 39*(3), 292–304. https://doi.org/10.1016/j.jbtep.2007.08.002

Stern, D. (2010). Partners in thoughts: working with unformulated, experienced, dissociation and enactment. London: Routledge.

Stolorow, R. D., Orange, D., & Atwood, G. E. (2001). World horizons: A post-Cartesian alternative to the Freudian unconscious. *Contemporary Psychoanalysis, 37*, 43–61.

Tarquinio, C., Brennstuhl, M. J., Rydberg, J. A., Bassan, F., Peter, L., Tarquinio, C. L., Auxéméry, Y., Rotonda, C., & Tarquinio, P. (2021). EMDR in telemental health counseling for healthcare workers caring for COVID-19 patients: A pilot study. *Issues in Mental Health Nursing, 42*(1), 3–14. https://doi.org/10.1080/01612840.2020.1818014

Taylor, P. J., & Saint-Laurent, R. (2016). Minding the body and embodying the mind: somatic experiencing the self in the group. The 2016 Annual Institute of the American Group Psychotherapy Association, 23–24, New York.

Thibaut, F. (2018). The mind-body Cartesian and psychiatry. *Dialogues in Clinical Neuroscience, 20*(1), 3. https://doi.org/10:31887/DCNS.2018.201/fthibaut

van Rooyen, K. (2016). What is traumatic stress? In A. Herbst & G. Reitsma (Eds.), *Trauma counselling: Principles and practice in South Africa today* (Chapter 9, pp. 157–182), Cape Town: Juta and Company (PTY), LTD.

Viner, R. M., Ross, D., Hardy, R., Kuh, D., Power, C., & Johnson, A. (2015). Life course epidemiology: Recognizing the importance of adolescence. *Journal of Epidemiological and Community Health 69*(8), 719–720. http://doi.org/10.1136/jech-2014-205300

Wachtel, P. L. (2010). *Relational theory and the practice of psychotherapy.* New York: The Guilford Press.

Watkins, L. E., Sprang, K. R., & Rothbaum, B. O. (2018). Treating PTSD: A review of evidence-based psychotherapy interventions. *Frontiers in Behaviour Neuroscience, 12,* 258. https://doi.org/10: 3389/fnbeh.2018.00258

Wekerle, C., Wolfe, D. A., Cohen, J. A., Bromberg, D. S., & Murray, L. (2019). Childhood Maltreatment. (2nd Ed.), Boston, MA: Hogrefe Publishers. https://doi.org/10.1027/00418-000

White, K. (2014). *Talking bodies: How do we integrate working with the body in psychotherapy from attachment and relational perspective?* London: Karnac.

Winblad, N. E., Changaris, M., & Stein, P. K. (2018). Effect of somatic experiencing resiliency-based trauma treatment training on quality of life and psychological health as potential markers of resilience in treating professionals. *Frontiers in Neuroscience, 70,* 1–10. https://doi.org/10.3389/ fnins.2018.00070

Wynn, G. H. (2015, August). Complementary and alternative medicine approaches in the treatment of PTSD. *Current Psychiatry Reports,* 17. https://doi.org/10.1007/s11920-015-0600-2.

Zandberg, L. J., Porter, E., & Foa, E. (2017. APA handbook of trauma psychology: Trauma practice. In S. N. Gold (Ed.), *APA handbook of trauma* (Vol. 2, pp. 169–192). Washington, DC: American Psychological Association. https://doi.org/10:1037/0000020-008

Zentgraf, H. R. (2018). Introduction to somatic experiencing therapy: Application to traumatic stress within the South African context. Psychology Honours Essay, University of Johannesburg.

Chapter 4

Theraplay for Children in South Africa

Therapists' Considerations for Its Use in the Local Context

Deidré du Toit[1] and Ahmed Riaz Mohamed[1,*]

[1]Department of Psychology, University of Pretoria, South Africa

Abstract

Attachment-based interventions and psychotherapies are targeted towards preventing and/or remediating relational challenges within caregiver–child dyads to facilitate child development and well-being. One such intervention is Theraplay, a dyadic attachment-focussed psychotherapeutic approach. Despite its popularity among practitioners, limited consideration has been given in the literature to the implementation of Theraplay in contexts outside of North America and other developed countries. Based on semi-structured interviews with six Theraplay-trained South African psychologists, this chapter explores therapists' perceptions regarding the implementation of Theraplay in South Africa. Through a thematic analysis, four main themes emerged: (1) Theraplay as a therapeutic modality; (2) South African perspective and Theraplay applicability; (3) considerations regarding resources in South Africa; and (4) caregiver accessibility and caregiver influence. A discussion of these themes is provided in this chapter pertaining to the facilitating factors and challenges regarding the implementation of Theraplay in South Africa. Furthermore, the chapter discusses findings concerning potential adaptations to Theraplay that may enhance its applicability in the South African context. In conclusion, the chapter consolidates pertinent practice recommendations and additionally offers recommendations for future research on Theraplay in South Africa.

Key Words: Theraplay, attachment-based therapy, caregiver–child relationship, South Africa

Introduction

Attachment theory has been highly influential in the field of child psychology, informing a growing body of attachment-based interventions and psychotherapies for children (Julian et al., 2017). Theraplay (Booth & Jernberg, 2010) is one such dyadic attachment-focussed psychotherapeutic approach. Despite its popularity among therapists, only limited consideration has been given in the literature to the implementation of Theraplay outside of the North American

* Corresponding Author's Email: ahmed.mohamed@up.ac.za.

context where it originated (Cooper et al., 2009), particularly in developing contexts such as South Africa. The purpose of this chapter is to explore the use of Theraplay for children in South Africa from the perspective of local practitioners. First, a brief discussion of attachment theory, the importance of caregiver–child attachment, attachment-based interventions, and the necessity of interventional adaptations for contextual and cultural relevance is provided. Following this, the remainder of the chapter discusses the findings from interviews conducted with South African Theraplay-trained therapists to explore their perceptions regarding the implementation of Theraplay in South Africa. The chapter concludes with recommendations for practice and further research regarding Theraplay for children in South Africa.

Attachment Theory and Caregiver–Child Relationships

Attachment theory posits that human infants have a biological proclivity from birth to establish attachments to their primary caregivers and use them as a secure base for exploration and as a safe haven for protection (Ludy-Dobson & Perry, 2010; Sullivan et al., 2011). Bowlby (1969) proposed that children's expectations of, and experiences with, their caregivers' degree of availability and responsiveness to their needs become the foundation for internal working models of relationships (Duschinsky, 2015). This contributes towards shaping their sense of self (i.e., as lovable or worthless) as well as their beliefs about others (i.e., as reliable or untrustworthy) and the world (i.e., as safe or dangerous) (Fonagy, 2018).

The work of Mary Ainsworth has informed the identification of secure as well as insecure patterns of attachment in children (Ainsworth, 1979; Ainsworth et al., 1978; Main & Solomon, 1990). Those with secure attachments have caregivers who are appropriately responsive to their needs (Pearce & Pezzot-Pearce, 2007) and serve as a secure base from which to explore their environment as well as a safe haven to return to in times of distress (Cooper et al., 2013). Those with insecure attachments have caregivers who are non-responsive (avoidant attachment), inconsistently responsive (ambivalent attachment), or simultaneously a source of safety and danger (disorganised attachment) (Duschinksy, 2015; Granqvist et al., 2017). Children with an ambivalent attachment tend to be more anxious and have a preoccupation about caregiver availability (Pearce & Pezzot-Pearce, 2007), while those with avoidant attachments tend to show excessive self-reliance (Cooper et al., 2013). Lastly, children with disorganised attachments may present with poor emotional regulation, bewildered behaviours (e.g., freezing), and behavioural stereotypies (e.g., rocking back and forth) reflecting the disorganisation of the attachment system (Cyr et al., 2010; Ludy-Dobson & Perry, 2010).

Meta-analytic evidence has supported theoretical propositions that secure attachment is strongly associated with social competence and adaptation in children (Groh et al., 2014), while attachment insecurity and disorganisation are firmly related to internalising and externalising problems (Groh et al., 2012), with disorganised attachment showing an elevated risk for externalisation (Fearon et al., 2010). Therefore, children with disorganised attachments—followed by those with ambivalent and avoidant attachments—are considered most at risk for developing psychopathology, which may extend into adulthood (Levendosky et al., 2011; Pascuzzo et al., 2015). Consequently, over the past two decades, there has been significant attention paid to the prevention and remediation of at-risk and insecure caregiver–child relationships to mitigate these mental health and developmental risks.

Given that there appeared to be a close relationship between attachment patterns and specific caregiving behaviours, Ainsworth et al. (1978) believed that it was the caregiver's degree of sensitive responsiveness towards the infant that was a notable precursor to attachment security or insecurity, which is a contention generally supported by research (Fearon & Belsky, 2016). Caregivers' sensitivity towards their infants' needs encapsulates the capacity to identify, as well as accurately and promptly respond to their child's needs (Ainsworth et al., 1991). Gerlach et al. (2022) have found that distal factors such as family risk status have an influence on attachment security but that this impact is mediated by the caregiver's sensitivity. As such, even in high-risk families, provided the caregiver is sensitive, children may develop secure attachments. Such findings suggest that the nature and quality of caregiving and, by extension, the caregiver–child relationship are highly influential in the mental health and well-being of children within the context of environmental risks (Fearon & Belsky, 2016; Shaver & Mikulincer, 2002). Considering the repercussions of non-optimal caregiving and possible environmental risk factors, there is a need for therapeutic interventions, such as Theraplay, targeting the caregiving relationship to promote improved outcomes for children (DeKlyden & Greenberg, 2016; Ludy-Dobson & Perry, 2010).

While the cross-cultural relevance of attachment theory has been critiqued (Meehan & Hawks, 2013), studies of attachment patterns conducted across several African countries since the 1970s have supported the cross-cultural applicability of attachment concepts (van IJzendoorn & Sagi-Schwartz, 2008). Furthermore, studies of attachment-based interventions in non-Western settings, such as South Africa, have demonstrated positive effects on maternal sensitivity and attachment security (Cooper et al., 2009; Mohamed et al., 2022). There has, however, been increasing recognition among the developers of attachment-based interventions that adaptation of original interventions is essential to their effective cross-cultural application and implementation (Carrera et al., 2022). Although attachment may be widely applicable, the behavioural expressions thereof may differ across contexts due to the influence of the environment and culture on conceptualisations of caregiving (Dawson, 2018; Keller & Chaudhary, 2017). Consequently, in order for attachment-based interventions to be transferable, it is crucial to take the influence of culture and the environment on caregiver–child relationships into account (Keller, 2016; Vicedo, 2017).

The developers of the Attachment and Biobehavioral Catch-up (ABC) intervention, for example, have noted the necessity of making interventional adaptations that retain its core identity while also strengthening its cultural sensitivity when implementing the intervention among Spanish-speaking, Latinx families in the USA (Carrera et al., 2022). Similarly, other attachment-based interventions, such as the Video-Feedback Intervention to Promote Positive Parenting and Sensitive Discipline (VIPP-SD), have been adapted to working with Turkish immigrant families in the Netherlands and have shown positive effects on maternal sensitivity (Yagmur et al., 2014). Hence, the question is not whether attachment-based interventions are cross-culturally applicable. Instead, the question is how attachment-based interventions can be applied in ways that are sensitive and responsive to context-, and culture-bound, differences in caregiving and caregiver–child relationships.

The Fundamentals of Theraplay

What Is Theraplay?

Theraplay is a structured intervention that incorporates dyadic play between caregivers and their children to enhance the quality of attachment relationships. This is accomplished through replicating healthy caregiver–child relationships using light-hearted and engaging interactions to promote favourable emotional modulation in children (Booth & Jernberg, 2010). Where there has been a lack of positive stimulation and validation, or fixation at a developmental stage due to trauma or previous caregiver–child attachment injuries, the purpose of Theraplay is to strengthen the self-confidence, trust, and attachment in the relational dyad (Munns, 2013).

Figure 4.1 reflects the four crucial virtues/domains around which Theraplay sessions are centred: structure, engagement, nurture, and challenge (Booth & Jernberg, 2010). Structure relates to the trustworthiness and predictability of the caregiver to promote security while setting appropriate boundaries for the child (Bojanowski & Ammen, 2011). Engagement fosters attunement, encouragement of autonomy, and shared joy between the caregiver and child (Booth & Jernberg, 2010). Nurturance involves the soothing response of a caregiver to the child's regulatory needs and the ability for the caregiver and child to empathetically interact with one another (Booth & Winstead, 2015). Lastly, challenge comprises children experiencing a sense of accomplishment through the ability of caregivers to set challenges that are developmentally appropriate for them (Booth & Jernberg, 2010).

The Marschak Interaction Method (MIM), an assessment of the caregiver–child interaction prior to the commencement of Theraplay, assists with the determination of which domains require therapeutic attention for each dyad (Bojanowski & Ammen, 2011). The sessions are planned and structured by the therapist according to the dimensions (Figure 4.1) that require remediation as determined by the MIM. Age-appropriate activities are chosen that are highly interactive and often involve physical contact aiming to imitate healthy caregiver–child interactions (Booth & Winstead, 2015). Table 4.1 contains a sample of activities available for selection by the therapist for inclusion in Theraplay sessions. Prominence is initially given to the interactivity between the therapist and the child, but the focus gradually shifts from therapist–child interactions to the caregiver working directly with the child to enhance the caregiver–child relationship (Munns, 2003). Generally, Theraplay processes involve approximately 18 to 26 weekly sessions, 30 to 45 minutes in duration (Bojanowski & Ammen, 2011). A further four, quarterly, follow-up sessions are recommended over the year following treatment to maintain therapeutic progress (Wettig et al., 2006); see Booth and Jernberg (2010) for a more detailed description of Theraplay.

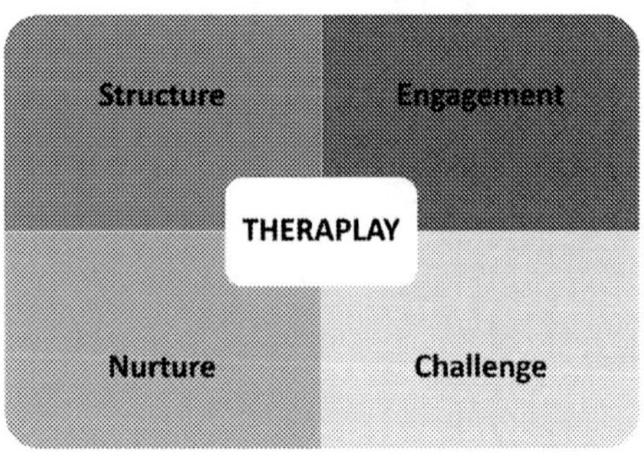

Figure 4.1 Theraplay dimensions.

Table 4.1 Examples of activities organised according to Theraplay dimension

Theraplay dimension	Examples of Theraplay activities[1]
Structure	*Cotton ball hockey*: Lie on the floor on our tummies (or sit with a pillow between you). Blow cotton balls back and forth trying to get the cotton ball under your partner's arm or off the edge of the pillow. Or you can cooperate and both blow hard enough to keep the ball in the middle.
Engagement	*Sticker match*: Put a colourful sticker on the child and have the child put stickers on you or their parent in just the same place until both are decorated in the same way. After the stickers are applied, child and parent touch matching stickers together, for example, nose to nose, elbow to elbow, before removing them.
Nurture	*Lotioning or powdering*: Put lotion or powder on the child's arms, hand, legs, or feet. You can sing a personalised song as you do this, 'Oh, lotion, oh lotion on Sarah's feet / It feel so good, it feels so sweet. Oh lotion, oh lotion on Sarah's hand / It feels so good, it feels so grand.' Attend to the child's sensory needs by using firm pressure, or choosing powder rather than lotion for the child who has tactile sensitivity.
Challenge	*Balloon tennis*: Keep balloon in the air using specified body parts; for example, heads, hands, no hands, shoulders. If you choose feet, everyone lies on the floor and keeps the balloon in the air by kicking it gently. To create more structure and focus, choose a goal for how long you can keep it in the air, for example 'Let's see if we can count to twenty'.

[1]Activity descriptions obtained from Booth and Jernberg (2010, pp. 525–545).

Indications for Theraplay Utilisation

Various studies have indicated that Theraplay interventions have beneficial effects for internalising and externalising difficulties in children with mental health challenges (Mohamed & Mkabile, 2015; Wettig et al., 2006). Research also suggests that Theraplay positively influences the personality characteristics of children regarding assertiveness, self-reliance, and self-confidence (Bundy-Myrow, 2005). Furthermore, studies have found that Theraplay has diminished symptom intensity in children with attentional problems and anxiety difficulties (Brendel & Maynard, 2014), as well as those on the autism spectrum (Simeone-Russell, 2011; Wettig et al., 2006), and with intellectual and developmental disabilities (Mohamed & Mkabile, 2015; Siu, 2014). Several studies have supported the effectiveness of Theraplay for various populations of children (Simeone-Russell, 2011). Such populations include those related to adoption (Shea, 2015; Weir et al., 2013), domestic violence (Bennett et al., 2006), social developmental skills difficulties (Siu, 2014), disruptive and conduct behavioural disorders (Foulkrod & Davenport, 2010; Weir, 2011), language disorders (Julian et al., 2017; Kupperman et al., 2005), and those at risk of developing internalising problems (Siu, 2009). Although the research briefly outlined here is not exhaustive, and much of the evidence does not yield from randomised controlled trials, the existing evidence is nonetheless broadly suggestive of the therapeutic benefit of Theraplay.

The South African Context

Internationally, the effectiveness of attachment-based interventions has been established (Bakermans-Kranenburg et al., 2003, 2005; Wright & Edgington, 2016). However, apart from a few exceptions (e.g., Dawson et al., 2021; Dekel et al., 2018; Meinck et al., 2017;

Tomlinson et al., 2005), there is a distinct lack of attachment research in South Africa. Even more limited is research on the effectiveness and feasibility of attachment-based interventions in South Africa, in general (e.g., Aspoas & Amod, 2014; Cooper et al., 2009; Mohamed et al., 2022), and regarding Theraplay, specifically (e.g., Mohamed & Mkabile, 2015). South Africa is unique regarding its cultural, linguistic, and ethnic diversity (Berg, 2012). This spans 11 official languages, multiple collectivistic and individualistic cultural groups as well as their increasingly complex intersections (Adams et al., 2014; Eaton & Louw, 2000). It is necessary, therefore, that psychologists develop cultural competence when working with individuals and families in South Africa. In addition to therapists understanding their own ethnic and cultural backgrounds and the implicit biases that accompany them, this involves an imperative to become conscientised to other cultures, to develop culturally conscious relational skills, and to implement therapeutic interventions that are culturally sensitive (Johnston, 2015; Lott, 2010). Due to the diversity in the South African population, critique has been levelled in response to the uncritical application of Westernised psychological interventions (Sher & Long, 2012). It is, therefore, imperative when considering the use or wider implementation of interventions developed elsewhere, that the relevance, applicability, and feasibility of such interventions be explored to inform if, and how, these should be adapted to meet the local context. The developers of Theraplay point out that consideration should be given to the cultural values of the families being treated and modifications to the therapeutic intervention should be made accordingly (Booth & Jernberg, 2010). However, research on the views that mental healthcare professionals have on the cross-applicability of using Theraplay and its vicissitudes in the context of South Africa has not been conducted.

Therapists' Perceptions of Theraplay in South Africa

The remainder of this chapter will address the use of Theraplay in the South African context. This will be achieved through the presentation and discussion of findings from a qualitative study conducted with a group of trained practitioners using Theraplay in South Africa (du Toit, 2020). Exploring the experiences of this group may offer insights into the applicability of Theraplay in a non-Western context with a variety of social, cultural, and economic factors that may impact the caregiver–child relationship. It may further assist in furthering efforts to develop relevant services to address the mental healthcare needs of a multicultural and contextually diverse South African population more effectively (Johnston, 2015). Therefore, the overarching aim of this study was to explore therapists' perceptions of the implementation of Theraplay in the South African context. The following research objectives were addressed:

- To explore therapists' perceptions regarding facilitating factors of implementing Theraplay in South Africa
- To explore therapists' perceptions regarding the challenges involved with implementing Theraplay in South Africa
- To obtain the professional opinion of therapists regarding suggestions and possible adaptions, where necessary, for Theraplay in South Africa

Research Methodology

Research Design

The study used an exploratory qualitative research design (Braun & Clarke, 2013) to better understand and develop insights into the use of Theraplay in South Africa. This was accomplished through exploring the perceptions of therapists who have used Theraplay in South Africa, which is an area that has to date not received attention in the literature.

Research Participants and Sampling Procedures

Purposive sampling was the primary sampling strategy and was supplemented by snowball sampling. The final sample consisted of six practicing psychologists, registered with the Health Professions Council of South Africa, who had at least Level 1 training in, and a minimum of three years' experience using, Theraplay. The rationale for this was to ensure that the participants had gathered sufficient experience using Theraplay to allow for meaningful commentary on the facilitators, challenges, and adaptations regarding its implementation locally.

Purposive sampling was carried out via an advertisement posted to an online professional referral network of mental healthcare professionals, to which prospective participants responded via email or telephonically. The snowball sampling involved requesting participating therapists to refer any other Theraplay-trained mental healthcare professionals who met the inclusion criteria (Willig, 2013). Subsequently, the researcher contacted potential research participants to explain the study in further detail, to answer any questions, and to schedule a time for obtaining informed consent and for data collection. Table 4.2 summarises the research participants.

Data Collection Procedures

Individual semi-structured interviews were conducted with each participant guided by an interview schedule developed in reference to the study objectives (Robson, 2002). The interview

Table 4.2 Summary of participants

Participant	Age range (years)	Gender	Race group	Years of independent practice (years utilising Theraplay)	Current practice type (previous experience) and level of training in Theraplay
1	35–40	Female	White	7 years (5 years)	Private (Public), Levels 1 and 2
2	25–30	Female	Black	3.5 years (3.5 years)	Both, Level 1
3	35–40	Female	White	11 years (11 years)	Private (Public), Levels 1 and 2
4	30–35	Female	White	6 years (4.5 years)	Private (Public), Level 1
5	30–35	Female	White	7 years (7 years)	Public (Private), Levels 1 and 2
6	40–45	Female	White	14 years (14 years)	Private (Public), Levels 1 and 2

schedule contained broad questions regarding the perceptions of the process of using Theraplay, how the therapists experienced implementing the approach in the local context, and possible recommendations regarding its implementation in South Africa. These open-ended questions guided the direction of the interviews and highlighted areas for further exploration through detail-oriented probing strategies to obtain rich data (Willig, 2013). Interviews ranged 60 to 90 minutes in duration and took place at the practice location of the participants. All interviews were conducted, audio-recorded, and subsequently transcribed by the first author.

Data Analysis

Using *Atlas.ti*, the data were analysed using Braun and Clarke's (2014) inductive thematic analysis to identify themes across the interviews. For the purposes of rigour, the data were analysed separately by the first author as well as an independent, second analyst. First, the analysts familiarised themselves with the content of the interview transcripts through multiple readings. Following this, open coding was applied by noting significant words, phrases, or segments in the transcripts that were relevant to the aims of the study. Thereafter, the codes were grouped according to their semantic similarity and preliminary themes were developed from this. This process was followed independently by each analyst. Subsequently, the analysts met to discuss the initial themes and any notable disagreements were resolved through consensus. Subsequently, the preliminary themes were revisited in an iterative process resulting in themes being merged, split, or eliminated. In a concluding discussion, the analysts met to finalise the themes presented in Table 4.3.

Ethical Considerations

The study was approved by the Faculty of Humanities Research Ethics Committee at the University of Pretoria (GW20180819HS). Verbal and written informed consent were obtained from each participant prior to the commencement of data collection.

Discussion of Noteworthy Findings

The aim of this study was to explore therapists' perceptions pertaining to the use of Theraplay in South Africa. This was achieved by exploring the facilitating factors, challenges involved, as well as possible suggestions and adaptations related to the utilisation of Theraplay, locally. The following four themes emerged: (1) Theraplay as a therapeutic modality, (2) South African perspective and Theraplay applicability, (3) considerations regarding resources in South Africa, and (4) caregiver accessibility and caregiver influence (see Table 4.3 for an overview). In the following, these themes are integrated into a discussion organised.

Factors Facilitating the Implementation of Theraplay in South Africa

The participants in this study agreed on the overall strengths of Theraplay. Participants appreciated its theoretical and empirical basis as well as the continual efforts to expand its evidence base.

Table 4.3 Themes and supporting interview extracts

Theme	Theme outline	Supporting interview extracts
Theraplay as a therapeutic modality	Theraplay was perceived as effective and practical for a range of diagnostic and age groups. Although its sound theoretical framework and structure were considered beneficial, there was some concern regarding possible rigidity. It was also valued that Theraplay seeks to remain updated and relevant through current research. Further consideration was highlighted regarding the goals of nurturing touch for when children become older or have experienced trauma.	'Theraplay can go right from neurodevelopmental disorders. […] I see ADHD as an attachment disorder. […] I use [Theraplay] to manage the relational difficulties […]. I definitely use it across the board for diagnoses'. 'I'm a bit ambivalent about how structured it is. […] I do think there's a lot to be said for formulation and preparation for therapeutic interventions. And what worries me […] it's starting to become exceptionally formulaic where it's sort of like, step one, step two, step three, […] each child needs an individualised plan, not just —oh this is session one, interview this parent, session two do the following […]'.
South African perspective and Theraplay applicability	Some aspects of Theraplay and its activities were perceived as culturally and contextually suitable to South Africa, such as its non-reliance on language. However, there were other factors that were regarded as needing revision to make Theraplay more culturally and contextually relatable. This included the need for additional context-specific activities and for some existing tasks to be revised.	'Being a very, very diverse country, something like Theraplay that is not so heavily reliant on language, comes in really, really handy […] And a lot of the times, especially in the public service, you find that there's a lot of language barriers […] And I think Theraplay comes in handy when it comes to, you know, working with that kind of difficulty in therapy […] as language isn't so important, you know, it's more about the [Theraplay] activity and the-the improving of the relationship'. 'In my [Theraplay] training, difficulties that […] came across in different countries, but which is also applicable to South Africa, is countries that [have] a lot of poverty. […] For example, one of the games is to throw marshmallows at one another […]. And that is extremely hard for children [where] food is very rare'.
Considerations regarding resources in South Africa	An advantage of Theraplay is that it is less demanding on resources, requiring only minimal space and inexpensive items. Although this is beneficial to a developing country such as South Africa, there are other resource obstacles. This includes financial difficulties, such as transportation expenses and limited or no medical aid coverage. Geographical and financial obstacles also influence access to Theraplay training and supervision opportunities for local therapists.	'[Theraplay activities] don't require a lot of money […] to-to-to buy the stuff needed, like the newspaper or cotton wool or whatever. […] it's easily accessible, I don't think anybody [in South Africa] gets denied access to any of the activities for financial reasons'. 'The ideal [number of prescribed sessions] is a really long time… Either for people to take off work […] because they-they [are] bringing the children to therapy or to pay trans-transport money […] for completion of the Theraplay sessions. […] We try to refer to closer to home, […] but there's not always a psychologist in the community or that is trained in Theraplay'.
Caregiver accessibility and caregiver influence	This theme included the impact that caregivers have on the Theraplay process in light of their expectations and perceptions thereof. Although Theraplay was considered comprehensible and accessible to caregivers, facilitating their understanding of its rationale, there were also barriers. These included lack of caregiver accessibility due to social circumstances, various life stressors, and resistance/avoidance.	'Parents can either make the therapy or break it. […] it is exceptionally difficult to manage two people in the room plus yourself, plus try and manage everything else. […] In my experience, [it] is the parents have to get on with you. So, your rapport has to be very strong with the parents in order for them not to feel, you know, criticised, hyper-vigilant, you know'. '…often work with single mothers although Theraplay encourage[s] that both parents should be there, but in […] South Africa, I think that is a reality that-that a lot of people are not together either because they never married or because they divorced or work […] or-or even death, maybe both are even dead'.

This aligns with the recognition of Theraplay by the California Evidence-based Clearinghouse (CEBC) for Child Welfare in the USA as an intervention supported by promising research evidence (CEBC, n.d.). This is likely to facilitate confidence in Theraplay, assisting practitioners—such as those in the current study—in selecting the most impactful clinical interventions (Fairburn & Cooper, 2011; Stewart & Chambless, 2007).

Participants also perceived Theraplay to be widely applicable across psychopathologies. This is consistent with studies which have found positive effects of Theraplay for attachment disorders (Foulkrod & Davenport, 2010) as well as behavioural (Wettig et al., 2006) and attentional (Brendel & Maynard, 2014) difficulties. This broad applicability was perceived as valuable in South Africa where exposure to domestic and community violence may place children at an elevated risk of disrupted attachments and psychological distress (Ludy-Dobson & Perry, 2010). This is particularly concerning given the limited focus on mental health, in general, and for children, specifically, in terms of both policy and service provision in South Africa (Turner & Honikman, 2016). Consequently, in this context, Theraplay was regarded as a useful therapeutic resource.

Theraplay was perceived to be accessible to caregivers, undercutting the influence of potential barriers to the therapeutic process, such as the level of education and language differences (Berg, 2012; Ntuli, 2012; Petersen & Lund, 2011). This was attributed to the focus in Theraplay on engaging the caregiver–child dyad through experiential and interactive play (Munns, 2003) and relying less on linguistic ability. With 11 official languages, linguistic barriers are commonplace in the South African context where most psychologists are still white and English-, or Afrikaans-speaking, while the majority of the population is black and for whom English is often a third or fourth language (Busch, 2010; Johnston, 2015). Although language is not absent from Theraplay, the process is not reliant on it, thus expanding its reach in a population where linguistic barriers between service providers and their users are a regular occurrence in clinical settings.

Participants also believed that the interactive, experiential nature of Theraplay may feel more familiar and 'natural' to caregivers as compared to insight-driven approaches. Novick and Novick (2011) noted that caregivers are likely to engage more actively in intervention processes when these are experiential. This may facilitate caregivers' relatability to the intervention, enhancing their openness to the therapeutic process. It is possible that due to feeling more included, caregivers may be able to identify more closely with the rationale of the intervention through experiencing it play out directly in real time. This might also influence their buy-in and commitment, facilitating the transferral of the therapeutic benefits into the home environment. This may further promote the generalisability of the relational skills developed in the Theraplay process to settings outside of the therapy room (Booth & Jernberg, 2010).

Theraplay was considered by participants to be cost-efficient because it makes use of everyday materials which are relatively inexpensive, facilitating implementation in under-resourced settings. This was also thought to allow greater transferability of activities and skills into the home setting. In addition, practically, Theraplay was considered flexible and versatile due to its non-reliance on a traditional playroom making it possible to implement in a range of settings not otherwise suitable for psychotherapy. The reality of poverty in South Africa makes help-seeking difficult for those who rely on public health services due, for example, to the prohibitive cost of public transportation (Petersen & Lund, 2011; Ruane, 2010). Therefore, the flexibility of Theraplay is advantageous as this increases its access to those who may otherwise be prevented—by circumstance—from receiving it. This has the potential to meet a need for the mental healthcare of children in difficult-to-access geographic locations or resource-limited institutional settings in South Africa by implementing the intervention in local clinics, schools, or even the home. This aspect of dyadic interventions has been promoted since the 1970s (Fraiberg et al., 1975) and has become a central feature of several attachment-based interventions (e.g., Dozier & Bernard, 2019; Juffer et al., 2017).

Challenges Involved in Implementing Theraplay in South Africa

Several challenges related to implementing Theraplay in South Africa were also noted. The participants reported that caregivers are often uncertain about their own role in the process because Theraplay requires their direct involvement, which is not a regular feature of traditional play therapy. Nock et al. (2007) found—for traditional therapies—that caregivers believe their role to be indirect, through seeking out treatment for their children, providing consent and payment and ensuring that their children attended sessions. Caregivers are, therefore, not accustomed to being directly involved in the therapeutic process beyond the traditional provision of periodic progress feedback (Nock et al., 2007; O'Connor & Zeanah, 2003). This departs from the Theraplay process where the focus on the caregiver–child relationship necessitates the direct involvement of the caregiver in sessions (Booth & Jernberg, 2010). Therapists, therefore, should take the time to ensure that caregivers clearly understand their direct role in the Theraplay process, helping them to realign their expectations of therapy (DeFife & Hilsenroth, 2011; Novick & Novick, 2011). This may contribute towards navigating potential resistance, or even practical considerations such as leave from work, that may impact the therapeutic process.

Once having started Theraplay, participants reported that caregivers may continue to have distorted impressions of what sessions should entail such as, for example, the belief that the therapist should be doing more than merely teaching them how to play with their children. This may relate to the possibility that caregivers may exhibit defensiveness stemming from guilt and shame rooted in feeling responsible for their child's challenges (Eaton et al., 2016; Sanders & Burke, 2014). As King et al. (2014) indicated, the therapist must build a strong rapport both with the child and with the caregiver as this provides an empathic holding environment. Through this, caregivers can experience non-judgemental understanding which may disarm defensiveness, positively influencing their willingness to engage in the therapeutic process as agents of change.

Ensuring that caregivers understand the rationale of the intervention may allow them to feel more supported, respected, and acknowledged for their integral part within the therapeutic process (DeFife & Hilsenroth, 2011; Nock et al., 2007). This may further influence caregiver involvement not only in sessions but also at home (King et al., 2014). Non-adherence by caregivers to practicing Theraplay skills at home was a challenge highlighted by participants. Although it is important for all child psychotherapies that practitioners ensure caregivers understand the rationale behind and intricacies of therapy, it is particularly vital for dyadic approaches where the treatment process and its success are hinged on caregivers' direct and active involvement. This may enhance the credibility of the Theraplay process for caregivers which could influence their expectations, motivation to engage within and beyond sessions, and possibly increase treatment adherence (Hawley & Garland, 2008; Naidu & Behari, 2010).

Caregiver unavailability, due to factors such as avoidance/resistance or work-related absences, was considered by the participants as challenging. This is consistent with previous research implicating stigmatisation, psychological turmoil, work responsibilities, exhaustion, and family worries in caregivers' lack of involvement in their children's psychotherapeutic processes (Watkins et al., 2013). However, in Theraplay, as with other dyadic approaches, the 'client' is neither the child nor the caregiver but, rather, is the caregiver–child relationship (Barlow et al., 2016). As such, optimally, Theraplay actively includes both parties in a highly interactive process. While Theraplay can proceed without the caregiver, with the therapist as the substitute, this is not ideal. There was concern among the participants that by caregivers not being involved in the process—even if this was unavoidable—their motivation and willingness to practice Theraplay skills at home would be diminished which may limit the therapeutic reach of the process.

Every aspect of the Theraplay process is highly structured, planned, and prescribed by the therapist in advance (Booth & Jernberg, 2010). This ensures that Theraplay is administered in a relatively uniform manner across settings and contexts. The participants in this study felt that, while such structure can be relieving to therapists, there was some concern that this may sacrifice the flexibility of a more personalised therapeutic process for individual caregiver–child dyads. In line with this, Norcross and Wampold (2011) found that efficient therapeutic relationships are those in which the therapeutic process is tailored according to the individual seeking treatment as it empowers patients and increases treatment adherence. Although the domains (Figure 4.1) requiring therapeutic attention and their corresponding Theraplay activities do vary depending on the needs of the dyad, there is seemingly little room for deviation from the planned weekly protocol.

Physical touch is a notable feature in many Theraplay activities. Despite nurturing touch being regarded as therapeutically beneficial (Harrison et al., 2012), the participants believed that greater consideration should be given to this aspect in South Africa where physical and sexual abuse against children is endemic (Artz et al., 2018; Statistics South Africa, 2018a). The participants expressed concern that the indiscriminate use of touch could be counter-therapeutic when associated with trauma due to the potential for re-traumatisation. This could have implications for Theraplay where touch is a component of many of the activities such as *lotioning/powdering* (see Table 4.1). Although Booth and Jernberg (2010) suggest the gradual introduction of nurturing touch to children who are tactile and defensive, present findings suggest that greater caution be used in a country such as South Africa given its significant rates of violence and abuse committed against children (Johnston, 2015).

Another challenge raised by the participants was that, although Theraplay is considered cost-effective regarding its required materials, it does not accommodate insufficient finances to cover the costs of treatment in the private sector or transport expenses for those accessing services in the public sector. The latter, particularly, is the reality for a significant proportion of the population in South Africa where approximately 75% of the population who require mental healthcare are not able to afford or access treatment, and consequently do not receive it (Schneider et al., 2016). Findings also highlighted that the lack of resources in South Africa poses a challenge as it impacts available funding for mental healthcare affecting human resources and training opportunities (Lund et al., 2011; Petersen & Lund, 2011), including Theraplay. Currently, Theraplay training is offered only by the Theraplay Institute in the USA or, alternatively, if the Institute is invited abroad, all of which may incur hefty costs for attendees. This opportunity has only been offered on a limited number of occasions in South Africa, the cost of which may have been prohibitive for some due to self-funding and the absence of other sources of funding for practitioners not in private practice. This may further restrict the pool of available practitioners who are trained in Theraplay, many of whom are exclusively in private practice and, therefore, not accessible to much of the population who are reliant on public health services.

Moreover, the study indicated that while the domains of Theraplay were considered relevant and applicable to the local context, further thought is needed to go into how these domains may manifest in the South African cultural landscape. Caregiving and caregiver responsibilities are situated within context-specific social and legal institutions (Knudsen & Andersen, 2014). In addition, variations can occur both inter- and intra-culturally (Tamis-LeMonda et al., 2008). This draws attention to how cultural dynamics influence caregiving and attachment behaviours (Johnston, 2015). For example, eye contact and maintaining proximity to caregivers are considered to indicate greater attachment security (Zeanah et al., 2011). However, these may be considered disrespectful within African cultures while they are accepted and expected under appropriate circumstances in Western cultures (Ntuli, 2012). As highlighted in the present study, such cultural influence on child-rearing practices in South Africa needs to be considered when using Theraplay activities. Although Booth and Jernberg (2010) do mention that the cultural values of a caregiver–child dyad are crucial to consider, it is more complex in the South African context given its ethnocultural diversity (Berg, 2012). Accordingly, greater consideration and guidance should be given to these aspects to increase the relevance of Theraplay to a broader pool of potential beneficiaries, locally. There is the potential need for adaptation of activities to align more closely with how the Theraplay domains are 'translated' in the local cultural landscape so that therapeutic outcomes may be maximised. In a meta-analysis of therapeutic interventions that have been culturally modified compared to interventions that have not, Benish et al. (2011) found that culturally adapted therapy has better therapeutic outcomes than psychotherapy that had not been adapted, which supports the perceptions expressed in the current study. Specifically, in the context of attachment-based interventions which emphasise the role of caregivers, acknowledging the influence of culture on caregiving practices is crucial in order to provide services that are aligned with, or sensitive to, cultural norms and variations (Keller, 2018).

Practitioners' Adaptations and Recommendations for the Implementation of Theraplay in South Africa

In response to some of the challenges experienced, the participants reflected on adaptations that they have made to Theraplay. Most South Africans do not have access to medical aid and rely on public services, and the coverage of those who do have medical aids is often limited (Statistics South Africa, 2018b). Participants in this study have, therefore, adapted their approach by deviating from the prescribed 18 to 26 Theraplay sessions (Booth & Jernberg, 2010). This is in response to the financial challenges, transportation struggles, and partial compensation for limited sessions covered by medical aids. Although it is acknowledged that reducing the number of sessions may not be ideal regarding the ultimate therapeutic outcomes that could be achieved, it is reasoned that fewer Theraplay sessions are more beneficial than no treatment.

The participants also made adaptations to the prescribed Theraplay activities, where applicable. These included, for instance, singing a Zulu song instead of twinkle-twinkle-little-star or using nurturing language instead of touch, if touch is problematic for a particular caregiver–child dyad. These adaptations were deemed necessary to make Theraplay activities more relatable to caregivers and their children to increase positive outcomes and treatment adherence

(Norcross & Wampold, 2011). Participants further recommended that a wider variety of culture-specific Theraplay activities be developed for use in specific contexts. They suggested that systematically observing local caregiver–child interactions could benefit adaptations to Theraplay activities based on an emic perspective of the family's culture-specific relational dynamics. This could include exploring with caregivers the everyday activities that they engage in that are nurturing, challenging, structuring, and engaging as a foundation from which to update existing, or develop new, Theraplay activities that would be more familiar to the South African context (Benish et al., 2011). This would enhance the relatability and familiarity of Theraplay activities for the caregivers and children, which may impact their willingness to engage in the therapeutic process and facilitate the transfer and generalisation thereof into the home environment.

Access to international trainers is also costly, limiting the number of trained Theraplay practitioners in South Africa, which in turn limits the number of dyads that can access this therapy. Therefore, it was unanimously recommended by all participants that the Theraplay Institute provides more frequent training workshops to increase the number of qualified Theraplay practitioners in South Africa. Ultimately, this would increase the human resources to improve Theraplay service delivery allowing more access to the intervention in a context where high rates of poverty, exposure to community violence, and various forms of abuse (Lund et al., 2011; Ward et al., 2014) increase the risk of caregiver–child relational ruptures and necessitates the need for dyadic interventions. This would further enable practitioners to refer caregiver–child dyads to clinics closer to home, easing the financial burden.

Recommendations for Theraplay in South Africa

Practice Recommendations

Based on the findings of the study, the following practice recommendations are offered:

- The scope of Theraplay activities should be broadened to include more culture-specific games and songs sung in local languages.
- Local musical instruments and dances that are applicable to certain local cultures should be considered for integration into Theraplay activities to make sessions more relatable to families from different cultural backgrounds.
- Parallel activities for those involving physical touch should be developed so that for children who are touch sensitive, or for whom touch is a traumatic trigger, the alternative parallel activity can be substituted. This could, for example, involve using verbal nurturance instead of physical nurturance to achieve an analogous outcome.
- While 18 to 26 sessions are the recommended duration of a Theraplay process, this is not set in stone. To account for the cost of therapy in the context of limited financial resources, capped medical aid coverage, transport costs, and overburdened public health services, shorter therapeutic processes must be considered. However, it may be necessary when using a much-shortened version of Theraplay that adaptations need to be made to how activities are organised, or the number of activities included in the sessions, to maximise intensity despite the shorter duration.
- An additional practice recommendation would be to establish a local affiliate of the Theraplay Institute that could serve to provide locally based and contextually sensitive

Theraplay training and supervision. This would serve to reduce the costs of accessing Theraplay training in South Africa, making it more available to practitioners and, therefore, increasing its availability as a service.

Recommendations for Future Research

One area that could serve to facilitate the practice of Theraplay in South Africa would be to develop, through further research, a set of culture-specific adaptations to Theraplay activities for each of the four dimensions based on detailed ethnographic observations of parent–child interactions. In addition, future research on the perceptions and opinions of Theraplay practitioners should utilise a larger and more diverse sample regarding gender, ethnicity, and culture. This might offer wider, and more in-depth, perceptions of the local implementation of Theraplay and may provide further insights into the cross-applicability of the intervention. Including more context-specific research pertaining to therapists' perceptions of implementing Theraplay in rural communities in South Africa would also potentially allow for more integrated and representative findings. Making use of focus groups and/or a Delphi procedure could be particularly beneficial here to obtain a professional consensus among participating mental health professionals on context-specific adaptations to Theraplay.

Increasing focus is being given to the significant role that caregivers play within interventions for children (Julian et al., 2017; Williford et al., 2016). Future research on caregivers' experiences of being part of the Theraplay process may be useful to identify factors that facilitate their involvement and active engagement as well as the barriers to this. This could assist in informing micro-interventions to address issues of avoidance, resistance, treatment adherence, and motivation on the part of the caregiver who is crucial to the success of the intervention and to optimise positive outcomes.

Future research might also consider exploring which attachment-based interventions mental healthcare providers prefer using and for what reasons. It could be enlightening to survey therapists in South Africa to understand the extent of their knowledge of Theraplay and their reasons for either choosing to use it or not. Such insight into reasons for preferring not to use this modality or to utilise other attachment-based approaches may be of value to the Theraplay Institute regarding possible improvements in training and interventional adjustments.

Study Limitations

A limitation of the current study is that, due to its small sample size, the opinions of the therapists may not represent the perceptions of all South African Theraplay practitioners. Replication with a larger and more diverse sample may well yield different results. The final sample included only female clinical psychologists and had five white participants with only one black participant. The limited cultural and racial diversity of the sample is likely to have restricted the participants' capacities to comment more meaningfully on the cross-cultural factors at play in the use of Theraplay in South Africa. Furthermore, none of the participants worked in a rural community context. Therefore, the perceptions explored in this study were rooted in professional experiences in both private practice and the urban public sector, which may not be directly applicable to rural settings that may require special consideration.

Summary and Conclusion

This chapter explored therapists' perceptions regarding their use of Theraplay in South Africa. Semi-structured interviews with six Theraplay-trained psychologists revealed several strengths which facilitated the local use of the approach. These included its established theoretical basis, emerging evidence base, suitability for a range of psychological problems and patient groups, its experiential nature, and its versatility. Nonetheless, a range of challenges emerged, including caregivers' misaligned expectations regarding their degree of direct involvement, caregiver defensiveness and avoidance due to guilt and self-blame, the rigidity of the approach, limited access to training and supervision, and potential for alienation due to activities that may be culturally unfamiliar. Practitioners responded to certain contextual realities by adapting the Theraplay process. This involved implementing a therapeutic process that was shortened to reduce the costs of treatment and transportation and using local songs and games to enhance the relatability of the activities. Theraplay is regarded as a useful and relevant therapeutic intervention in South Africa. However, it is also evident that—despite this relevance—there are context-specific considerations that are required to enhance the cross-cultural and contextual applicability of Theraplay in a way that responds to the realities of the South African setting. This would promote Theraplay in making its mark in the broader landscape of psychotherapeutic interventions to address much-needed mental health services for children in the country.

References

Adams, B. G., van der Vijver, F. J. R., de Bruin, G. P., & Torres, C. B. (2014). Identity in descriptions of others across ethnic groups in South Africa. *Journal of Cross-Cultural Psychology, 45*(9), 1411–1433. https://doi.org/10.1177/0022022114542466

Ainsworth, M. D. S. (1979). Infant-mother attachment. *American Psychologist, 34*(10), 932–937. https://doi.org/10.1037/0003-066X.34.10.932

Ainsworth, M. D. S., Bell, S. M., & Stayton, D. J. (1991). Infant-mother attachment and social development: 'Socialisation' as a product of reciprocal responsiveness to signals. In M. Woodhead, R. Carr, & P. Light (Eds.), *Child development in social context: Becoming a person* (pp. 30–55). Routledge.

Ainsworth, M. D. S., Blehar, M. C., Waters, E., & Wall, S. (1978). *Patterns of attachment: A psychological study of the strange situation.* Lawrence Erlbaum.

Artz, L., Ward, C., Leoschut, L., Kassanjee, R., & Burton, P. (2018). The prevalence of child sexual abuse in South Africa: The optimus study South Africa. *South African Medical Journal, 108*(10), 791–792. https://doi.org/10.7196/SAMJ.2018.v108i10.13533

Aspoas, B., & Amod, Z. (2014). A South African study on caregiver perceptions of a parent-infant intervention implemented to foster a secure attachment. *Infant Mental Health Journal, 35*(6), 580–590. https://doi.org/10.1002/imhj.21458

Bakermans-Kranenburg, M. J., van IJzendoorn, M. H., & Juffer, F. (2003). Less is more: Meta-analyses of sensitivity and attachment interventions in early childhood. *Psychological Bulletin, 129*(2), 195–215. https://doi.org/10.1037/0033-2909.129.2.195

Bakermans-Kranenburg, M. J., van IJzendoorn, M. H., & Juffer, F. (2005). Disorganized infant attachment and preventive interventions: A review and meta-analysis. *Infant Mental Health Journal, 26*(3), 191–216. https://doi.org/10.1002/imhj.20046

Barlow, J., Bennett, C., Midgley, N., Larkin, S.K., & Wei, Y. (2016). Parent–infant psychotherapy: A systematic review of the evidence for improving parental and infant mental health. *Journal of Reproductive and Infant Psychology, 34*(5), 464–482. https://doi.org/10.1080/02646838.2016.1222357

Benish, S. G., Quintana, S., & Wampold, B. E. (2011). Culturally adapted psychotherapy and the legitimacy of myth: A direct-comparison meta-analysis. *Journal of Counseling Psychology*, *58*(3), 279–289. https://doi.org/10.1037/a0023626

Bennett, L., Shiner, S. K., & Ryan, S. (2006). Using Theraplay® in shelter settings with mothers and children who have experienced violence in the home. *Journal of Psychosocial Nursing and Mental Health Services*, *44*(10), 38–48. https://doi.org/10.3928/02793695-20061001-06

Berg, A. (2012). *Connecting with South Africa: Cultural communication and understanding*. Texas A&M University Press.

Bojanowski, J. J., & Ammen, S. (2011). Discriminating between pre- versus post-Theraplay treatment Marschak interaction methods using the Marschak interaction method rating system. *International Journal of Play Therapy*, *20*(1), 1–11. https://doi.org/10.1037/a0022668

Booth, P. B., & Jernberg, A. M. (2010). *Theraplay: Helping parents and children build better relationships through attachment-based play* (3rd ed.). Jossey-Bass.

Booth, P. B., & Winstead, M. L. (2015). *Theraplay: Repairing relationships, helping families heal*. Guilford Press.

Bowlby, J. (1969). *Attachment and loss: Vol. 1. Attachment*. Basic Books.

Braun, V., & Clarke, V. (2013). *Successful qualitative research: A practical guide for beginners*. Sage.

Braun, V., & Clarke, V. (2014). What can thematic analysis offer health and wellbeing researchers? *International Journal of Qualitative Studies on Health and Well-being*, *9*(1), 2652–2654. https://doi.org/10.3402/qhw.v9.26152

Brendel, K. E., & Maynard, B. R. (2014). Child-parent interventions for childhood anxiety disorders: A systematic review and meta-analysis. *Research on Social Work Practice*, *24*(3), 287–295. https://doi.org/10.1177/1049731513503713

Bundy-Myrow, S. (2005). Theraplay for children with self-regulation problems. In C. Schaefer, J. McCormick, & A. Ohnogi (Eds.), *International handbook of play therapy: Advances in assessment, theory, research, and practice* (pp. 35–64). Jason Aronson.

Busch, B. (2010). School language profiles: Valorizing linguistic resources in heteroglossic situations in South Africa. *Language and Education*, *24*(4), 283–294. https://doi.org/10.1080/09500781003678712

California Evidence-based Clearinghouse for Child Welfare. (n.d.). *Theraplay*. https://www.cebc4cw.org/program/theraplay/

Carrera, P., Benito-Gomez, M., Zablah, F. M., Schein, S.S., Costello, A. H., Roben, C. K. P., & Dozier, M. (2022). Adapting with sense: An update on culturally responsive efforts of the attachment & biobehavioral catch-up intervention with Spanish-speaking, Latinx families. *Global Implementation Research and Applications*. Advance online publication. https://doi.org/10.1007/s43477-022-00049-0

Cooper, P. J., Pauletti, R. E., Tobin, D. D., Menon, M., Menon, M. K., Spatta, B. C., … Perry, D. G. (2013). Mother-child attachment and gender identity in preadolescence. *Sex Roles*, *69*(11–12), 618–631. https://doi.org/10.1007/s11199-013-0310-3

Cooper, P. J., Tomlinson, M., Swartz, L., Landman, M., Molteno, C., Stein, A., … Murray, L. (2009). Improving quality of mother-infant relationship and infant attachment in socioeconomically deprived community in South Africa: Randomised controlled trial. *British Medical Journal*, *338*(142), Article b974. https://doi.org/10.1136/bmj.b974

Cyr, C., Euser, E. M., Bakermans-Kranenburg, M., & van IJzendoorn, M. (2010). Attachment security and disorganization in maltreating and high-risk families: A series of meta-analyses. *Development and Psychopathology*, *22*(1), 87–108. https://doi.org/10.1017/S0954579409990289

Dawson, N. (2018). From Uganda to Baltimore to Alexandra Township: How far can Ainsworth's theory stretch? *South African Journal of Psychiatry*, *24*(1), Article a1137. https://doi.org/10.4102/sajpsychiatry.v24i0.1137

Dawson, N., Bain, K., & Mesman, J. (2021). Observing maternal sensitivity in a South African township: An exploratory study into behavioral features using different measures. *Attachment & Human Development*, *23*(2), 150–163. https://doi.org/10.1080/14616734.2020.1828531

DeFife, J. A., & Hilsenroth, M. J. (2011). Starting off on the right foot: Common factor elements in early psychotherapy process. *Journal of Psychotherapy Integration*, *21*(2), 172–191. https://doi.org/10.1037/a0023889

Dekel, B., Abrahams, N., & Andipatin, M. (2018). Exploring adverse parent-child relationships from the perspective of convicted child murderers: A South African qualitative study. *PLoS One*, *13*(5), Article e0196772. https://doi.org/10.1371/journal.pone.0196772

DeKlyden, M., & Greenberg, M. T. (2016). Attachment and psychopathology in childhood. In J. Cassidy & P. R. Shaver (Eds.), *Handbook of attachment: Theory, research, and clinical applications* (3rd ed., pp. 639–666). Guilford Press.

Dozier, M., & Bernard, K. (2019). *Coaching parents of vulnerable infants: The attachment and biobehavioral catch-up approach.* Guilford Press.

du Toit, D. A. (2020). *Therapists' perceptions on the implementation of Theraplay in the South African context* (Master's dissertation). University of Pretoria.

Duschinsky, R. (2015). The emergence of the disorganized/disoriented (D) attachment classification, 1979–1982. *History of Psychology*, *18*(1), 32–46. https://doi.org/10.1037/a0038524

Eaton, L., & Louw, J. (2000). Culture and self in South Africa: Individualism-collectivism predictions. *Journal of Social Psychology*, *140*(2), 210–217. https://doi.org/10.1080/00224540009600461

Eaton, K., Ohan, J. L., Stritzke, W. G. K., & Corrigan, P. W. (2016). Failing to meet the good parent ideal: Self-stigma in parents of children with mental health disorders. *Journal of Child and Family Studies*, *25*(10), 3109–3123. https://doi.org/10.1007/s10826-016-0459-9

Fairburn, C. G., & Cooper, Z. (2011). Therapist competence, therapy quality, and therapist training. *Behavioural Research and Therapy*, *49*(6–7), 373–378. https://doi.org/10.1016/j.brat.2011.03.005

Fearon, R. M. P., Bakermans-Kranenburg, M. J., van IJzendoorn, M. H., Lapsley, A. M., & Roisman, G. I. (2010). The significance of insecure attachment and disorganization in the development of children's externalizing behavior: A meta-analytic study. *Child Development*, *81*(2), 435–456. https://doi.org/10.1111/j.1467-8624.2009.01405.x

Fearon, R. M. P., & Belsky, J. (2016). Precursors of attachment security. In J. Cassidy & P. R. Shaver (Eds.), *Handbook of attachment: Theory, research, and clinical applications* (3rd ed., pp. 291–313). Guilford Press.

Fonagy, P. (2018). *Attachment theory and psychoanalysis.* Routledge.

Foulkrod, K., & Davenport, B. R. (2010). An examination of empirically informed practice within case reports of play therapy with aggressive and oppositional children. *International Journal of Play Therapy*, *19*(3), 144–158. https://doi.org/10.1037/a0020095

Fraiberg, S., Adelson, E., & Shapiro, V. (1975). Ghosts in the nursery: A psychoanalytic approach to the problems of impaired infant-mother relationships. *Journal of the American Academy of Child Psychiatry*, *14*(3), 387–421. https://doi.org/10.1016/S0002-7138(09)61442-4

Gerlach, J., Fößel, J. M., Vierhaus, M., Sann, A., Eickhorst, A., Zimmermann, P., & Spangler, G. (2022). Family risk and early attachment development: The differential role of parental sensitivity. *Infant Mental Health Journal*, *43*(2), 340– 356. https://doi.org/10.1002/imhj.21964

Granqvist, P., Sroufe, L. A., Dozier, M., Hesse, E., Steele, M., van Ijzendoorn, M., … Duschinsky, R. (2017). Disorganized attachment in infancy: A review of the phenomenon and its implications for clinicians and policy-makers. *Attachment & Human Development*, *19*(6), 534–558, https://doi.org/10.1080/14616734.2017.1354040

Groh, A. M., Fearon, R. P., Bakermans-Kranenburg, M. J., van IJzendoorn, M. H., Steele, R. D., & Roisman, G. I. (2014). The significance of attachment security for children's social competence with peers: A meta-analytic study. *Attachment & Human Development*, *16*(2), 103–136. https://doi.org/10.1080/14616734.2014.883636

Groh, A. M., Roisman, G. I., van IJzendoorn, M. H., Bakermans-Kranenburg, M. J., & Fearon, R. P. (2012). The significance of insecure and disorganized attachment for children's internalizing symptoms: A meta-analytic study. *Child Development*, *83*(2), 591–610. https://doi.org/10.1111/j.1467-8624.2011.01711.x

Harrison, C., Jones, R. S. P., & Huws, J. C. (2012). "We're people who don't touch": Exploring clinical psychologists' perspectives on their use of touch in therapy. *Counselling Psychology Quarterly*, *25*(3), 277–287. https://doi.org/10.1080/09515070.2012.671595

Hawley, K. M., & Garland, A. F. (2008). Working alliance in adolescent outpatient therapy: Youth parent and therapist reports and associations with therapy outcomes. *Child & Youth Care Forum*, *37*(2), 59–74. https://doi.org/10.1007/s10566-008-9050-x

Johnston, E. R. (2015). South African clinical psychology's response to cultural diversity, globalisation and multiculturalism: A review. *South African Journal of Psychology, 45*(3), 374–385. https://doi.org/10.1177/0081246315575648

Juffer, F., Bakermans-Kranenburg, M. J., & van IJzendoorn, M. H. (2017). Pairing attachment theory and social learning theory in video-feedback intervention to promote positive parenting. *Current Opinion in Psychology, 15*, 189–194. https://doi.org/10.1016/j.copsyc.2017.03.012

Julian, M. M., Lawler, J. M., & Rosenblum, K. L. (2017). Caregiver-child relationships in early childhood: Interventions to promote well-being and reduce risk for psychopathology. *Current Behavioral Neuroscience Reports, 4*(2), 87–98. https://doi.org/10.1007/s40473-017-0110-0

Keller, H. (2016). Attachment. A pancultural need but a cultural construct. *Current Opinion in Psychology, 8*, 59–63. https://doi.org/10.1016/j.copsyc.2015.10.002

Keller, H. (2018). Universality claim of attachment theory: Children's socioemotional development across cultures. *Proceedings of the National Academy of Science of the United States of America (PNAS), 115*(45), 11414–11419. https://doi.org/10.1073/pnas.1720325115

Keller, H., & Chaudhary, N. (2017). Is mother essential for attachment? In H. Keller & K. A. Bard (Eds.), *Models of care in different cultures. Contextualizing attachment: The cultural nature of attachment* (pp. 109–138). MIT Press.

King, G., Currie, M., & Petersen, P. (2014). Child and parent engagement in the mental health intervention process: A motivational framework. *Child and Adolescent Mental Health, 19*(1), 2–8. https://doi.org/10.1111/camh.12015

Knudsen, H., & Andersen, N. A. (2014). Playful hyper responsibility: Toward a dislocation of parents' responsibility? *Journal of Education Policy, 29*(1), 105–121. https://doi.org/10.1080/02680939.2013.791929

Kupperman, P., Bligh, S., & Goodban, M. (2005). Theraplay with articulation disorders. In G. L. Landreth, D. S. Sweeney, D. C. Ray, L. E. Homeyer, & G. J. Glover (Eds.), *Play therapy interventions with children's problems: Case studies with DSM-IV-TR diagnoses* (2nd ed., pp. 219–221). Jason Aronson.

Levendosky, A. A., Bogat, G. A., & Huth-Bocks, A. C. (2011). The influence of domestic violence on the development of the attachment relationship between mother and young child. *Psychoanalytic Psychology, 28*(4), 512–527. https://doi.org/10.1037/a0024561

Lott, B. (2010). *Multiculturalism and diversity: A social psychological perspective*. John Wiley & Sons.

Ludy-Dobson, C. R., & Perry, B. D. (2010). The role of healthy relational interactions in buffering the impact of childhood trauma. In E. Gil (Ed.), *Working with children to heal interpersonal trauma: The power of play* (pp. 26–43). Guilford Press.

Lund, C., Kleintjies, S., Cooper, S., Petersen, I., Bhana, A., & Flisher, A. J. (2011). Challenges facing South Africa's mental health care system: Stakeholders' perceptions of causes and potential solutions. *International Journal of Culture and Mental Health, 4*(1), 23–38. https://doi.org/10.1080/17542863.2010.503039

Main, M., & Solomon, J. (1990). Procedures for identifying infants as disorganized/disoriented during the Ainsworth Strange Situation. In M. T. Greenberg, D. Cicchetti, & E. M. Cummings (Eds.), *Attachment in the preschool years: Theory, research, and intervention* (pp. 121–160). University of Chicago Press.

Meehan, C. L., & Hawks, S. (2013). Cooperative breeding and attachment among the Aka foragers. In N. Quinn & J. Mageo (Eds.), *Attachment reconsidered: Cultural perspectives on a Western theory* (pp. 85–113). Palgrave.

Meinck, F., Cluver, L. D., Orkin, F. M., Kuo, C., Sharma, A. D., Hensels, I. S., & Sherr, L. (2017). Pathways from family disadvantage via abusive parenting and caregiver mental health to adolescent health risks in South Africa. *Journal of Adolescent Health, 60*(1), 57–64. https://doi.org/10.1016/j.jadohealth.2016.08.016

Mohamed, A. R., & Mkabile, S. (2015). An attachment-focused parent-child intervention for biting behaviour in a child with intellectual disability: A clinical case study. *Journal of Intellectual Disabilities, 19*(3), 251–265. https://doi.org/10.1177/1744629515572711.

Mohamed, A. R., Sterkenburg, P., Yeatman, J. G., van Rensburg, E., & Schuengel, C. (2022). Using attachment and biobehavioral catch-up with young children with developmental delays: A

multiple-baseline trial of attachment, sensitivity, and cortisol. *Journal of Intellectual Disabilities*. Advance online publication. https://doi.org/10.1177/17446295221104614
Munns, E. (2003). Theraplay: Attachment-enhancing play therapy. In C. E. Schaefer (Ed.), *Foundations of play therapy* (pp. 156–174). John Wiley & Sons.
Munns, E. (2013). Filial therapy and Theraplay. In N. R. Bowers (Ed.), *Play therapy with families: A collaborative approach to healing* (pp. 147–160). Jason Aronson.
Naidu, T., & Behari, S. (2010). The parent-child-therapist alliance: A case study using a strategic approach. *Journal of Child & Adolescent Mental Health*, *22*(1), 41–50. https://doi.org/10.2989/17280583.2010.493674
Nock, M. K., Ferriter, C., & Holmberg, E. (2007). Parent beliefs about treatment credibility and effectiveness: Assessment and relation to subsequent treatment participation. *Journal of Child and Family Studies*, *16*(27), 27–38. https://doi.org/10.1007/s10826-006-9064-7
Norcross, J. C., & Wampold, B. E. (2011). What works for whom: Tailoring psychotherapy to the person. *Journal of Clinical Psychology*, *67*(2), 127–132. https://doi.org/10.1002/jclp.20764
Novick, K. K., & Novick, J. (2011). *Working with parents makes therapy work*. Rowman & Littlefield.
Ntuli, C. D. (2012). Intercultural misunderstanding in South Africa: An analysis of nonverbal communication behaviour in context. *Intercultural Communication Studies*, *21*(2), 20–31. https://web.uri.edu/iaics/files/02CynthiaDanisileNtuli.pdf
O'Connor, T. G., & Zeanah, C. H. (2003). Attachment disorders: Assessment strategies and treatment approaches. *Attachment & Human Development*, *5*(3), 223–244. doi:10.1080/14616730310001593974
Pascuzzo, K., Moss, E., & Cyr, C. (2015). Attachment and emotion regulation strategies in predicting adult psychopathology. *SAGE Open*, *5*(3). https://doi.org/10.1177/2158244015604695
Pearce, J. W., & Pezzot-Pearce, T. D. (2007). *Psychotherapy of abused and neglected children* (2nd ed., pp. 17–20). Guilford Press.
Petersen, I., & Lund, C. (2011). Mental health service delivery in South Africa from 2000 to 2010: One step forward, one step back. *South African Medical Journal*, *101*(10), 751–757. https://www.ajol.info/index.php/samj/article/view/70342/58675
Robson, C. (2002). *Real world research*. Blackwell Publishers.
Ruane, I. (2010). Obstacles to the utilisation of psychological resources in a South African township community. *South African Journal of Psychology*, *40*(2), 214–225. https://doi.org/10.1177/008124631004000211
Sanders, M. R., & Burke, K. (2014). The "hidden" technology of Effective Parent Consultation: A guided participation model for promoting change in families. *Journal of Child and Family Studies*, *23*(7), 1289–1297. https://doi.org/10.1007/s10826-013-9827-x
Schneider, M., Baron, E., Breuer, E., Docrat, S., Honikman, S., Onah, M., … Tomlinson, M. (2016). Integrating mental health into South Africa's health system: Current status and way forward. *South African Health Review*, *2016*(1), 153–163. https://journals.co.za/docserver/fulltext/healthr/2016/1/healthr_2016_a15.pdf?expires=1574691368&id=id&accname=guest&checksum=D928728F098401F3398E19079364F018
Shaver, P. R., & Mikulincer, M. (2002). Attachment-related psychodynamics. *Attachment & Human Development*, *4*(2), 133–161. https://doi.org/10.1080/14616730210154171
Shea, S. E. (2015). Finding parallels: The experiences of clinical social workers providing attachment-based treatment to children in foster care. *Clinical Social Work Journal*, *43*(1), 62–76. https://doi.org/10.1007/s10615-014-0488-z
Sher, D., & Long, W. (2012). Historicising the relevance debate: South African and American psychology in context. *South African Journal of Psychology*, *42*(4), 564–575. https://doi.org/10.1177/008124631204200410
Simeone-Russell, R. (2011). A practical approach to implementing Theraplay for children with autism spectrum disorder. *International Journal of Play Therapy*, *20*(4), 224–235. https://doi.org/10.1037/a0024823
Siu, A. F. Y. (2009). Theraplay in the Chinese world: An intervention program for Hong Kong children with internalizing problems. *International Journal of Play Therapy*, *18*(1), 1–12. https://doi.org/10.1037/a0013979b

Siu, A. F. Y. (2014). Effectiveness of group Theraplay on enhancing social skills among children with developmental disabilities. *International Journal of Play Therapy, 23*(4), 187–203. https://doi.org/10.1037/a0038158

Statistics South Africa. (2018a). *Men, women and children: Findings of the living conditions survey 2014/15* (Report no. 03-10-02). Statistics South Africa.

Statistics South Africa. (2018b). *Public healthcare: How much per person?* (Report no. 06-13-02). Statistics South Africa.

Stewart, R. E., & Chambless, D. L. (2007). Does psychotherapy research inform treatment decisions in private practice? *Journal of Clinical Psychology, 63*(3), 267–281. https://doi.org/10.1002/jclp.20347

Sullivan, R., Perry, R., Sloan, A., Kleinhaus, K., & Burtchen, N. (2011). Infant bonding and attachment to the caregiver: Insights from basic and clinical science. *Clinics in Perinatology, 38*(4), 643–655. https://doi.org/10.1016/j.clp.2011.08.011

Tamis-LeMonda, C. S., Way, N., Hughes, D., Yoshikawa, H., Kalman, R. K., & Niwa, E. Y. (2008). Parents' goals for children: The dynamic coexistence of individualism and collectivism in cultures and individuals. *Social Development, 17*(1), 183–209. https://doi.org/10.1111/j.1467-9507.2007.00419.x

Tomlinson, M., Cooper, P., & Murray, L. (2005). The mother–infant relationship and infant attachment in a South African peri-urban settlement. *Child Development, 76*(5), 1044–1054. https://doi.org/10.1111/j.1467-8624.2005.00896.x

Turner, R. E., & Honikman, S. (2016). Maternal mental health and the first 1000 days. *South African Medical Journal, 106*(12), 1164–1167. https://doi.org/10.7196/SAMJ.2016.v106i12.12129

van IJzendoorn, M. H., & Sagi-Schwartz, A. (2008). Cross-cultural patterns of attachment: Universal and contextual dimensions. In J. Cassidy & P. R. Shaver (Eds.), *Handbook of attachment: Theory, research, and clinical applications* (pp. 880–905). Guilford Press.

Vicedo, M. (2017). Putting attachment in its place: Disciplinary and cultural contexts. *European Journal of Developmental Psychology, 14*(6), 684–699. https://doi.org/10.1080/17405629.2017.1289838

Ward, C., Mikton, C., Cluver, L., Cooper, P., Gardner, F., Hutchings, J.,... & Wessels, I. (2014). Parenting for lifelong health: From South Africa to other low-and middle-income countries. *Early Childhood Matters, 122*. https://cafo.org/wp-content/uploads/2015/08/Parenting-for-Lifelong-Health1.pdf

Watkins, D. C., Pittman, C. T., & Walsh, M. J. (2013). The effects of psychological distress, work, and family stressors on child behavior problems. *Journal of Comparative Family Studies, 44*(1), 1–16. https://doi.org/10.3138/jcfs.44.1.1

Weir, K. N. (2011). Playing for keeps: Integrating family and play therapy to treat reactive attachment disorder. In A. A. Drewes, S. C. Bratton, & C. E. Schaefer (Eds.), *Integrative play therapy* (pp. 243–254). John Wiley & Sons.

Weir, K., Lee, S., Cansoa, P., Rodrigues, N., McWilliams, M., & Parker, L. (2013). Whole family Theraplay: Integrating family systems theory and Theraplay to treat adoptive families. *Adoption Quarterly, 16*(3/4), 175–200. https://doi.org/10.1080/10926755.2013.844216

Wettig, H. H. G., Franke, U., & Fjordbak, B. S. (2006). Evaluating the effectiveness of Theraplay®. In C. E. Schaefer & H. G. Kaduson (Eds.), *Contemporary play therapy: Theory, research, and practice* (pp. 103–135). Guilford Press.

Williford, A. P., Carter, L. M., & Pianta, P. C. (2016). Attachment and school readiness. In J. Cassidy & P. R. Shaver (Eds.), *Handbook of attachment: Theory, research, and clinical applications* (3rd ed., pp. 966–982). Guilford Press.

Willig, C. (2013). *Introducing qualitative research in psychology* (3rd ed.). Open University Press.

Wright, B., & Edgington, E. (2016). Evidence-based parenting interventions to promote secure attachment: Findings from a systematic review and meta-analysis. *Global Pediatric Health, 3*. https://doi.org/10.1177/2333794x16661888

Yagmur, S., Mesman, J., Malda, M., Bakermans-Kranenburg, M. J., & Ekmekci, H. (2014). Video-feedback intervention increases sensitive parenting in ethnic minority mothers: A randomized control trial. *Attachment & Human Development, 16*(4), 371–386. https://doi.org/10.1080/14616734.2014.912489

Zeanah, C. H., Berlin, L. J., & Boris, N. W. (2011). Practitioner review: Clinical applications of attachment theory and research for infants and young children. *Journal of Child Psychology and Psychiatry, 52*(8), 819–833. https://doi.org/10.1111/j.1469-7610.2011.02399.x

Chapter 5

Process-Based Therapy and Its Potential in Accommodating a Diverse Post-apartheid South Africa

Nevern Subermoney*

Secunda, Gauteng, South Africa

Abstract

Post-apartheid South Africa brings with it the challenge of how to train and practice as a psychotherapist with a diversity of individuals while being sensitive to their unique history, context, and goals. This chapter proposes that a novel meta-framework for understanding evidence-based psychotherapy, process-based therapy (PBT), offers guidance on how to use the science of psychotherapy in a way that is tailored to the unique individual, their context, and their goals for therapy. A multiple case study method is used to show how three different cases from the author's psychotherapy practice can be formulated with three different therapeutic modalities, while using PBT as a meta-framework. Future research on the effectiveness and efficacy of PBT in the South African context is needed to validate the preliminary potential of this approach.

Key Words: evidence-based psychotherapy, process-based therapy, case studies, efficacy

Introduction

Post-apartheid South Africa brings with it the challenge of how to train and practice as a psychotherapist with a diversity of individuals while being sensitive to their unique history, context, and goals. This chapter proposes that a novel meta-framework for understanding evidence-based psychotherapy, process-based therapy (PBT), offers guidance on how to use the science of psychotherapy in a way that is tailored to the unique individual, their context, and their goals for therapy. In this chapter, PBT will be introduced, along with its core tenets. The chapter will then go on to propose three ways in which PBT may be useful to a diverse, post-apartheid South African context, namely theoretical integration of many psychotherapeutic modalities, accommodation of a diversity of clients, and prioritising treatment utility over theoretical commitment. How PBT fulfils its utility in these three domains will be illustrated through the use of three case studies in which different therapeutic modalities are used, with PBT serving as a meta-framework that unifies all three modalities. The chapter will then

* Corresponding Author's Email: nevern.subermoney@gmail.com.

conclude with a discussion of PBT's three potential uses in the diverse post-apartheid South African context.

Process-Based Therapy

Process-based therapy (PBT) is a new definition of what evidence-based therapy means (Hoffman et al., 2021). It aims to allow the psychotherapist to use therapeutic techniques that have been found through scientific research to be helpful in general, while applying this knowledge in an individualised way that respects the uniqueness of the individual, their context, and their goals for therapy. The way it aims to do this is by replacing our default mode of treating psychiatric syndromes using therapeutic protocols, with the alternative of linking evidence-based psychological processes to evidence-based treatment kernels (Hayes et al., 2020).

Evidence-Based Processes

Traditionally psychological science has attempted to conceptualise human suffering in terms of diagnostic criteria that identify which psychiatric syndrome an individual has (Hayes et al., 2020). This has meant that human suffering is today understood through dominant psychiatric diagnostic guides such as the *International Classification of Diseases* (*ICD*-10) and *Diagnostic and Statistical Manual* (*DSM*-5) (Hayes et al., 2020). PBT instead focuses on the common human processes that lead to suffering and well-being, respectively, also known as evidence-based processes (Hofmann et al., 2021). In moving the field's focus from psychiatric syndromes and toward evidence-based processes, PBT opens the door to tailoring treatment to the individual's specific problem. This helps avoid the problem of boxing clients into diagnostic silos that are not specific enough to treat the actual problem, as new research is beginning to show (Hayes et al., 2020).

Outside of the psychiatric domain, the shift from psychiatric diagnoses to evidence-based processes also begins to break down the boundaries between different psychotherapeutic traditions (Hayes et al., 2020). This allows well-researched processes of suffering and well-being, regardless of which therapeutic school they stem from, to be used to enrich the clinician's understanding of their client. Because these evidence-based processes cut across different psychotherapeutic traditions, PBT also opens the door to understanding psychotherapeutic treatment in novel ways.

Evidence-Based Treatment Kernels

Just as PBT acknowledges that there are many therapeutic modalities with evidence-based processes that lead to suffering and well-being, it also acknowledges that many therapeutic modalities possess techniques that are useful and have been empirically validated (Hayes et al., 2020). According to Hoffman et al. (2021), "PBT needs to be based on a view of intervention that accommodates any evidence-based change processes, regardless of the specific therapeutic orientation" (p. 10). This means that PBT allows the psychotherapist more flexibility in choosing a psychotherapeutic technique that fits the specifics of the case.

It also allows the clinician freedom in using specific evidence-based treatment kernels without having to learn and train in an entire name–brand protocol (Hayes et al., 2020). PBT acknowledges that no clinician has the time, money, or intellectual capacity to train in the entire plethora of evidence-based treatments: a list that is continuously growing (Hofmann et al., 2021). Rather, PBT encourages clinicians to sift out the therapeutic kernel within protocols that have been empirically validated and that fit the specifics of the case that they are currently working with.

As Hoffman et al. (2021) state, the focus of PBT is not what treatments work, but rather, how treatments work. Said in a different way, PBT does not focus on the scientific research that pits one therapeutic modality against another in randomised controlled trials (Hofmann et al., 2021). Rather, it focuses on process-based research that endeavours to understand how treatments work, because if you understand how a treatment works, you can apply it to unique cases more appropriately. For example, understanding the effectiveness of cognitive restructuring as a treatment kernel allows non-cognitive behavioural therapy (CBT) practitioners to make use of this evidence-based technique, without having to follow an entire CBT protocol that might not be relevant to the individual being seen (Hayes et al., 2020).

Psychological Formulation of Clients within the PBT Framework

PBT identifies the evidence-based processes at play for a specific client and implements the most appropriate evidence-based treatment kernel to help the client achieve their specific goals for therapy. The question that then needs to be asked is how best to link evidence-based processes to evidence-based treatment kernels. For this purpose, PBT uses two main theoretical foundations: evolution science and network analysis.

First, evolution science is used as a meta-framework that is comprehensive enough to accommodate the potential vastness of evidence-based processes that could lead to human suffering and human flourishing. Evolution science is the study of how biological life adapts to its environment over time through the variation, selection, and heritability of its characteristics (Hayes et al., 2020). It was previously understood that only genes were heritable, and so evolution science came to focus primarily on genetic characteristics. However, evolution scientists have recently provided evidence of the fact that human beings evolve along other dimensions, such as epigenetics, behaviour, and culture (Hayes et al., 2020). This more comprehensive understanding of the evolution of human beings is what allows psychological science to be nested within it.

PBT assumes that any psychological process that forms part of human existence must fit within the context of evolution science (Hayes et al., 2020). Hence, PBT is an attempt to extend evolution science into the behavioural sciences. Early research from the originators of the PBT approach shows that it is possible to categorise evidence-based processes within six broad domains of psychological functioning: cognition, affect, attention, motivation, self, and overt behaviour (Hofmann et al., 2021). Each process can then be analysed in terms of the evolutionary principles of variation, selection, and retention (Hofmann et al., 2021). Variation refers to the variety of instances of a specific psychological phenomenon, selection refers to the function of the phenomenon, and retention refers to the process through which the phenomenon sustains itself. For example, the feeling of social anxiety could fall within the domain of affect but then could be analysed in terms of variation (turning down social invites restricts variation), selection (feeling relieved when I turn down social invites), and retention (the anxiety grows stronger over time because of this).

The second theoretical foundation of PBT is network analysis, which is used to visually illustrate the way in which psychological processes are linked with each other within the specifics of a case. Network analysis is a way of thinking "often used to make sense of dynamic and interconnected systems" (Hofmann et al., 2021, p. 16). It has been used with great success in a variety of fields such as climate science and stock market analysis but has only recently been introduced into the field of clinical psychology (Hofmann et al., 2021).

Within PBT, network analysis is used as a visual illustration of how the client's different parts of psychological functioning all link up and influence one another. The visual illustration is made up of nodes and arrows, where nodes represent an aspect of the client's psychological functioning, and arrows represent how different nodes influence one another. Later in this chapter, three case studies will be formulated using network analysis, which will provide more clarity on the specifics of how this way of thinking applies to the psychotherapeutic context.

PBT gives the psychotherapist a common language to speak about the evidence-based processes that lead to human suffering and human flourishing through the use of the extended evolutionary model. It also allows us to illustrate these processes effectively, in context, and with unique individuals, through the use of network analysis. The next section will speak specifically to the South African context and how PBT can be advantageous within this context in three specific ways.

The Advantage of PBT in a Diverse Post-apartheid South Africa

The Integration of Different Therapeutic Modalities

Depending on the South African tertiary institution you attend as a psychologist in training, you could be trained in one specific therapeutic modality or a set of therapeutic modalities chosen by that specific tertiary institution. The specific therapeutic modalities that you are trained in will depend on the tertiary institution's discretion and can be identified in the documentation their psychology department provides online or by contacting them about this directly.

The problem is that these therapeutic modalities often have contradictory sets of assumptions, prioritise different aspects of human psychology, and use different therapeutic techniques for the treatment of their clients (Hofmann et al., 2019). In cases where the student is trained in multiple theoretical modalities, the integration of these modalities is ultimately left to the discretion of the student, regardless of the degree to which guidelines for integration are provided. This too can often be problematic, as is highlighted by research which shows that students trained in a single theoretical modality often have better outcomes with their clients than those who take an eclectic approach (Eysenck, 1970). This demonstrates that even when clinicians attempt to integrate different sources of wisdom for the client's benefit, they do so ineffectually.

In a South African context where budding psychotherapists are trained in different therapeutic modalities, an evidence-based path of integration is needed to allow clinicians to extract maximal value from what the science of psychotherapy has to offer. PBT offers the opportunity for the integration of different therapeutic modalities by focusing on linking evidence-based processes to evidence-based treatment kernels.

The Accommodation of a Diversity of Clients

It is no secret that South Africa holds a very diverse population of individuals. While racial diversity is the most readily pertinent, diversity lies across many other dimensions, including socioeconomic status, religious beliefs, ethnic identities, sexual orientations, age groups, etc. Over and above social diversity, clients bring a range of unique presenting problems and life goals to the therapeutic process. This is a challenge for newly trained clinicians because it requires tremendous flexibility, critical thinking, social awareness, and open-mindedness.

PBT allows for the accommodation of diversity because it understands and treats clients in a truly individualised way (Hofmann et al., 2021). Through network analysis, PBT formulates a client's internal and external context from the bottom-up. This means that a specific therapeutic modality is not decided a priori and assumed to fit the individual. Rather, the network analysis formulation allows the psychotherapist to understand the uniqueness of the individual, in their unique context, and with their unique goals for therapy integrated into the formulation. In a country where psychological theories have been used to oppress specific racial groups (Hook et al., 2004), it is of the utmost importance to understand clients in their uniqueness.

Prioritising Treatment Utility over Theoretical Commitments

With a diversity of theoretical modalities comes a theoretical war between opposing therapy camps. This is often best illustrated through the excessive emphasis on research that pits different therapeutic modalities against one another in randomised controlled trials (Hofmann et al., 2021). Fortunately, this conflict between theoretical camps is not always present, as is illustrated by the many attempts at more integrative models (Hayes et al., 2020). However, when this kind of research is emphasised within the field of clinical psychology, it can make newly trained clinicians feel obliged to side with a specific therapeutic camp. This can in turn lead to the clinician blinding themself to the weaknesses of their own theoretical modality and negating the value of other therapeutic modalities.

PBT provides the opportunity to sidestep theoretical commitment by emphasising the treatment utility of whatever approach the clinician adopts. This is important because the ultimate aim of the clinician is to effectively assist the client. According to PBT, the ultimate arbiter of our therapeutic endeavours should be whether the chosen treatment is effective in moving our clients toward their goals or not (Hofmann et al., 2021). On a technical level, this is accomplished through the constant assessment of the outcomes that are important to the client, along with a constant evaluation of how the client's network is shifting over time (Hofmann et al., 2021). In a country as diverse as South Africa on so many dimensions, PBT's commitment to verifiable progress during treatment allows clinicians to hold themselves accountable.

The following sections will illustrate the above-mentioned advantages of PBT for the South African context in a more detailed manner, using a multiple case study method. This will be done through the illustration of three case studies from the author's own private practice, with each case study using a different theoretical modality that will be formulated within the meta-approach of PBT. The cases were chosen based on the criteria of whether the client was willing to share the content of their session, and whether the case strongly emphasised a specific theoretical modality (for the purposes of illustrating how PBT can accommodate a wide range of theoretical modalities). The aim is to outline the potential of PBT to draw from many theoretical modalities while putting the individual first and giving clinicians a common language with which to speak about psychotherapy. The three most commonly used therapeutic modalities in the South African context were chosen for the three case studies that are to follow: person-centred therapy (PCT), CBT, and psychodynamic therapy (PDT).

PCT and the Case of SB

The following section will discuss the use of PCT, as formulated within the meta-approach of PBT, in the case of a client who will be known as SB. The section begins with a brief discussion of SB's demographics, her relevant history, and the presenting problem. The general principles of PCT are then outlined and applied to the case using a process-based approach.

The Case of SB

SB is a white female in her thirties who identifies as a cultural Jew and lives by herself in the Western Cape. She completed her BA and now works for a company in the education and learning space, a job she describes as busy but engaging. Her initial presenting problem in therapy was learning how to deal with feelings of shame and loneliness, and she also spoke about how harsh she can be on herself. SB elaborated on the latter point by explaining how she always feels the need to be perfect, and how she feels that if she could improve herself, then she would be worthy of love. Furthermore, she discussed a sense of disconnection from her emotions and the parts of herself that do not fit her idea of perfection. My sense during the assessment phase was that the therapeutic modality of PCT would be beneficial to her.

Psychological Processes and Treatment Kernels in PCT

PCT originated in the 1940s with Carl Ransom Rogers, a psychologist who believed that people naturally have vast resources for self-understanding and self-direction (Raskin et al., 2019). The following is a summary only of the general principles of PCT that will be relevant to the current case study.

According to the PCT framework, all human beings have a need for positive regard from caregivers. However, many children grow up constantly experiencing specific conditions that need to be fulfilled before they are deemed worthy of positive regard by their caregivers. According to PCT, the individual internalises these conditions of worth, imposes them on themselves, and thus becomes incongruent. Hence, the aim of PCT is to help the client internalise a sense of unconditional positive self-regard so that they can become congruent within themselves (Raskin et al., 2019). Being a whole person is important within the PCT framework because it allows the individual to have all the information they need about themselves to make the best decisions for themselves.

According to PCT, the internal resources of self-understanding and self-direction that an individual possesses can be accessed by the psychotherapist who is congruent within themselves and provides unconditional positive regard and empathic understanding (Raskin et al., 2019). This kind of therapeutic relationship is what allows for the change in psychotherapy and is known as three therapeutic attitudes.

The first attitude is congruence, which involves the psychotherapist being aware of their moment-to-moment internal experience, and communicating that openly and authentically (Raskin et al., 2019). Rogers regarded this therapeutic attitude as more fundamental than the other two, because if the psychotherapist is not seen as genuine and authentic, then the client cannot trust that the psychotherapist does in fact hold the empathic understanding and unconditional positive regard toward them (Raskin et al., 2019). Furthermore, congruence is there to avoid the temptation of the therapist to hide behind a mask of professionalism (Raskin et al., 2019).

Empathic understanding involves showing curiosity in understanding the client's experience. It involves actively keeping the client's experience at the centre of the process and constantly expressing this through "cognitive processes, affective processes, and expressive behaviour" (Raskin et al., 2019, p. 123). This attitude is important to the process of therapy, because it allows the client to know that when the psychotherapist accepts them, they are being accepted on the basis of first being fully understood.

Unconditional positive regard is the final therapeutic attitude and entails showing the client warmth and acceptance, regardless of their current state (Raskin et al., 2019). Therapeutically, this is where the rubber meets the road. Congruence and empathic understanding are necessary preconditions, but it is the unconditional positive regard of the psychotherapist that allows the client to find acceptance for themselves, and begin to move in a direction of prioritising the actual self versus the idea of who they are (Raskin et al., 2019).

As therapy progresses, there are two major shifts that occur within the client. Firstly, the client begins to view themselves in a more positive light, also known as positive self-regard (Raskin et al., 2019). Secondly, clients begin to derive the standards for their life from their own experience rather than from the judgments of others (Raskin et al., 2019). This means that their locus of evaluation shifts from being externally rooted to being internally rooted, thus allowing them to be more self-determining. Rogers described this kind of person as fully functioning. He defined the fully functioning person as someone who is "able to experience all of their feelings, are afraid of none of them, and allow awareness to flow freely in and through their experience" (Raskin et al., 2019).

According to PCT, "the act of voicing a preference or a feeling or an opinion is the first step in establishing selfhood and personal identity" (Raskin et al., 2019, p. 126). This is progress within the PCT framework, and after feeling safe enough to embody this self in the therapeutic context, the client can then begin to embody this self in other contexts (Raskin et al., 2019).

The following section will now describe how the PCT processes and treatment kernels were applied in the case of SB.

PCT Psychological Processes in the Case of SB

After our initial sessions, SB began to open up about how critical and punitive her father was during her early childhood. According to her, he did not praise her when she did things well but criticised her very harshly when his high standards were not met. From a PCT perspective, her father was imposing harsh conditions of worth on her. Some of these conditions included the expectation that she always succeeds academically, that she is competent at things before having tried them, and that she never fails (Figure 5.1).

During our sessions, she would often describe a part of her that she termed "Make-Sure SB". According to her, this was the internal voice that kept her in line when it came to academics,

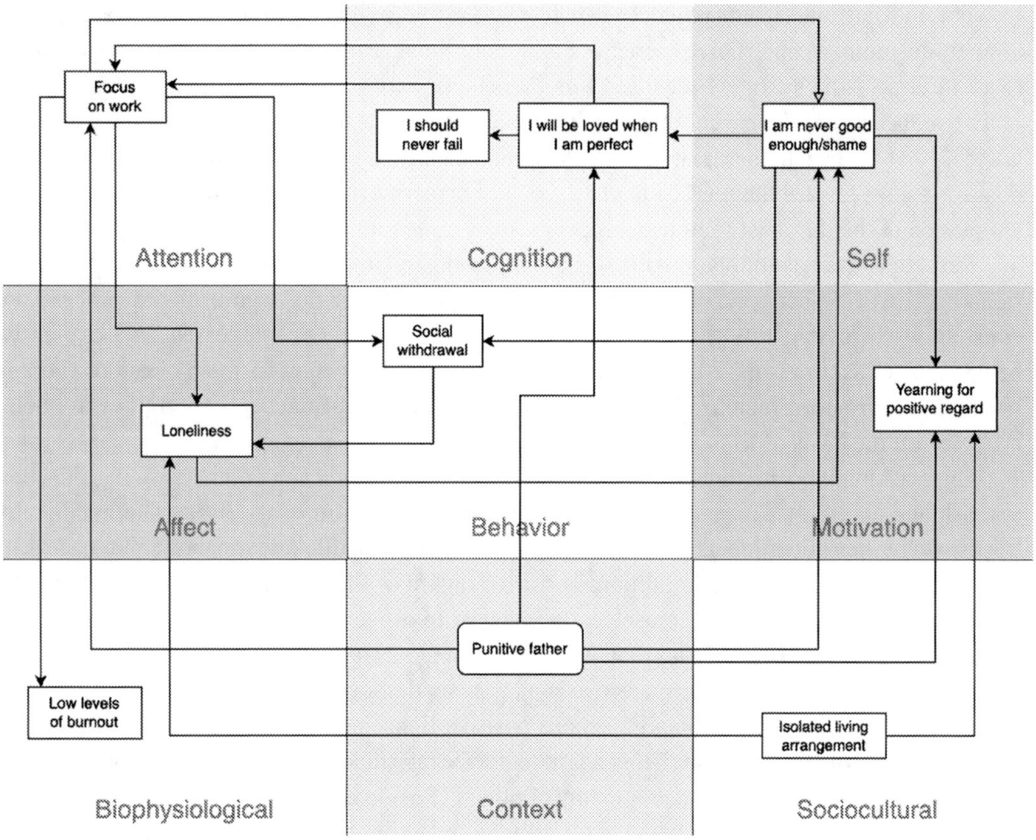

Figure 5.1 SB's initial network analysis formulation.

occupational success, and personal development. From a PCT perspective, this part of her can be understood as the incongruent self that was formed while growing up. This is the self she assumed would give her the best chance of fulfilling her conditions of worth and thus achieving positive self-regard from those around her.

Throughout our sessions together, she described her occupation as fulfilling but also stressful. She explained on several occasions how tired and burned out she felt. She also alluded to a lack of fulfilment outside of the occupational domain. From a PCT perspective, the other parts of herself unrelated to Make-Sure SB had been devalued over time because of the demanding nature of her conditions of worth. Over time, these conditions of worth became more important than her basic human needs, such as rest, hobbies, socialising, and intimacy.

The PBT formulation allowed me to formulate her yearning for positive regard as a core motivation, and to understand how this motivation is not inherently bad, but that it is its interaction with the arbitrary conditions of worth that cause her to not have this yearning fulfilled ultimately. The PBT formulation highlights the centrality of the feelings of shame and unworthiness, which was one of the deciding factors in choosing the PCT framework for SB. Finally, the attentional domain is not explicitly highlighted in PCT, but the PBT formulation allows us to see how her attention on work and self-development can actually perpetuate social withdrawal and loneliness. According to PCT, this is an example of how the yearning for positive regard can take precedence over the actualising tendency of the organism.

PCT Treatment Kernels in the Case of SB

During therapy, I listened for any emotions that were pushed aside for not aligning with the pursuit of her conditions of worth. An emotion that often came up was loneliness. Reflecting this back to her in an empathic way allowed her to acknowledge and integrate this emotion into her conceptualisation of what she yearns for. Through contact with this emotion, she acknowledged her desire for more friendship and intimacy in her social life, which allowed her to move towards a more congruent understanding of her identity (Figure 5.2).

During one of our sessions together, SB showed a glimmer of frustration towards having to take a lot of responsibility during one of her religious meetings. I tried to understand this emotion empathically and without judgment, which allowed her to acknowledge this frustration for herself. She thereafter decided that she in fact did not want to be in the role of responsibility that she had taken on. At that moment, her locus of evaluation shifted from the external to the internal. In other words, she made a decision based on her own experience of the situation, rather than to avoid the assumed judgment of the group: a sign of progress in PCT.

During the course of treatment, I continued to provide her with a context where the parts of herself that she was ashamed of were welcome. I did this by providing the three therapeutic conditions, and SB leaned into this space and used it to explore vulnerability and the kinds of authenticity that do not usually feel safe for her. A sign of progress in later sessions was that

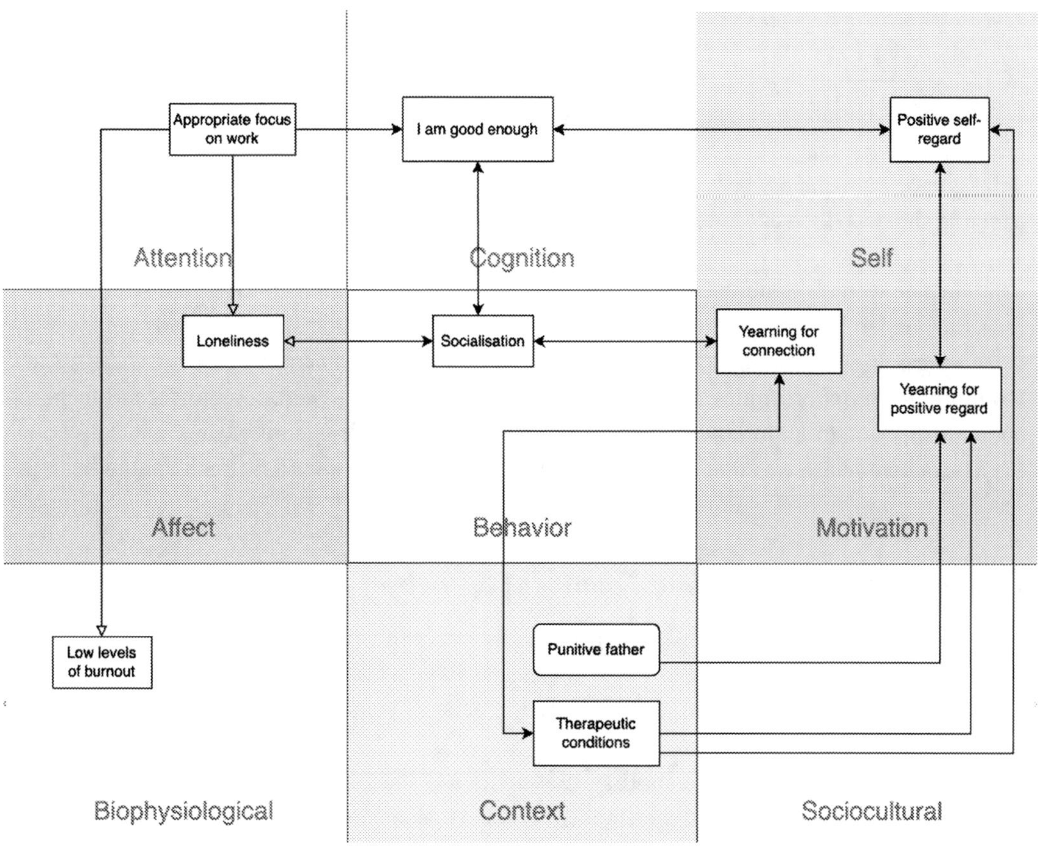

Figure 5.2 SB's evolving network analysis formulation as treatment progresses.

she had spontaneously decided to go out for drinks with her colleagues on a Friday after work: a situation she would usually avoid. Furthermore, she described herself as having been more authentic and vulnerable during that encounter. From a PCT perspective, this is an indication of her getting in touch with her true self. It was a sign that she was behaving in ways that are more congruent with what she yearns for as a whole human being.

Given that SB has devoted so much time to occupational success given her strong conditions of worth, an important part of the therapeutic work was allowing her the space to explore what she wants from life outside of work. She was able to intuitively identify many yearnings that were outside the domain of work. Through this process of uncovering these yearnings, SB slowly became more in touch with her full identity, which according to PCT, allows one to behave in ways that are good for themselves.

CBT and the Case of OM

The following section will discuss the use of CBT, as formulated within the meta-approach of PBT, in the case of a client who will be known as OM. The section begins with a brief discussion of OM's demographics, her relevant history, and the presenting problem. The general principles of CBT are then outlined and applied to the case using a process-based approach.

The Case of OM

OM is a black female in her early twenties who lives in the Northern Cape. OM is currently unemployed due to the fact that she was unable to study the course that she initially intended on, and is still figuring out what her occupational future will involve. Her presenting problem in therapy was a feeling she described as "inner turmoil" that she was struggling to understand. She further spoke about how she feels out of touch with her emotions and is often confused about what she is feeling and why she would possibly feel that way. In later sessions, OM began to open up about how she feels the need to be perfect around her friends and family, and that she often finds it necessary to wear a mask in social settings. She described this process as problematic because it causes her to withdraw from opportunities to socialise. Her goals for therapy were to connect to others more authentically and to learn how to process her emotions in more adaptive ways. My sense during the assessment phase was that the therapeutic modality of CBT would be beneficial to her.

Psychological Processes and Treatment Kernels in CBT

CBT posits that our ways of thinking influence the ways in which we feel and the ways in which we behave (Beck & Weishaar, 2019). Over the past 50 years, CBT has evolved into many forms, and thus the following is a summary of only the general principles of CBT relevant to the current case study.

CBT aims to "explore and modify dysfunctional interpretations, chiefly through logical examination and behavioural experiments" (Beck & Weishaar, 2019, p. 239). This means that there are both cognitive treatment kernels and behavioural treatment kernels that are relevant to CBT.

Some of the behavioural treatment kernels include skills training, role-playing, and exposure therapy (Beck & Weishaar, 2019). Skills training is self-explanatory and involves helping the client identify and acquire the psychological and behavioural skills needed to achieve their goals. Role-playing involves playing out challenging scenarios during sessions so that the client is better equipped to deal with them in scenarios outside of the therapeutic space. Exposure therapy involves systematically exposing the client to the thing that they fear so that their fear can diminish over time.

There are also various cognitive techniques that are used in CBT. These techniques are "directed primarily at correcting errors and biases in information processing and modifying the core beliefs that promote faulty conclusions" (Beck & Weishaar, 2019, p. 240). One such technique involves "identifying and testing the patients beliefs" (Beck & Weishaar, 2019, p. 240). These core beliefs have to be tested for both validity and adaptiveness (Beck & Weishaar, 2019). If they do not pass these tests, the client is encouraged to try new beliefs that may be more accurate or more functional (Beck & Weishaar, 2019). Another cognitive technique involves the identification of cognitive distortions that are contributing to the client's dysfunction. Cognitive distortions are systematic errors in thinking that come in many varieties. Examples include thinking in extremes (dichotomous thinking), attributing external events to oneself (personalisation), and abstracting a general rule from a few isolated incidents (overgeneralisation) (Beck & Weishaar, 2019).

The following section will now describe how the CBT processes and treatment kernels were applied in the case of OM.

CBT Psychological Processes in the Case of OM

CBT calls for the identification and modification of core beliefs that are leading to dysfunction, so this was explored with OM in therapy. The client and I collaboratively identified a core belief that was roughly, "If I am imperfect, I will be abandoned". According to OM, this belief was largely constructed in her mind due to her early experiences with her father, where she was often abandoned by him (Figure 5.3).

Early on in our sessions, OM explained that she struggles to know how she is feeling. As mentioned above, she described her internal world as an inner turmoil that was difficult to pin down. She also elaborated by saying that it feels uncomfortable to allow her feelings to arise and that she does not want to appear like she is not well put together. From a CBT perspective, the continual avoidance of specific emotions caused her fear of her emotions to grow over time. Furthermore, from a third-wave CBT perspective, the continual avoidance of emotion can often lead to an individual slowly losing touch with what they are feeling from moment to moment.

Another important point that OM brought up early in our sessions was that because of her need to appear perfect, she often struggled to have difficult conversations or to communicate her own needs to those around her. From a CBT perspective, she had never acquired the skillset of communication and boundary setting. However, rather than focusing on why these skills were never acquired, CBT's present-moment focus emphasises the need to acquire these skills so that she can achieve her own goals in her life.

She elaborated on her need to be perfect by stating that many of her social interactions felt like performances because of the mask that she feels pressured to use in social settings. She explained that the pressure associated with having to perform would often lead to her

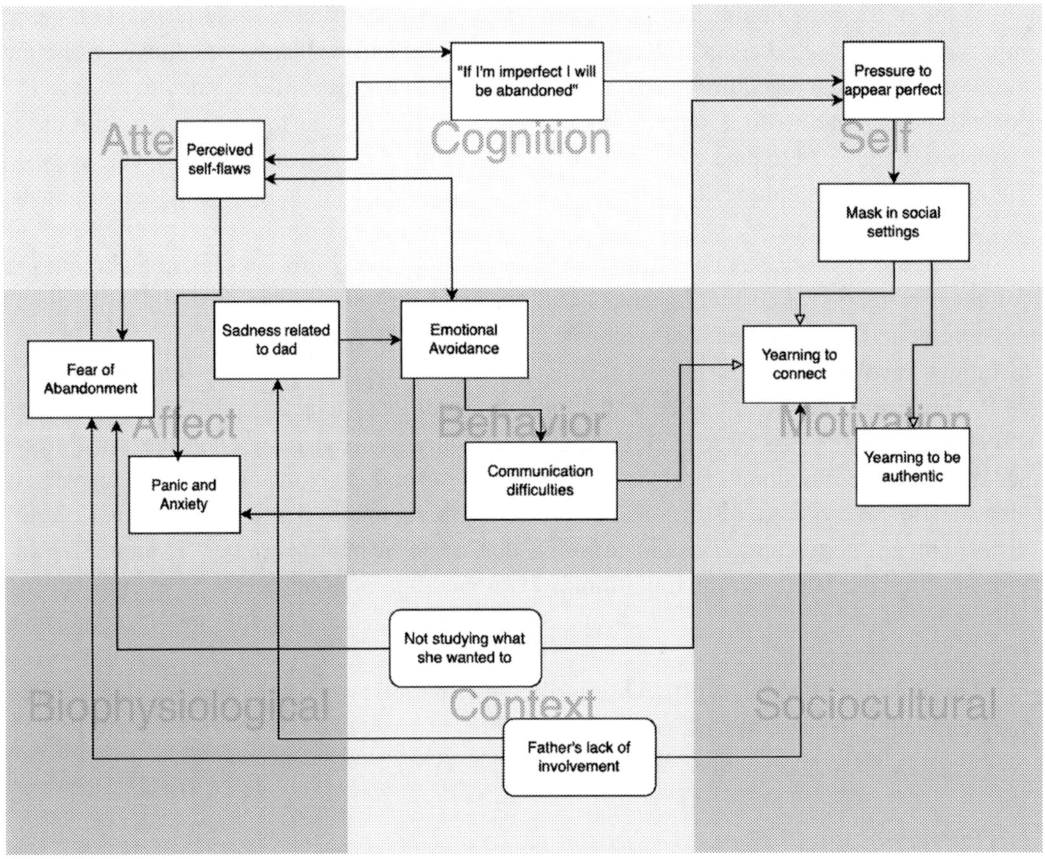

Figure 5.3 OM's initial network analysis formulation.

withdrawing from social interactions entirely. This was another instance in which the CBT process of behavioural avoidance and the consequent increased fear was relevant to the case. Furthermore, a CBT perspective also allowed us to investigate her cognitions related to these situations and identify the common cognitive errors of maximisation and minimisation. Individuals who are anxious maximise the likelihood of harm and minimise the likelihood that they will cope, which we identified as the way OM too was processing her current social situation.

CBT Treatment Kernels in the Case of OM

Together, we challenged the validity of her belief that she will be abandoned if she is imperfect, and I also helped her understand the ways in which this belief perpetuated dysfunction in her own life. Furthermore, we collaboratively designed a behavioural experiment to see if she really would be rejected for being herself. OM carried out this experiment and in the follow-up session described being vulnerable with a friend that she had not seen in a long time. She explained to me that she was in fact not rejected and that the lack of rejection for her vulnerability was emotionally relieving. It was the opportunity she needed to modify her core belief, "If I am imperfect, I will be abandoned" (Figure 5.4).

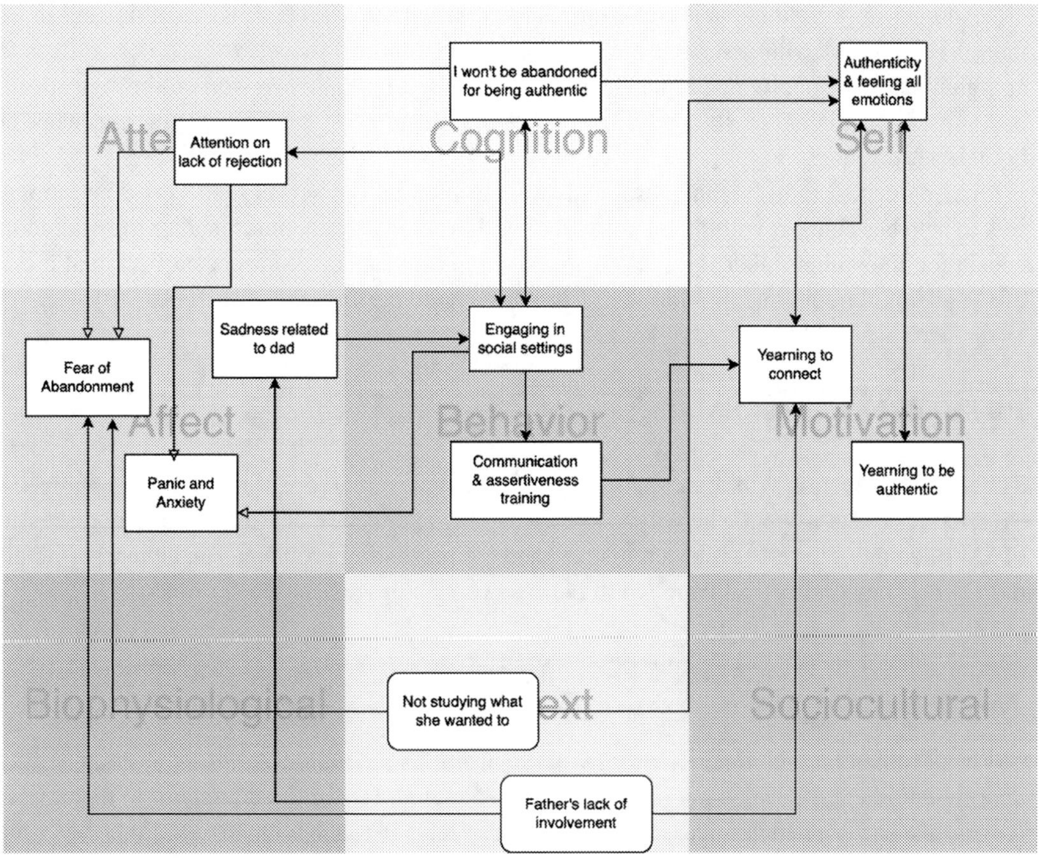

Figure 5.4 OM's evolving network analysis formulation as treatment progresses.

In terms of behavioural treatment kernels, I found the use of modelling and positive reinforcement helpful in helping OM become more authentic, which was one of her goals for therapy. Firstly, modelling vulnerability and authenticity in sessions was helpful because it made her feel more comfortable in bringing these parts of her to the therapy session too. I also modelled these traits in an explicit way by self-disclosing when I had a thought or feeling that was not necessarily the "perfect" behaviour of a clinician. Secondly, I positively reinforced the gains made in terms of her vulnerability and authenticity when that did occur. By simply pointing out and congratulating her on these occasions, she became more enthusiastic and self-assured in embodying these traits.

In terms of increasing her emotional awareness, I used labelling and experiential exposure. Firstly, research into affective neuroscience has shown that labelling emotions can help us better identify them. I explained this to OM and we often began labelling emotions together to help her get more in touch with them. As therapy progressed, I noticed that she became better at identifying her own emotions and using labels that we had previously discussed in therapy. Secondly, I assisted with experiential exposure during the session to the thing she feared, which was feeling emotions. I provided a context where it was safe to do so, and where I only exposed her to her own emotions to the degree at which she was comfortable. I reinforced the safety of the space by always reassuring her that she does not have to go further than she is willing, an important component of successful exposure treatments.

Another important behavioural treatment kernel within CBT is skills training, and in this vain, I helped OM with assertiveness training. The intent of this was to help her address the communication difficulty node that she had been struggling with. We worked through specific techniques and dialogues she could use to communicate how she was feeling and what her boundaries are.

I also decided to use behavioural activation as a treatment kernel with OM. The rationale was to help her connect with others instead of withdrawing, by encouraging her to speak to her cousin for enjoyment rather than to put on a good performance. OM reported back that the act of socialising for enjoyment rather than to put on a good performance was relieving to her.

PDT and the Case of SM

The following section will discuss the use of PDT, as formulated within the meta-approach of PBT, in the case of a client who will be known as SM. The section begins with a brief discussion of SM's demographics, her relevant history, and the presenting problem. The general principles of PDT are then outlined and applied to the case using a process-based approach.

The Case of SM

SM is an Indian female in her twenties who identifies as a Hindu. She works in the renewable energy sector and described her job as busy but engaging. Her initial complaint in therapy was feeling like she is a people-pleaser and that she also feels in touch with her emotions. SM spoke about how this has led to her being quite harsh on herself and has also led to difficulties in her expressing herself with others. Furthermore, she discussed how growing up there was not much room for her emotions in her family context, and that when she felt emotional in anyway, she would often withdraw and spend time alone in her room. My sense during the assessment phase was that the therapeutic modality of PDT would be beneficial to her.

Psychological Processes and Treatment Kernels in PDT

PDT is a distinctive form of psychological treatment and a model of psychological functioning. It originated with Sigmund Freud at the dawn of the 20th century but has since evolved in many fundamental ways (Safran et al., 2019). The following is a summary of only the general principles of PDT that will be relevant for the purposes of the current case study.

According to PDT, all human beings are "motivated in part by wishes, fantasies, or tacit knowledge that is outside of awareness" (Safran et al., 2019, p. 22). This is generally referred to as the unconscious and a principle shared by most psychodynamic thinkers is that the psychotherapist should assist in making the unconscious conscious (Safran et al., 2019). The rationale for this is that the client's growing awareness of the connection between symptoms, as well as their own contribution to those symptoms, affords the client more agency and choice in their own life (Safran et al., 2019).

Interpretation is a useful tool that the psychodynamic psychotherapist can use to make the unconscious conscious. Interpretation is "the therapist's attempt to help clients become aware of aspects of their intrapsychic experience and relational patterns that are unconscious" (Safran et al., 2019, p. 42). Later developments in PDT began to emphasise the importance of the interpretation having an emotional component and having utility in the process of change (Safran et al., 2019).

Interpretation within PDT often involves helping the client understand their defence mechanisms: the intrapsychic processes that the client engages in to avoid painful experiences (Safran et al., 2019). There is no exhaustive list of defence mechanisms that all psychodynamic thinkers subscribe to, but the idea that we avoid painful experiences in systematic ways is non-controversial.

Another general principle shared by many psychodynamic theorists is that childhood and early family contexts influence the way that individuals feel and behave later in life (Safran et al., 2019). For this reason, historical reconstruction is often an important component of PDT. This involves the creation of narratives where there are none and changing narratives where they are maladaptive (Safran et al., 2019).

Therapeutically, much of the change that occurs during PDT is the result of the therapeutic alliance. According to Safran et al. (2019), the therapeutic alliance refers to the quality of the relational bond between the psychotherapist and client, as well as the degree to which they are aligned regarding the tasks and goals of therapy. It is important for the psychotherapist to stay empathic to allow the client to see that relationships are flexible and that both perspectives can be recognised without either dismissing the other (Safran et al., 2019).

Because of the intersubjective nature of the therapeutic relationship, the psychotherapist cannot avoid being an active participant in the therapeutic process. Hence, enactments will occur: the playing out of complementary roles in relationships that are the result of relational patterns that developed during childhood (Safran et al., 2019).

During enactments, the psychotherapist can rely on both transference and countertransference to aid in making sense of the experience. Transference involves the client's emotional reaction to the psychotherapist, and countertransference is the resultant emotional reaction that the psychotherapist has toward the client (Safran et al., 2019). Both of these reactions can be a source of information in understanding the client's interpersonal and intrapsychic processes.

The following section will now describe how the PDT processes and treatment kernels were applied in the case of SM.

PDT Psychological Processes in the Case of SM

Since our first session together, a recurring complaint had been that SM was quite stressed and fatigued. The initial conceptualisation of this stress was obvious; her work was very stressful. However, it was later discovered that the stress that she had been experiencing was also linked to not wanting to disappoint others. Whether it be occupationally or personally, she explained that she often overworked or over-extended herself to meet the needs of others, even when this was at a detriment to her own well-being: a pattern that she had recognised from childhood (Figure 5.5).

Furthermore, during our sessions together, SM would often anticipate that I would judge her for expressing negative emotions. She explained that this anticipation also had its roots in her childhood, explaining that she was often punished for expressing any emotions perceived by her parents as negative.

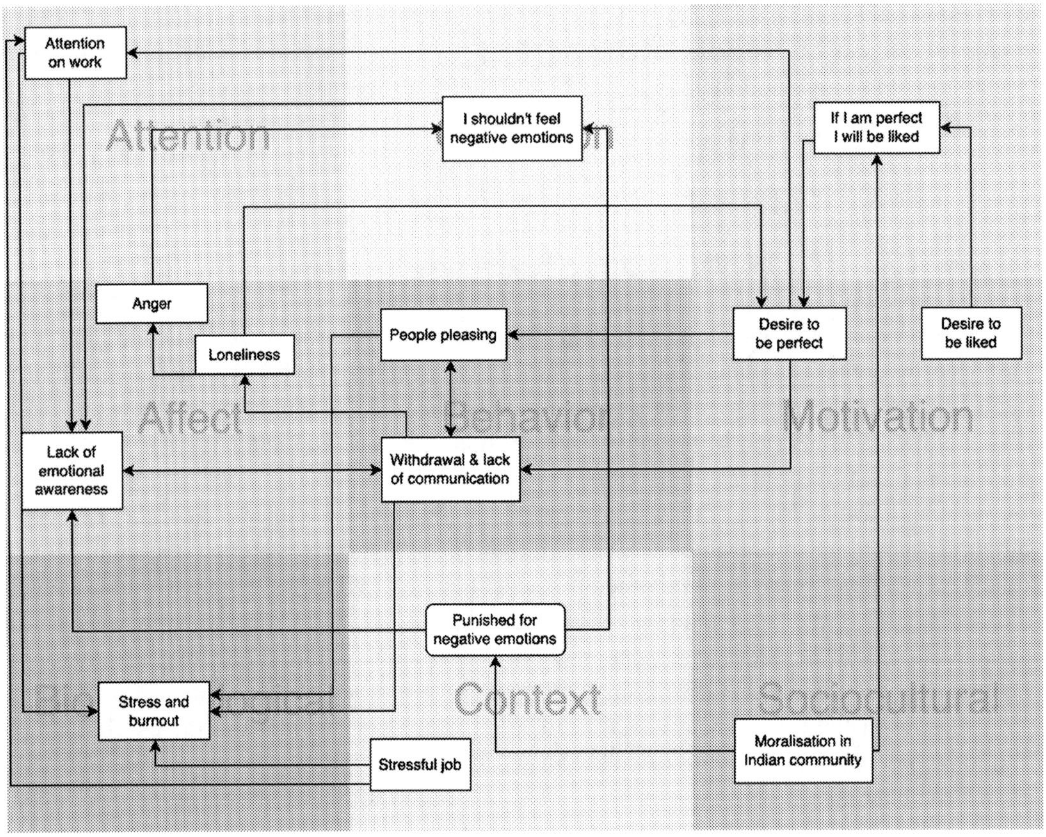

Figure 5.5 SM's initial network analysis formulation.

On the occasions when SM's parents did not punish her for negative emotions, they often emotionally neglected her. SM recounted several experiences when she would feel emotionally distressed and her parents would not empathise with her emotions. She explained that this would often lead to her crying alone in her room. She explained that this interpersonal dynamic has stayed with her, meaning that even in her adult life, she often withdraws when what she actually needs is support.

During our sessions, I often felt a liking for SM. I identified this as countertransference, as this is how she unconsciously intends to make those around her feel. I noticed in sessions that I usually felt pleased to see her, and noticed the similarity between this feeling within myself, and the people-pleasing dynamic that she had verbally reported. Her verbal reports about her people-pleasing indicated that upsetting those around her made her very uncomfortable. She linked this to her early childhood context, explaining that if she did not please those around her, she was afraid that she would not be liked.

As stated above, another of SM's presenting complaints was that she felt out of touch with her emotions. Early on in our sessions together, it was evident that a prominent defence mechanism for SM was repression. I noticed in our sessions that she often smiled and chuckled when beginning to confront any negative emotion during the session, which even SM identified as a way to cope with how she really feels. The link between this defence mechanism and her lack of emotional awareness became clearer with each session.

Also related to her difficulty with emotional awareness, SM explained that she would often feel angry but neither knew how to make sense of the anger, nor how to communicate that anger. On occasions when she did feel angry, she felt wrong for feeling that way. She also explained that despite feeling angry, she struggled to set the boundaries needed to ensure that she did not feel that same anger on a regular basis. From a psychodynamic perspective, she struggled to understand and formulate her own boundaries because her anger was never allowed to be felt or expressed. She also explained that she anticipates upsetting those around her with her boundaries, which clarified the fact that there was also a link between her people-pleasing tendencies and her difficulty communicating her boundaries.

PDT Treatment Kernels in the Case of SM

Her growing awareness of her unconscious yearning to be liked and the consequences of her stress and burnout allowed our stress management techniques to be more tailored to her. Instead of focusing on generalised stress management techniques, the psychodynamic perspective allowed us to focus on her desire to not disappoint others and help her manage her stress by managing this need (Figure 5.6).

During sessions, I overtly encouraged her to experience her emotions. This allowed her to learn on an experiential level that it was okay to experience a full range of emotions, even

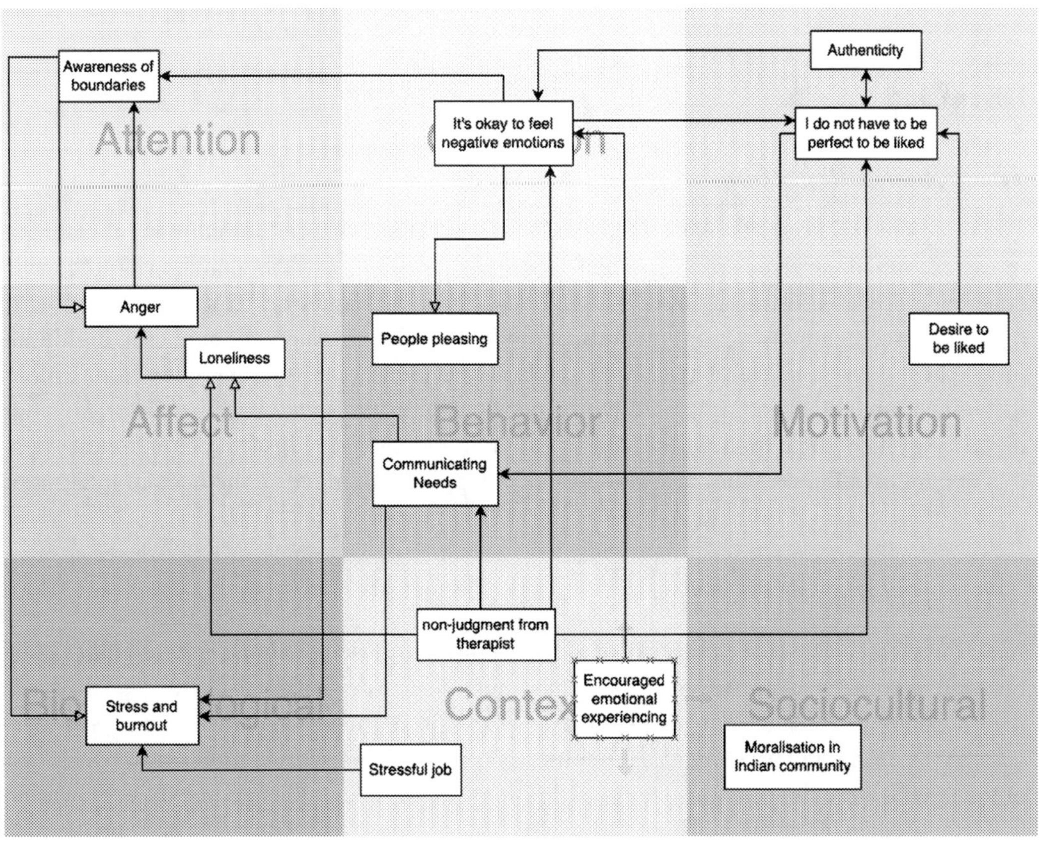

Figure 5.6 SM's evolving network analysis formulation as treatment progresses.

those that were deemed negative during her childhood. Furthermore, it allowed the surfacing of those negative emotions, which in turn increased her awareness of her own boundaries. Related to this point, I explicitly made the interpretation that she seemed to be finding it difficult to set boundaries because she was not allowing the communications of her anger to surface. I further explained that by not allowing herself to feel anger, she was also stopping herself from understanding what boundaries had been violated and thus what boundaries to set.

The therapeutic alliance is an important aspect of PDT, and it was important for SM that I do not show her the judgement that she received in childhood for expressing human emotion. During the enactments where she projected her parents onto me, I made sure that she had the corrective emotional experience of not being judged while expressing negative emotions. This experience of non-judgement is an important component of PDT that is additional to the verbal encouragement that I gave her. It was especially important for her to be shown that she could still be liked even when experiencing negative emotions, because this was one of the main reasons that she felt that she could not feel these emotions. This in turn began reinforcing her thought that she does not have to be perfect to be liked. In the third session already, SM explained that she had grown increasingly comfortable with expressing her emotions during our sessions together.

Related to her difficulty with her emotional awareness, I made the interpretation that her parents would often not allow space for her emotions, which is why she may now struggle to understand her own emotions and why she withdraws when struggling emotionally. By using an interpretation that highlights where her relationship to her own emotions and coping mechanisms come from, she was able to recognise that this way of coping need not be her future.

Discussion

Theoretical Integration

The three preceding case studies were used to show PBT's potential for allowing the clinician to extract maximal value from different theoretical modalities while maintaining theoretical coherence. It was illustrated how PBT provides a general framework that can be used across different cases that use different theoretical modalities. Even though not explicitly highlighted in any of the cases above, it is easy to see how the integration of techniques from different theoretical modalities could be used with any of the cases presented in this chapter. Given the diversity of theoretical modalities that are taught at most tertiary institutions in South Africa, it is of paramount importance that students be equipped with practical methods of integration.

Accommodation of Diversity

In all three cases above, the clients differed on many axes. Racial, ethnic, and religious diversities were all obviously portrayed in the demographics sections, but these clients also differed in their presenting problems and goals for therapy. SB's presenting problem was shame and loneliness, OM's presenting problem was inner turmoil, and SM's presenting problem was feeling out of touch with her emotions. Despite these different and unique problem contexts, PBT was able to accommodate all of them. These three case studies collectively illustrate PBT's potential in being flexible enough to be of clinical use to a diverse set of individuals.

Treatment over Theory

Finally, it was shown that PBT prioritises clinical value over theoretical commitment, something that is very important for the South African context, given that psychological theories have been used to marginalise groups in our collective past. Oftentimes, psychiatric diagnoses prioritise general diagnostic labels that are highly descriptive but do not lend themselves to the therapeutic steps that are required. Through the above case studies, it was shown how the network analysis formulation of each client allowed the clinician to intuitively identify the evidence-based treatment kernels that were needed to address the identified psychological processes. It is this emphasis on creating the kind of formulation that allows for maximal treatment utility and that a South African context with many psychological camps could potentially benefit from.

Conclusion

Post-apartheid South Africa brings with it the challenge of how to train and practice as a psychotherapist with a diversity of individuals while being sensitive to their unique history, context, and goals. This chapter proposed that a novel meta-framework for understanding evidence-based psychotherapy, PBT, offers guidance on how to use the science of psychotherapy in a way that is tailored to the unique individual, their context, and their goals for therapy. PBT was introduced, along with its core tenets. The chapter then went on to propose three ways in which PBT may be useful to a diverse, post-apartheid South African context, namely theoretical integration of many psychotherapeutic modalities, accommodation of a diversity of clients, and prioritising treatment utility over theoretical commitment. How PBT fulfils its utility in these three domains was illustrated through the use of three case studies in which different therapeutic modalities are used, with PBT serving as a meta-framework that unifies all three modalities. The chapter then concluded with a discussion of PBT's three potential uses in the diverse post-apartheid South African context.

References

Beck, A. T., & Weishaar, M. E. (2019). Cognitive therapy. In D. Wedding & R. J. Corsini (Eds.), *Current psychotherapies* (pp. 237–272). Cengage Learning.

Eysenck, H. J. (1970). A mish-mash of theories. *International Journal of Psychiatry*, *9*, 140–146.

Hayes, S. C., Hofmann, S. G., & Ciarrochi, J. (2020). A process-based approach to psychological diagnosis and treatment: The conceptual and treatment utility of an extended evolutionary meta model. *Clinical Psychology Review*, *82*, 101908.

Hofmann, S. G., & Hayes, S. C. (2019). The future of intervention science: Process-based therapy. Clinical Psychological Science, *7*(1), 37–50.

Hofmann, S. G., Hayes, S. C., & Lorscheid, D. N. (2021). *Learning process-based therapy: A skills training manual for targeting the core processes of psychological change in clinical practice*. New Harbinger Publications.

Hook, D., Mkhize, N., Collins, A., Kiguwa, P., Parker, I., & Burman, E. (Eds.). (2004). *Critical psychology*. Juta and Company Ltd.

Raskin, N. J., Rogers, C. R., & Witty, M. C. (2019). Client-centered therapy. In D. Wedding & R. J. Corsini (Eds.), *Current psychotherapies* (pp. 101–156). Cengage Learning.

Safran, J. D., Kriss, A., & Foley, V. K. (2019). Psychodynamic psychotherapies. In D. Wedding & R. J. Corsini (Eds.), *Current psychotherapies* (pp. 22–59). Cengage Learning.

Chapter 6

Grief

(The Lack of) Training of Psychologists in Postapartheid South Africa

Bêne Otto*

Department of Psychology, Faculty of Humanities, University of Johannesburg

Abstract

Grief is arguably the most universal human experience. This reality has been brought closer to consciousness with the COVID-19 pandemic and unprecedented loss of life, leaving behind hundreds of thousands of bereaved individuals. Death and grief further remains a taboo topic, which often results in misconceptions and misinformation that leads to the disenfranchising of the experience of loss. Despite the number of individuals affected by grief, the training that psychologists receive in post-apartheid South Africa is minimal across universities. This chapter seeks to address this disconnect by highlighting grief theory from the current thanatological literature.

Key Words: grief, loss, psychotherapy, thanatology, training

Introduction

There are few things that can be held as absolute truth. Life is filled with nuance and coloured with grey areas; few things are ever really black and white. But if there is one thing that is undeniably true, it is that human existence is finite. All that live will eventually die. Death is an inevitable fact of life.

It goes without saying that all humans will, at some point in their lifetime, become acquainted with death, either through the loss of a loved one or through their own eventual demise. When faced with death and loss, our natural response is the experience of mourning and grief. Because none of us are immune to death or the impacts of loss, grief is arguably the most universal human experience.

Although death is a reality of life, humans are biologically wired to survive and the finitude of our existence can be terrifying to hold in mind. Awareness is often avoided at all costs

* Corresponding Author's Email: beneotto1@gmail.com

as we, often unconsciously, push our fears of death and loss down on a daily basis (Albuquerque et al., 2021). However, with the unprecedented loss of life from the COVID-19 pandemic that has left hundreds of thousands bereaved in its wake, the reality of human mortality and fragility has been brought closer to consciousness. This awareness and the resulting death anxiety have been striking, particularly at the height of the pandemic where we saw panic buying in attempts to secure resources and aid chances of survival (David et al., 2021).

Within the context of the pandemic, the global awareness and fear of death are not surprising. Since the start of the pandemic, over 565 million cases and 6.37 million deaths worldwide and 4 million cases and 102 thousand deaths in South Africa have been reported. The magnitude of these numbers is intensified by the short period of time in which these deaths occurred. From an academic standpoint, it seems prudent and significant to discuss the statistics of death, but it is important to recognise that each number is an individual human being who lived and was connected to family and community (Borgstrom & Mallon, 2021). Each death is further likely to impact more than one person, whose loss may ripple across the wider community in which the individual lived. For each of these individual deaths, Verdery et al. (2020) estimate that at least nine bereaved individuals are deeply impacted by the loss. That is 918,000 individuals grieving the loss of a loved one to COVID-19 in South Africa alone.

While the COVID-19 pandemic has certainly brought the reality of death and loss to the forefront, the truth is that hundreds of thousands of people die yearly even in the absence of a pandemic. In 2018, South Africa registered 454,014 deaths – more than double the yearly estimated COVID-19 deaths (Statistics South Africa, 2013). Based on the same estimation of how many individuals are impacted by each death (Verdery et al., 2020), this would have left approximately 4 million people bereaved in just 2018. To put that into context, that is four times the amount of bereaved individuals impacted by COVID-19.

Yet, despite the exponential number of grieving individuals both before and after the pandemic, the topics of death and grief remain taboo and cause great discomfort and shame if raised. The taboo of death contributes to an individualised and isolated experience (Bauer, 2011), as well as misconceptions and misinformation that lead to the disenfranchising of the experience of loss and grief. Grief is disenfranchised when the experience falls outside of the socially accepted norms and expectations or is poorly witnessed, dismissed, or invalidated by others (Doka, 1989; Bauman, 2022). Coined by Doka (1989), disenfranchised grief has up until recently been believed to be highly contextual. However, Barney and Yoshimura (2020) argue that the experience of grief is perpetually disenfranchised, regardless of the circumstances surrounding the death, the individual, or their expressions of grief.

The consequences of grief not being witnessed and instead being disenfranchised by the people around the bereaved, as well as society at large, can be significant and can have long-term effects on the individual that may lead them to seek professional intervention (St. Clair, 2013). However, despite the number of individuals affected by grief and disenfranchised grief, the training that psychologists receive in post-apartheid South Africa is minimal across universities. This chapter explores the dominant narrative of grief in the South African context and describes the impact that this narrative can have on disenfranchised grief. It looks at the lack of training of psychologists in this subject matter and explores what is covered. Finally, this chapter makes future recommendations that include grief theory from current thanatological literature as well as therapeutic perspectives, so as to better equip psychologists when facing grieving clients.

Grief: The South African Context

When we hear the word 'grief', our minds imagine the loss of a loved one – we automatically think of the most commonly feared and denied the reality of the human condition: death (Borgstrom & Mallon, 2021). In this chapter, grief is conceptualised as a "natural human response to separation, bereavement or loss … describing an individual's personal response to loss and having emotional, physical, behavioral, cognitive, social and spiritual dimensions" (Buglass, 2010, p. 44). Grief is thus a normal reaction to the death of a loved one that can further be understood as a highly individual, all-encompassing experience (Doka, 2002). While often misconceived as a solely emotional experience of mere sadness, grief can manifest cognitively, behaviourally, interpersonally, spiritually, physiologically, and affectively (Bauman, 2022). Grieving the loss of a loved one can therefore affect an individual in all aspects of their being. Manifestations of grief can and do persist for long periods of time as the individual adapts to life after loss (Barney & Yoshimura, 2020). In recent years, and within the context of the COVID-19 pandemic, the overwhelming experience of the loss of a loved one has become a focus in both the academic and general spheres. The interest in death and grief can partially be explained by the development of modern medicine and technology which has allowed Western societies of the 21st century to live much longer than previous generations.

That being said, South Africa is a particular context. The country is divided into 9 provinces and has 11 official languages. Each of the nine provinces has unique health and social challenges such as a high occurrence of HIV/AIDS in the Kwa-Zulu Natal, Limpopo, and Eastern Cape provinces (Statistics South Africa, 2010). In some rural areas in South Africa, adult life expectancy is low and infant mortality is high (Drenth et al., 2013). The main causes of natural deaths in both rural and urban areas are epidemics such as tuberculosis and HIV/AIDS, whereas violence and motor vehicle accidents account for a high number of non-natural causes of death in the country (Statistics South Africa, 2010). Prior to the COVID-19 pandemic, the life expectancy of South Africans from birth was estimated to be 62.4 years for males and 68.4 for females (Statistics South Africa, 2021). Compared to life expectancy in more developed countries, this is a 10- to 20-year difference with the United Kingdom averaging on 77.2 years for males and 81.5 years for females (National Statistics, 2007). This would suggest that South Africans are more likely to experience the death of a loved one a lot earlier in life than people in developed countries.

While the experience of grief is unique to the individual, all grieving occurs within a social and cultural context, and more specifically within a dominant narrative. The dominant narrative of grief stipulates the norms, rules, and expectations around what is accepted as appropriate grieving: not too much and not too little (Moran, 2016). This narrative mirrors and emphasises the cultural norms around death and grief and provides the bereaved with a script for the performance and expression of their grief (Barney & Yoshimura, 2020). As Walter (1999) states, "all societies have rules for how the emotions of grief are to be displayed and handled" (p. 120). Society polices grief in at least three components of grief: how grief is expressed, for how long, and how the bereaved manage their continuing relationship with their dead (Neimeyer et al., 2014). The distinction between the use of the term *society* rather than *culture* is intentional. A society consists of an economic, social, and industrial infrastructure that includes people from a variety of different cultural and ethnic backgrounds (Harris, 2009–2010). This chapter focuses on the dominant narratives around death and grief rather than the narratives that exist within specific cultural traditions or ethnic groups that form a part of South African society. Even with death having been front row and centre more recently the COVID-19 pandemic, both globally and in South Africa, death continues to be viewed as a failure of modern medicine and a great source of shame rather than a natural and expected outcome of life (Reynolds, 2002). This sets the stage for how grieving individuals are perceived and expected to perform their experience of grief in the South African context.

With the exception of a few minority groups, South African society follows the same pattern of death-denying as other Western, capitalist, and patriarchal societies (Drenth et al., 2013). It is constructed on the foundational assumption that grief is time-limited and should not surpass the scope of typical or expected reactions such as shock, longing, and then healing. In most cultural groups, death is thought of as a taboo topic that is not discussed (Dlukuku, 2010; Marcus, 2002), which contributes to a solitary experience of grief. There are further many social rules that are widely known and recognised, but often not explicitly stated (Harris, 2009–2010). It is the bereaved individual's responsibility to 'work through' their grief on their own behind closed doors or, in some cases, with professional intervention. Like in many Western societies, the bereaved are expected to find their way in an environment that often does not support them or their loss, as well as to manage this process on their own (Souza, 2017). In order for grief to be deemed 'healthy', it must reach a resolution within a socially acceptable timeframe. This centres on the bereaved breaking bonds with their deceased loved one so as to effectively "move on" and "get over" the loss, while simultaneously finding a positive meaning in the loss. Failure to complete the 'grief work' may lead to the diagnosis of pathological grief (van Heerden, 2002). Where death is an expected outcome, the grief work should begin prior to the loss and result in a reduced intensity of grief experience after the death, as well as a quicker resolution. These sets of acceptable conditions of grieving prescribed by the dominant narrative of grief, while enduring and persistent, rarely align with the realities of both the experience and expression of grief (Barney & Yoshimura, 2020).

Neimeyer et al. (2014) maintain that individuals are both subjected to and subjugated by the dominant narrative of grief. It both informs their identity as bereaved individuals and regulates the performance of the role, suggesting that a proper way of grieving exists and should be adhered to. Expectations of grieving serve as the script which is modelled and reinforced when the bereaved perform grief in accordance with these expectations over time (Barney & Yoshimura, 2020). However, when individuals are either unable or unwilling to follow this scripted process of grieving, stigmatisation and disenfranchisement follow.

Disenfranchised Grief

Stigmatisation occurs when grief performance falls outside of the dominant prescriptions and socially accepted customs of grieving, or when grieving individuals are not able or willing to follow a given scripted process for grief. Doka (2002) coined the term *disenfranchised grief*, using it to describe grief that is "experienced when a loss cannot be openly acknowledged, socially sanctioned or publicly mourned" (p. 160). Disenfranchised grief is thus experienced when an individual's grief is not seen to fit within socially accepted norms of the dominant narrative of grief. The stigmatisation of grief is consistent with properties that define disenfranchised grief such as the exclusion of the griever, denial of the loss as meaningful, and invalidation of the griever's emotions and behaviours following the loss (Reimer, 2019). In the context of a dominant narrative of grief, the bereaved may even disenfranchise themselves by refusing to share their experience of loss and grief out of fear, shame, or blame (Kauffman, 2002). Whether grief is disenfranchised interpersonally or intrapsychically, grief that is unacknowledged and unsupported can leave the bereaved feeling isolated and alienated in their experience (Thompson et al., 2016).

According to Doka (2009), disenfranchised grief results from a variety of reasons:

1. Lack of acknowledgement

The relationship is not recognised as meaningful or valuable. For example, loss in the context of LGBTQIA+ relationships, extramarital relationships, and other relationships that aren't socially sanctioned or lack social validation can result in the invalidation of the consequent grief experienced. According to Green and Grant (2008), queer and same-sex relationships still face disapproval, scrutiny, and discrimination. When an individual in the relationship dies, the surviving partner's grief may be seen as less significant than heterosexual widowhood (Barney & Yoshimura, 2020).

2. The nature of the loss

In some cases, loss may not be recognised and acknowledged as a legitimate loss of life, for example, perinatal deaths (e.g., miscarriage, stillbirth, or abortion), the loss of a pet, or the 'social' or 'psychological deaths' that result from individuals being institutionalised, in a coma, or lacking awareness of existence (Doka, 2009).

3. Attributes of the griever

The griever may not be socially recognised as capable of experiencing grief due to their perceived lack of awareness, cognitive capacity, or involvement with the deceased (Barney & Yoshimura, 2020). For example, children, the elderly, or intellectually disabled are believed to lack the cognitive ability to comprehend the death of a loved one. Within the dominant narrative of grief, children may be perceived as being too young to understand the concepts of death, loss, and grief, oblivious to the significance and nuances, as well as in need of protection by indirect or direct avoidance. In the case of older persons, the loss of a significant other or partner may be viewed as normal and thus not require much support (Kusmaul & Anderson, 2018). Similarly to children, adults with symptoms of cognitive decline may be seen as vulnerable by others and in need of protection through avoidance (Doka, 2009). These narratives dismiss the reality that both younger and older individuals are equally capable of experiencing grief (Barney & Yoshimura, 2020).

4. The cause of death

Similarly to how societies have normative expectations of what comprises appropriate performances of grief, values, and norms develop around what constitutes acceptable causes of death. According to van der Geest (2004), this is often centred around the degree to which the cause of death is evaluated as voluntary or involuntary with respect to the deceased. 'Good' deaths are seen to conform to the dominant narrative of grief, whereas 'bad' deaths are perceived as disobeying it. The circumstances or cause of death can be seen as a source of stigma or embarrassment, resulting in disenfranchisement. For example, death from AIDS-related complications, suicide, substance overdose, or crime may be viewed as the result of moral failure and result in the blaming and shaming of the deceased. The surviving loved ones are often subjected to exclusionary treatment, their grief devalued or invalidated and denied the opportunity to be shared (Valentine et al., 2016). Both to protect the reputation of the deceased and their right to grieve the loss, families sometimes feel the need to misrepresent the cause of death to others (Pitman et al., 2018; Barney & Yoshimura, 2020).

5. The performance of grief

Corr (2002) argues that the way in which grievers express and perform their experience of grief may be another source of disenfranchisement. The dominant narrative of grief stipulates that for grief to be socially appropriate, it must be expressed within the Goldilocks principle: not too much and not too little. For example, if grief expression is not perceived as 'just right', grievers may be told by society that their experience or expression of grief is inappropriate or that their way of coping with the loss and their reactions to the loss is unacceptable (Corr, Nabe & Corr, 2009). Grievers may then try to mask their grief in stoicism or find ways to grieve that keep their experience out of sight of others so as to be more socially acceptable or prevent social isolation and exclusion, and as a result internalise the disenfranchisement (Harris, 2009–2010). Furthermore, the dominant narrative assumes that one can and should aspire to return to a pre-loss way of being within a socially acceptable amount of time. This timeframe of grief asserts the unrealistic expectation that grief resolution should occur anywhere between a few weeks and a few months but must be resolved and overcome within the first year after the loss. Yet, the reality of grief is that the experience is ongoing, dynamic, and unlikely to reach a recognisable end that aligns with the dominant narrative (Barney & Yoshimura, 2020). Just as the experience of grief is ongoing, so is the process in which the bereaved adapt to life after loss in which new roles, rituals, and ways of relating are developed.

Whatever the cause of disenfranchised grief, the phenomenon is a paradox. The very nature of disenfranchised grief creates further psychological challenges for the bereaved while simultaneously minimising or removing sources of social support (Doka, 1989). Doka's original theory of disenfranchised grief assumes that the experience of disenfranchisement is highly contextual. However, Barney and Yoshimura (2020) argue that because the dominant narrative turns a blind eye to the contextual aspects of grief, all grief experiences are disenfranchised through the widespread assumption that grief is a linear and temporary experience separate from the individual's sense of self.

In attempts to align their performance of grief to the expectations of the dominant narrative, grievers increasingly experience isolation, feeling misunderstood or invalidated as a result of the mismatch between reality and the social expectations of grieving. This is because bereaved individuals are unlikely to ever completely return to their pre-loss state. Instead, the loss, the consequent grief, and the post-loss narrative become integrated over time as important parts of the individual's identity (Barney & Yoshimura, 2020).

Even when grief occurs after a socially acceptable death and the bereaved express their experience of grieving in accordance with the dominant narrative, disenfranchisement may occur over time (Bonanno et al., 2008). Grief can be disenfranchised through empty platitudes and recycled phrases such as "at least they are no longer suffering" or "they are in a better place now" (Funk et al., 2018). However, well-intended comments like these, along with the many that may come to your own mind, further permutate the misconception that grief is temporary, should be experienced in a certain way, and can reach a conclusion. In the absence of an understanding of grief that allows for the reality that the experience is an ongoing part of an individual's identity, grief will continue to be perpetually disenfranchised (Barney & Yoshimura, 2020).

(The Lack of) Grief Training of Psychologists in Post-apartheid South Africa

Death impacts everyone in South Africa regardless of age, race, culture, creed, or socio-economic status (Drenth, 2008). Given the universality of death, loss, and grief, and the silent but widespread experience of disenfranchised grief, we can assume that many grieves will seek out the assistance of a psychologist. Psychologists are, amongst other things, committed to enhancing human well-being. In their attempts to do this, they face South Africans from all walks of life who find them when they are often at their most vulnerable. The grieving is no exception, and it is almost guaranteed that all psychologists will work with clients dealing with loss and grief (Doughty et al., 2011). Yet, the training that psychologists receive in post-apartheid South Africa is limited, if present at all, across universities. This is not a novel observation with an article published 23 years ago, suggesting that "more intensive training could be offered in loss and grief therapy" (Viljoen et al., 1999).

While very little literature on the topic exists in the South African context, in general, psychologists do not receive specific scheduled training in the areas of death, loss, and grief. Grief training is instead offered in supervision and during case presentations if students treat grieving individuals in their placements, or in passing as part of trauma or crisis intervention workshops. According to Demmer (2006), South African healthcare professionals, including psychologists, received a single workshop on grief in their training, which lasted roughly two hours and involved making a 'memory box'. None of the many grief theories in the thanatological literature or relevant therapeutic approaches were explored. Participants reported feeling uncomfortable dealing with issues around grief and death both during and after their training. Like other healthcare professionals in South Africa, psychologists are often not empowered with the training or knowledge regarding the impact of grief or how to support the grieving while holding the dominant narrative of grief in mind.

Many practising psychologists therefore continue to rely on and utilise outdated models. Existing literature on grief ranges from the older grief work, attachment, stages, phases, and tasks to the more recent conceptualisations of continuing bonds and dual-processing (Drenth, 2008). Training of psychologists in South Africa often involves being taught only a few of these theories, if any at all dependent on the university, and not in great depth. The most popular of which are stage theories, taught at the undergraduate level, and Freud, taught at some universities during Master's training. These theories are considered to be outdated in the current thanatological study (Barney & Yoshimura, 2020; O'Connor, 2019), yet are heavily subscribed to in post-apartheid South Africa.

Stage/Phase Theories

Widely disseminated stage theories, particularly the five-stage model proposed by Kübler-Ross (1969), have been the most influential theories due to their simplicity and have thus become universally adopted and accepted as truth (Hall, 2014). Fifty-three years ago, Kübler-Ross (1969) published a seminal book in which she described her observations of terminally ill patients facing their own death. At the time, this filled a great gap in the literature, since Freud's publication of *Mourning and Melancholia* in 1917 (Beckett & Dykeman, 2017). Kübler-Ross' observations of the terminally ill consisted of five stages including "denial and isolation", "anger", "bargaining", "depression", and "acceptance" (p. 9). She found that individuals first experience a phase of disbelief in which 'it can't be true', followed by anger, resentment, or frustration that may be directed at others; then a stage of bargaining in which the patient recognises the severity of their illness but attempts to negotiate for more time. This is followed by a phase of depression where the patient may mourn losses they may have already incurred, such as loss of good health or physical ability, and anticipates future loss. Finally, the patient reaches the acceptance stage where they are able to accept the inevitability of their impending death and prepare for it, resulting in a sense of peace (Bell & Taylor, 2011).

Kübler-Ross' five-stage model was echoed in further stage and phase models (Beckett & Dykeman, 2017). Bowlby (1980) described four phases that result from the separation from an attachment figure, numbness, yearning, despair, and eventually reemergence into life. Parkes' (1972) theory of grief delineated a set of reactions to loss: numbness, searching/pining, depression, and recovery. The premise of these models shares a few commonalities: grief is experienced as a set of distinct stages or phases, and failure to move through these stages or phases in a timely fashion is problematic, resulting in pathology or dysfunction (Beckett & Dykeman, 2017).

Despite the fact that the five-stage model had not empirically reviewed or tested, Kübler-Ross was revered as something of a 'guru' and her stages were generalised by both professionals and popular culture to adapt to cover all kinds of loss and grief experiences across individuals (Beckett & Dykeman, 2017; Kohler, 2011). Similarly, the five-stage model has become familiar and accepted amongst South African professionals and laypeople alike as a template for the experience of grief are frequently included in published works, self-help guides, the media, and information on grief found through internet searches (Calderwood, 2011). While this theory has in many ways been helpful in understanding the experience of being terminally ill and preparing for one's own death, it was not developed or intended to be applied to people who have experienced the death of a loved one. According to Neimeyer (2012), the misappropriation of research on the dying to apply to the bereaved serves as a cause to debunk the model of grief. Other critiques of the theory include the suggestion that grief progresses in a linear fashion with an eventual ending, the theory lacks quantitative or qualitative support, and it is overly simplistic, ignoring the complexity and individuality of the grief experience (Neimeyer, 1999; Robinson, 2011). The five-stage model, as well as other stage/phase theories, have further been rejected by a number of mourners, primarily on the grounds that their experience did not progress on a simple, linear path as is often depicted in popular media (Walter, 2000).

Freud's "Mourning and Melancholia"

In some universities, particularly those that are more psychodynamically inclined, trainee psychologists are exposed to the work of Freud (1917), specifically selective readings from the book *Mourning and Melancholia*. In this work, he argues that grief, particularly emotional responses, must be 'worked through', that is lived through, acted out, and expressed, in order for mourning to be 'complete' (Corr et al., 2009). The primary goal of 'grief work' is to sever all ties and bonds with the deceased loved one so as to have the space and energy to reinvest in new attachments (Valentine, 2006). Once ties with the deceased have been severed, grief can reach a distinct ending so that the individual can move forward with their life (Rossenblatt, 1996). Modern research now supports the notion that continuing bonds with the deceased is a normal part of adaptation to loss (Barney & Yoshimura, 2020).

While Freud (1917) may never have intended to pathologise grief, his work has been widely used in the field of psychology to justify the concepts of 'grief work' and 'pathological mourning' (Granek, 2008). It has further resulted in variations of a universalised model that conceptualises grief as a "goal-directed activity" or a temporary "state of being" that involves processes of "letting go" of the deceased so as to return to "normal" functioning (Valentine, 2006). Although Freud's original emphasis was to explore the differences between grief and depression, interpretations of his work have led to viewing the normal, though painful, part of life as a condition that needs to be treated.

Despite these theories being considered outdated in the current thanatological literature, and only a minority being based on empirical research, they are resistant to change because of maintained universal, long-standing, and uncritical acceptance, as well as the limited dissemination of more contemporary conceptualisations of grief (Lindstrøm, 2002). Though these grief theories have ceased to be taken seriously in scholarly circles (Balk, 2011), to this day they are commonly known, taught, and applied in clinical practice (Stroebe et al., 2017). Since the birth of these theories, the idea of grief being a staged process has become deeply ingrained in popular and professional beliefs about loss and grief. Even with the movement away from stage/phase and Freudian theories in thanatological literature, the foundational premise of these outdated models remains the dominant narrative of grief maintained by and taught to healthcare professionals in South Africa (Breen, 2010–2011).

Medicalisation and Pathologising of Grief

A consequence of being taught outdated grief theory is the medicalisation and pathologising of grief. Medicalisation is described as the process of certain behaviours and conditions being defined as medical conditions or disorders that then become examined and treated by members of the medical profession (Bandini, 2015). Medical views consider grief to have a starting point, a middle, and an end, in which it is the grievers' task to do "grief work" to heal, return to productive lives, and aspire to a healthy outcome after loss (Stillion & Attig, 2014).

In the medical model, the complex and wide range of grief is commonly separated into two binary categories: normal and abnormal grief (Walter, 2005). Proponents of this model agree that normal and pathological grief look almost identical in terms of presentation and symptoms, but differ in terms of duration and intensity (Harris & Bordere, 2016). The term "complicated grief" appears to be the most commonly used in describing patterns of grief that do not conform to "normal" grieving in South African research (Drenth, Herbst & Strydom, 2013). Prigerson et al. (1995, p. 23) refer to complicated grief as "the failure to return to pre-loss levels of performance or states of emotional well-being".

The psychiatric terminology used to describe grief represents a manifestation of its medicalisation, such as "morbid", "unresolved", "abnormal", "complicated", "chronic", and "prolonged" (Valentine, 2006, p. 61). These terms are constructions of the medical profession and carry further connotations of healing and recovery. Thus, the medicalisation of grief attempts to place borders around normal grieving without considering the uniqueness and variability of grief experiences, including factors such as culture, gender, age, previous experiences of loss, and individual idiosyncrasies (Harris & Bordere, 2016). This construction of grief is thoroughly looped through mainstream media and perpetuates the narrative that one is obligated to express one's grief 'normally'; to evaluate oneself in terms of what is considered normal and pathological grieving; to attempt to follow stages of the grieving process and do the necessary grief work to reach resolution or healing; to turn one's grief into an experience of personal growth; and in the event that one cannot do this on one's own, to seek professional psychological or psychiatric help (Granek, 2015).

Conceptualising grief as an illness that can be cured with a positive attitude, therapy, or medication is to privatise what used to be a communal responsibility and creates a culture in which these expectations and narratives become the norm, regardless of whether or not they are realistic or helpful (Granek, 2015). Despite the bulk of thanatological literature having "moved on" from the uncritical acceptance of these assumptions in the dominant narrative of grief, the prevailing construction remains a stage-based response where recovery can be expected after a short period of time, imposing the idea that there are normal and pathological reactions to loss rather than encouraging acceptance and acknowledgement of each individual's unique grieving process (Cowan & Wilson, 2007).

Current Understanding of Grief

The predominant view of grief in the current thanatological literature recognises that grief is a complex and highly individual experience influenced by personality, experience, and culture (Doughty et al., 2011). Emphasis is placed on the idea that there is a wide range of normal and healthy reactions to a loss that are found in these individual differences. There is a general shift away from the conceptualisation of grief as a solely private and internal process that is experienced alone, with the notion that grief is a social and communicative phenomenon gaining support (Barney & Yoshimura, 2020). Firstly, grief can be seen as inherently social as it is born from the loss of an individual with which a relationship is shared and often inspires the bereaved to create meaningful social interactions. Archer (2008) notes that grief may serve a number of social functions that require emotional regulations in order for the effect of these social functions to be maximised. From this perspective, the separation from attachment figures that occur when loved ones are lost can be considered normal responses that have likely evolved as an adaptive mechanism to signal social animals the need to reunite with their attachment figures (Bowlby, 1980).

Secondly, the notion that grief is a communicative phenomenon is supported by the link between loss, grief, and the sense of self throughout the narratives that the bereaved both create and share about their loss (Barney & Yoshimura, 2020). Grief often manifests in a wide range of responses and communicated messages (Bonanno, 2001), partially due to the fact that the affective experience is long-lasting and not equivalent to temporary emotional experiences such as sadness. Furthermore, grief is deeply connected with the individual's identity and the loss and subsequent responses of grief become a part of it. For example, changes in identity occur when an individual loses their spouse after many years of marriage; where for a good many years "wife" has been a part of their identity, they now grapple with accepting membership to widowhood, a part of their identity that did not exist before the loss (Phipps, 2018). As such, grief is an evolving, continuing personal narrative and affective experience (Goldie, 2011).

According to Neimeyer, Klass, and Dennis (2014),

> our sense of self is established through the stories that we tell about our lives, the stories that others tell about us, and the stories that we enact in their presence. It is this self-narrative that can be profoundly shaken by the 'seismic' life events such as the death of a loved one and … narrating grief instigates the processes of reaffirmation, repair, or replacement of the basic plot and theme of the life story of the bereaved. (p. 489)

In other words, the identity of the bereaved is constructed through stories and language. This suggests that there is a communicative element to both the construction of identity and the associated narrative and that experiencing a loss equates to experiencing a change in identity which occurs during the development and sharing of long-term narratives about the experience of loss (Barney & Yoshimura, 2020).

Thirdly, Niemeyer et al. (2014) describe the loss of a loved one as an interpretative experience in which making meaning is both psychological and interactive. Park (2010) notes that these meanings may include global, such as worldviews, values, beliefs, and goals around justice control and predictability, and situational, such as meaning in the context of a particular event. Therefore, similarly to the way in which emotions are prompted by appraisals and meaning is made in social situations, grief involves making meaning around the loss of a loved one (Barney & Yoshimura, 2020). The meanings that are constructed around the life and death of a loved one are developed through social interaction between the family and friends that remain. Using a biological perspective of grief, Walter (1996) suggests that the shared grief and mourning of a deceased loved one offers a stable space for the deceased individual among the survivors. Research suggests that the bereaved need to be able to talk about their deceased loved one as this both include them in their present lives and helps keep their memory alive (Hogan et al., 1996). This is along the same vein, in the continuing bonds model of grief, the bereaved maintain their connection with their dead through sensing their presence; speaking to them; using them as a guide or role model; and talking about them (Klass et al., 1996). Walter (1996) asserts that grief is not a "matter, as the bereavement literature so often portrays, of friends 'supporting' the bereaved but of a number of bereaved persons working out together who Corina [the deceased] was and what she meant to them" (p. 13). This involves many communicative and social activities such as attending ritual ceremonies, creating shared rituals over time, and receiving and providing support. Grief performances vary greatly in content which both reflects and enables meaning-making around grief by reflecting the diversity of scripts that cultures adapt to and promote (Barney & Yoshimura, 2022).

Lastly, grieving involves the seeking of, reception to, or proving of social support. This is the "interpersonal transaction involving one or more of the following: (1) emotional concern (liking, love, empathy), (2) instrumental aid (goods or services), (3) information (about the environment), or (4) appraisal information relevant to self-evaluation" (House, 1981, p. 39). In the weeks that follow the loss of a loved one, the bereaved are often offered significant amounts of support from others in the form of words of condolences, sympathy cards, flowers, meals, and memorial services. Some of the bereaved seek support in the form of grief support groups, while others go on to offer support to others who are grieving both in support groups or within their interpersonal relationships. These acts are indicative of the value of the amount and quality of function and structural support available to bereaved individuals (Barney & Yoshimura, 2020). Perhaps this is why Jakoby (2014) argues that "talking about grief is considered to be one of the most helpful remedies in the case of bereavement" (p. 13).

It is however important to note that the social support offered to the bereaved often falls short and misses the mark altogether. Research has concluded on many occasions that people simply do not say much to grievers (Herkert, 2000; Ziegler, 1996; Sunoo & Soloman, 1996). It is often apparent that people, even those who are intimately familiar with one another, have difficulty communicating about death and grief and often avoid speaking about it altogether. Sadly, "in our culture of denial, we don't know what to say … We fall all over ourselves saying the wrong things" (Gould, 1995, p. 61).

While it is certain that not all grief will be expressed socially and in the presence of others, grief that is socially shared is governed by display rules (Barney & Yoshimura, 2020). For example, display rules may dictate that anger, sadness, and sometimes even excitement be expressed through silence and avoidance. The bereaved must also adjust their expression of grief according to display rules so as to achieve numerous social goals (Barney & Yoshimura, 2020). Simultaneously, the bereaved often hold the belief that they were not 'doing this grieving thing right' sharing comments such as 'I don't know how to get over it; I don't know how much to show', which implies they are sensitive to the gaze of the people around them (Moules et al., 2004, p. 102). If the purpose of regulating one's emotional experience of grief is to maximise the social functions of the emotional experience itself, then this would include procuring further support and reducing experiences of loneliness and social isolation (Fischer & Manstead, 2016). In some cases, censoring and concealing grief expressions may be the best way to achieve this.

Current grief literature offers many suggestions on how to communicate about grief, but this is often easier spoken of than done. Jakoby (2014) highlights that "there is a discrepancy between the scientific notion of the importance of talking about grief as the practical guidelines on the one hand, and the everyday reality of bereaved people, who have to deal with various difficulties of communicating grief, on the other" (p. 13). It is in this inconsistency that the disenfranchisement of grief exists (Barney & Yoshimura, 2020).

Recommendations

Given the shortage of research and existing literature on the training of psychologists in death, loss, and grief, the opening recommendation of this chapter is for this to be the focus of future research. With the current focus of South African thanatological research being largely on 'complicated grief', there is little to provide an understanding of what the potential reasons are for the lack of grief training of psychologists in post-apartheid South Africa. It would be helpful to explore this to both gain a deeper understanding and provide further support for the need for this to change. While it is comprehensible that not all topics can be covered in the one year of academic training that psychologists receive, given the COVID-19 pandemic and the general South African context of loss, it would seem that up-to-date training on death, loss, and grief should be of relevant importance.

With the prevalence of the experience of grief, particularly in the South African context, it is imperative that psychologists be trained and prepared to work with diverse individuals and their unique grief experiences, while fostering an awareness of the dominant narrative of grief and how this results in disenfranchisement. This includes contextualising an individual's experience of grief within the social rules of the dominant narrative in South African society and facilitating the understanding that grief is the natural response to loss, it has a broad range of normal responses, and it is valid, regardless of invalidating societal norms, rules, and regulations. Often grievers feel that there is something wrong with them when their reality does not align with what the dominant narrative stipulates as socially correct. These subjective experiences need to be reframed as what is "right" for the individual in their unique experience of grief against the social norms, rules, and expectations of society that are "wrong" (Harris, 2009–2010).

Expanding the knowledge of the idiosyncratic nature of loss and grief is crucial in the development of strategies tailored to the needs of the griever as they adapt to their new reality rather than cope with it. This gives grievers the space to continually adjust to the ongoing nature of loss. In contrast, coping implies that their response to loss is transitory and involves the use of specific skills (Corr & Doka, 2001). While often thought of as an affective experience, most often being sad, grief is an all-encompassing experience that can impact every aspect of the individual's being. Psychologists should be taught to encourage grieving clients to explore affective, cognitive, behavioural, physical, and spiritual adaptive strategies that align with their individuality and experience.

Given the dominant narrative of grief, it is unlikely that navigating grief identity will be smooth but rather that this part of the griever's identity will be silenced (Barney & Yoshimura, 2020). Understanding the many ways that grief identity is navigated, and the challenges that lead to disenfranchisement could better equip psychologists in supporting their grieving clients both in navigating their grief identity and in finding their voice in an otherwise silencing environment. A big part of this can simply be meeting the client where they are in their grief, without imposing any time limits, should's or should not's, and focusing on normalising, acknowledging, and validating their reality as it is. Normalising the multitude of grief experiences challenges both the unrealistic notion that one 'normal' way of grieving exists and thus the dominant narrative of grief. Here it is important to be cautious with labelling grieving individuals with disorders by using pathology-based diagnostic systems or by subtly aligning with social rules that undermine normal grief responses and pressure clients to suppress their grief (Harris, 2009–2010).

Failing to acknowledge the reality that grief is a lifelong experience creates barriers to the interpersonal and societal communication of grief (Barney & Yoshimura, 2020). It is important to remind bereaved individuals that the societal pressure to quickly overcome and "get over" grief is highly unrealistic, given the adaptation and reconstruction that a significant loss required (Harris, 2009–2010). Having a broader understanding of the actual experience of grief may allow psychologists to better support their clients, increase awareness of how unrealistic social rules and expectations oppress the bereaved, and redefine the dominant narrative of grief in South Africa. The role of psychologists working with grieving individuals in Western societies is clear: we must normalise death as a natural consequence of life and reframe grief as an adaptive response to the losses we experience as a result of human connection, rather than a source of shame.

References

Albuquerque, S., Teixeira, A. M., & Rocha, J. C. (2021). COVID-19 and disenfranchised grief. *Frontiers in Psychiatry, 12*, 638874. https://doi.org/10.3389/fpsyt.2021.638874

Archer, J. (2008). Theories of grief: Past, present, and future perspectives. In M. S. Stroebe, R. O. Hansson, H. Schut, & W. Stroebe (Eds.), *Handbook of bereavement research and practice: Advances in theory and intervention* (pp. 45–65). Washington, DC: American Psychological Association. https://doi.org/10.1037/14498-003

Archer, J. (1999). *The nature of grief: The evolution and psychology of reactions to loss*. Florence, KY: Routledge.

Attig, T. (2001a). *How we grieve: Relearning the world*. Oxford: Oxford University Press.

Attig, T. (2001b). Relearning the world: Making and finding meanings. In R. A. Neimeyer (Ed.), *Meaning reconstruction and the experience of loss* (pp. 33–53). New York, American Psychological Association.

Bandii, J. (2015). The medicalization of bereavement: (Ab)normal grief in the DSM-5. *Death Studies, 39*(6), 323–333. https://doi.org/10.1080/07481187.2014.951498

Bauer, J. C. (2011). *Working through grief: Tensions, tales and taboos in how working people experience personal loss* (Doctoral dissertation, UMI Dissertation Pubishing). Ann Arbor, MI.

Bauman, A. (2022). Attachment, avoidance, and disenfranchised grief in college students during the Covid-19 pandemic (Order No. 29167670). Available from ProQuest Dissertations & Theses Global. (2661062957). https://www.proquest.com/dissertations-theses/attachment-avoidance-disenfranchised-grief/docview/2661062957/se-2

Barney, K. A., & Yoshimura, S. M. (2020). Death-related grief and disenfranchised identity: A communication approach. *Review of Communication Research, 8*, 78–95. https://doi.org/10.12840/ISSN.2255-4165.024

Barney, K. A., & Yoshimura, S. M. (2022). Communicative elements of meaning-making in grief: A qualitative analysis. *Omega-Journal of Death and Dying, 85*(3), 225–247.

Beckett, C., & Dykeman, C. (2017). A metatheory of grief: Implications for counselors. *VISTAS Online, 30*, 1–10.

Bell, H., & Taylor, R. (2011). Rituals and grief: An exploratory study. *Omega: Journal of Death and Dying, 63*(4), 351–370. https://doi.org/10.2190/OM.63.4.c

Bonanno, G. A. (2001). Grief and emotion: A social-functional perspective. In M. S. Stroebe, R. O. Hansson, W. Stroebe, & H. Schut (Eds.), *Handbook of bereavement research: Consequences, coping, and care* (pp. 493–515). Washington, DC: American Psychological Association.

Borgstrom, E., & Mallon, S. (Eds.). (2021). *Narratives of COVID: Loss, dying, death and grief during COVID-19*. Milton Keynes, The Open University.

Boerner, K., & Wortman, C. B. (2008). Consequences of parental loss and childhood maltreatment on psychological distress: Implications for grief therapy. *Journal of Traumatic Stress, 21*(2), 190–197. https://doi.org/10.1002/jts.20319

Bonanno, G. A. (2001). Grief and emotion: A social-functional perspective. In M. S. Stroebe, R. O. Hansson, W. Stroebe, & H. Schut (Eds.), *Handbook of bereavement research: Consequences, coping, and care* (pp. 191–210). Washington, DC: American Psychological Association.

Borgstrom, E., & Mallon, B. (2021). *Death studies: A critical guide*. London: Routledge.

Buglass, E. (2010). Grief and bereavement theories. *Nursing Standard, 24*(41), 44–47. https://doi.org/10.7748/ns2010.06.24.41.44.c7834

Calderwood, K. A. (2011). Adapting the transtheoretical model of change to the bereavement process. *Social Work, 56*(2), 107–118. https://www.proquest.com/scholarly-journals/adapting-transtheoretical-model-change/docview/863249319/se-2

Clair, J. S. St. (2013). The witnessing of disenfranchised grief: Reliability and validity. *Journal of Nursing Measurement, 21*(3), 401–414. https://doi.org/10.1891/1061-3749.21.3.401

Cowan, J., & Wilson, J. (2007). Complaints in primary care arising from bereavement. *Clinical Governance, 12*(4), 296–304. https://doi.org/10.1108/14777270710828964

Corr, C. A., & Doka, K. J. (2001). Introduction: Grief, spirituality, and end-of-life care. In K. J. Doka (Ed.), *Death and dying, life and living* (5th ed.). Wadsworth: Belmont.

David, J., Visvalingam, S., & Norberg, M. M. (2021). Why did all the toilet paper disappear? Distinguishing between panic buying and hoarding during COVID-19. *Psychiatry Research, 303*, 114062. https://doi.org/10.1016/j.psychres.2021.114062

Demmer, C. (2004). Aids and bereavement in South Africa. *Social Work/Maatskaplike Werk, 40*(3), 296–317.

Doka, K. J. (1989). *Disenfranchised grief: Recognizing hidden sorrow*. Lexington, MA: Lexington Books.

Doka, K. J. (2002a). Disenfranchised grief. In Doka, K. J. (Ed.), *Living with grief: Loss in later life* (pp. 159–168). Washington, DC: The Hospice Foundation of America.

Doka, K. J. (2002b). *Disenfranchised grief: Recognizing hidden sorrow*. Lanham, MD: Lexington Books.

Doka, K. J. (2009). Disenfranchised grief. *Bereavement Care, 18*(3), 37–39. https://doi.org10.1080/02682629908657467

Doka, K. J. (Ed.). (2018). *Living with grief: Spiritual dimensions* (pp. xv–xxiii). Washington, DC: Hospice Foundation of America.

Doughty, E. A., Wissel, A., & Glorfield, C. (2011). Current trends in grief counseling. Retrieved from http://counselingoutfitters.com/vistas/vistas11/Article_94.pdf

Drenth, C. M. (2008). Complicated grief in the South African context: A therapeutic intervention programme. Ph.D. dissertation, North-West University, Potchefstroom.

Drenth, C., Bleijenberg, N., Boelen, P. A., Stroebe, M. S., & Schut, H. A. (2013). Perceived limitations to participation in grief research: Adverse effects, ethical considerations, and practice implications. *Death Studies, 37*(5), 398–417. https://doi.org/10.1080/07481187.2012.663925

Dlukulu, P. M. (2010) Black urban widows: Their experience of and coping with be-reavement in a transitional society. Ph.D. dissertation, University of Pretoria, Pretoria.

Fischer, A. H., & Manstead, A. S. R. (2016). Social functions of emotion and emotion regulation. In M. Lewis, J. Haviland, & L. Feldman Barrett (Eds.), *Handbook of emotion* (4th ed., pp. 456–469). New York: Guilford.

Freud, S. (1917). Mourning and melancholia. *Collected Papers IV*, 288–317; 152–170.

Funk, L. M., Michael, S. T., & Utley, A. (2018). Bereavement support groups for children: A systematic review. *Death Studies, 42*(7), 427–435. https://doi.org/10.1080/07481187.2017.1351706

Granek, L. (2015). The psychologization of grief and its depictions within mainstream North American media. In J. M. Stillion & T. Attig (Eds.), *Death, dying, and bereavement: Contemporary perspectives, institutions, and practices* (pp. 105–120). Washington, DC: Springer Publishing Co.

Goldie, R. S. (2011). Grief education in social work curricula: A survey of programs in the United States. *Journal of Social Work Education, 47*(1), 25–41. https://doi.org/10.5175/JSWE.2011.200900065

Gould, D. (1995). An exploration of the experience of bereavement in childhood. *Journal of Child Psychology and Psychiatry, 36*(5), 849–859. https://doi.org/10.1111/j.1469-7610.1995.tb01357.x

Granek, L. (2008). Bereaved parents' experiences of support: A qualitative study. *Death Studies, 32*(4), 352–375. https://doi.org/10.1080/07481180801972149

Granek, L. (2015). *The grief of infertility: Disenfranchised and unresolved*. New York: Routledge.

Green, L., & Grant, V. (2008). 'Gagged grief and beleaguered bereavements?' An analysis of multidisciplinary theory and research relating to same sex partnership bereavement. *Sexualities, 11*(3), 275–300. https://doi.org/10.1177/1363460708089421

Hall, M. (2014). *Counselling and spirituality: Integrating spirituality into counselling practice*. London: SAGE Publications Ltd.

Harris, D. (2009–2010). Oppression of the bereaved: A critical analysis of grief in western society. *OMEGA, 60*(3), 241–253.

Harris, D. L., & Bordere, T. C. (2016). African American grief. In N. A. Stroebe, R. O. Hansson, W. Stroebe, & H. Schut (Eds.), *Handbook of bereavement research and practice: Advances in theory and intervention* (2nd ed., pp. 409–429). American Psychological Association. https://doi.org/10.1037/14694-023

Herbst, M., & Strydom, H. (2013). Exploring the meaning of a good death for terminally ill patients: A South African perspective. *Journal of Psychology in Africa, 23*(1), 65–73. https://doi.org/10.1080/14330237.2013.10820672

Herkert, B. M. (2000). Communicating grief. *Journal of Death and Dying, 41*(2), 93–115. https://doi.org/10.2190/M7G5-XQGN-K3NN-U8AQ

Hogan, N. S., Morse, J. M., & Tason, M. C. (1996). Toward an experiential theory of bereavement. *Omega, 27*, 43–65.

House, J. S. (1981). *Work stress and social support*. Reading, MA: Addison-Wesley.

Jakoby, N. R. (2014) Talking about grief: Conversational partners sought by bereaved people. *Bereavement Care, 33*(1), 13–18. https://doi.org/10.1080/02682621.2014.902611

Kauffman, J. (2002). The psychology of disenfranchised grief: Liberation, shame and self-disenfranchisement. In K. J. Doka (Ed.), *Disenfranchised grief: New directions, challenges, and strategies* (pp. 61–78). Champaign, IL: Research Press.

Klass, D., Silverman, P. R., & Nickman, S. L. (Eds.). (1996). *Continuing bonds: New understandings of grief.* Philadelphia, PA: Taylor & Francis.

Kohler, C. G. (2011). The experience of grief and mourning in schizophrenia. *Schizophrenia Bulletin, 37*(3), 546–555. https://doi.org/10.1093/schbul/sbp115

Kübler-Ross, E. (1969). *On death and dying.* London: Tavistock/Routledge.

Kusmaul, N., & Anderson, K. (2018). Applying a trauma-informed perspective to loss and change in the lives of older adults. *Social Work in Health Care, 57*(5), 355–375. https://doi.org/10.1080/00981389.2018.1447531

Lindstrom, T. C. (2002). It ain't necessarily so: Challenging mainstream thinking about bereavement. *Family and Community Health, 25*(1), 11–21.

Marcus, T. (2002). W0! Zaphela Izingane: It is destroying the children: Living and dying with AIDS (2nd ed.). Johannesburg: Blesston Printing.

Moran, L. S. (2016). Men in mourning: Depiction of masculinity in young and older widowers in contemporary film. *Men and Masculinities, 19*(1), 85–104. https://doi.org/10.1177/1097184X15588591

Moules, N. J., Simonson, K., Prins, M., Angus, P., & Bell, J. M. (2004). Making room for grief: Walking backwards and living forward. *Nursing Inquiry, 11*, 99–107. https://doi.org/10.1111/j.1440-1800.2004.00204.x

Nabe, C. M., & Corr, C. A. (2009). Grief as an intense emotional experience. In M. S. Stroebe, R. O. Hansson, H. Schut, & W. Stroebe (Eds.), *Handbook of bereavement research and practice: Advances in theory and intervention* (pp. 21–38). American Psychological Association. https://doi.org/10.1037/11864-002

National Statistics. (2007). Mortality statistics: Deaths registered in 2006. Author.

Neimeyer, R. A. (1999). Searching for the meaning of meaning: Grief therapy and the process of reconstruction. *Death Studies, 23*(6), 541–558. https://doi.org/10.1080/074811899200925.

Neimeyer, R. A. (2012). *Techniques of grief therapy: Creative practices for counselling the bereaved.* New York: Routledge.

Neimeyer, R. A. (2014). The changing face of grief: Contemporary directions in theory, research, and practice. *Progress in Palliative Care, 22*(3), 125–130. https://doi.org/10.1179/1743291X13Y.0000000075

Neimeyer, R. A., Klass, D., & Dennis, M. R. (2014). A social constructionist account of grief: Loss and the narration of meaning. *Death Studies*, 1–14. https://doi.org/10.1080/07481187.2014.913454

O'Connor, M. F. (2019). Grief: A brief history of research on how body, mind, and brain adapt. *Psychosomatic Medicine, 81*(8), 731–738. https://doi.org/10.1097/PSY.0000000000000717

Park, C. L. (2010). Making sense of the meaning literature: An integrative review of meaning making and its effects on adjustment to stressful life events. *Psychology Bulletin, 136*(2), 257–301. https://doi.org/10.1037/a0018301

Parkes, C. M. (1972). *Bereavement: Studies of grief in adult life.* London: Tavistock Publications.

Phipps, C. B. (2018). Metamorphosis: An autoethnographic journey through loss, grief, and perceived identity changes. *Journal of Loss and Trauma.* https://doi.org/10.1080/15325024.2018.1475138

Prigerson, H. G., Maciejewski, P. K., Reynolds 3rd., C. F., Bierhals, A. J., Newsom, J. T., Fasiczka, A., Frank, E., Doman, J., & Miller, M. (1995). Inventory of complicated grief: A scale to measure maladaptive symptoms of loss. *Psychiatry Research, 59*(1–2), 65–79. https://doi.org/10.1016/0165-1781(95)02757-2

Pitman, A. L., Stevenson, F., Osborn, D. P. J., & King, M. B. (2018). The stigma associated with bereavement by suicide and other sudden deaths: A qualitative interview study. *Social Science & Medicine, 198*, 121–129. https://doi.org/10.1016/j.socscimed.2017.12.035

Reimer, J. E. (2019). College students' disenfranchised grief following a breakup: The effect of relationship closeness and perceived stigma on grief. [Doctoral thesis, California Polytechnic State University].

Reynolds, J. J. (2002). *Disenfranchised grief and the politics of helping: Social policy and its clinical implications.* In Doka K. J. (Ed.), *Disenfranchised grief: New directions, challenges, and strategies for practice* (pp. 351–387). Champaign, IL: Research Press.

Robinson, L. (2011). The complexities of grief and mourning in childhood. *Bereavement Care, 30*(1), 14–18. https://doi.org/10.1080/02682621.2011.9733951

Rosenblatt, P. C. (1996). *Grief across the lifespan: A biopsychosocial perspective.* New York, NY: Routledge.

Rossenblatt, P. C. (1996). The loss of a therapist: A personal account of grief and recovery. *Psychotherapy, 33*(2), 234–243. https://doi.org/10.1037/h0087709

Souza, M. (2017). Bereavement: An anthropological approach. *Death Studies, 41*(1), 61–67. http://doi.org/10.1080/07481187.2016.1257888

Statistics South Africa. (2010). Mortality and causes of death in South Africa, 2008: Findings from death notification. Author.

Statistics South Africa. (2013). Causes of death 2013. Retrieved from https://www.statssa.gov.za/?page_id=737&id=3

Statistics South Africa. (2021). Mid-year population estimates 2021. Author.

Stillion, J. M., & Attig, T. (2014). *Death, dying, and bereavement: Contemporary perspectives, institutions, and practices* (2nd ed.). Springer Publishing Company. https://doi.org/10.1891/9780826198228.0001.

Stillion, J. M., & Attig, T. (2015). *Death, dying, and bereavement: Contemporary perspectives, institutions, and practices.* New York: Springer.

Stroebe, M. S., Hansson, R. O., Stroebe, W., & Schut, H. (2017). *Handbook of bereavement research and practice: Advances in theory and intervention* (5th ed.). American Psychological Association. https://doi.org/10.1037/0000100-000

Stroebe, M. S., Stroebe, W., & Schut, H. (2008). Bereavement research: Methodological issues and ethical concerns. *Palliative Medicine, 22*(7), 823–828.

Sunoo, B. P., & Soloman, C. M. (1996). Facing grief: How and why to help people heal. *Personnel Journal, 75*, 78–89.

Thompson, N., Allan, J., Carverhill, P. A., Cox, G. R., Davies, B., Doka, K., … Wittkowski, J. (2016). The case for a sociology of dying, death, and bereavement. *Death Studies, 40*(3), 172–181. https://doi.org/10/1080/07481187.2015.1109377

Valentine, C. (2006). Academic constructions of bereavement. *Mortality, 11*(1), 57–78. https://doi.org/10.1080/13576270500439274

Valentine, C., Bauld, L., & Walter, T. (2016). Bereavement following substance misuse: A disenfranchised grief. *Omega: The Journal of Death and Dying, 72*(4), 283–301. https://doi.org/10.1177/0030222815625174

van der Geest, S. (2004). Good and bad death: Introduction. *Social Science & Medicine,* 58, 883–885. https://doi.org/10.1016/j.socscimed.2003.10.034

van Heerden, B. (2002). Coping with trauma: The role of meaning. *South African Journal of Psychology, 32*(2), 16–25.

Verdery, A. M., Smith-Greenway, E., Margolis, R., & Daw, J. (2020). Tracking the reach of COVID-19 kin loss with a bereavement multiplier applied to the United States. *PNAS, 117*(30), 17695–17701. https://www.pnas.org/cgi/doi/10.1073/pnas.2007476117

Viljoen, D. J., Beukes, R. B. I., & Louw, D. A. (1999). An evaluation of the training of psychologists at the university of the free state. *South African Journal of Psychology, 29*(4), 201–208.

Walter, T. (1996). A new model of grief: Bereavement and biography. *Mortality, 1*(1), 7–25. https://doi.org/10.10980/713685822

Walter, T. (Ed.). (1999). *The mourning for Diana.* Oxford and New York: Berg.

Walter, T. (2000). Modern death: Taboo or not taboo? *Sociology, 34*(2), 365–382.

Walter, T. (2005). *The revival of death.* London: Routledge.

Ziegler J. (1996). How corporations cope when death intrudes. *Business & Health, 14*, 31–42..

About the Editor

Zelda G. Knight has been a senior professor of psychology for 20 years. She is an experienced counselling psychologist and runs a part-time private practice. She has taught psychodynamic psychotherapy to student psychologists for almost 30 years. She has published many articles and book chapters in psychotherapy, training and practice in high-impact, peer-reviewed and accredited journals. As a participant at more than 30 international conferences, she has been a guest speaker on numerous occasions. She has been on the editorial board for several years for an international Italian journal on psychotherapy, as well as a visiting professor at the University of Valencia, Spain, and the Sigmund Freud University, Vienna, Austria. She is the vice-president of the World Council for Psychotherapy (WCP) African Chapter, a worldwide organization that promotes psychotherapy through networking, workshops, seminars and conferences. To this end, she has been on the organizing committee for two international WCP conferences for psychotherapy – in Moscow and South Africa.

Index

Note: Page numbers followed by 'n' refer to notes.

N

O

P

R

S